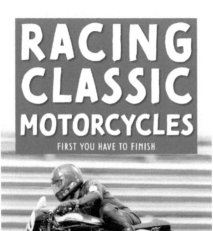

RACING CLASSIC MOTORCYCLES

FIRST YOU HAVE TO FINISH

SpeedPro Series
Harley-Davidson Evolution Engines, How to Build & Power Tune (Hammill)
Motorcycle-engined Racing Cars, How to Build (Pashley)
Secrets of Speed – Today's techniques for 4-stroke engine blueprinting & tuning (Swager)

Enthusiast's Restoration Manual Series
Beginner's Guide to Classic Motorcycle Restoration, The (Burns)
Classic Large Frame Vespa Scooters, How to Restore (Paxton)
Classic Small Frame Vespa Scooters, How to Restore (Paxton)
Classic Off-road Motorcycles, How to Restore (Burns)
Ducati Bevel Twins 1971 to 1986 (Falloon)
Honda CX500 & CX650, How to restore – YOUR step-by-step colour illustrated guide to complete restoration (Burns)
Honda Fours, How to restore – YOUR step-by-step colour illustrated guide to complete restoration (Burns)
Kawasaki Z1, Z/KZ900 & Z/KZ1000, How to restore (Rooke)
Norton Commando, How to Restore (Rooke)
Triumph Trident T150/T160 & BSA Rocket III, How to Restore (Rooke)
Yamaha FS1-E, How to Restore (Watts)

Essential Buyer's Guide Series
BMW Boxer Twins (Henshaw)
BMW GS (Henshaw)
BSA 350, 441 & 500 Singles (Henshaw)
BSA 500 & 650 Twins (Henshaw)
BSA Bantam (Henshaw)
Choosing, Using & Maintaining Your Electric Bicycle (Henshaw)
Ducati Bevel Twins (Falloon)
Ducati Desmodue Twins (Falloon)
Ducati Desmoquattro Twins – 851, 888, 916, 996, 998, ST4 1988 to 2004 (Falloon)
Harley-Davidson Big Twins (Henshaw)

Hinckley Triumph triples & fours 750, 900, 955, 1000, 1050, 1200 – 1991-2009 (Henshaw)
Honda CBR FireBlade (Henshaw)
Honda CBR600 Hurricane (Henshaw)
Honda SOHC Fours 1969-1984 (Henshaw)
Kawasaki Z1 & Z900 (Orritt)
Moto Guzzi 2-valve big twins (Falloon)
Norton Commando (Henshaw)
Piaggio Scooters – all modern two-stroke & four-stroke automatic models 1991 to 2016 (Willis)
Royal Enfield Bullet (Henshaw)
Triumph 350 & 500 Twins (Henshaw)
Triumph Bonneville (Henshaw)
Triumph Thunderbird, Trophy & Tiger (Henshaw)
Triumph Trident & BSA Rocket III (Rooke)
Velocette 350 & 500 Singles 1946 to 1970 (Henshaw)
Vespa Scooters – Classic 2-stroke models 1960-2008 (Paxton)

Those Were The Days ... Series
Café Racer Phenomenon, The (Walker)
Drag Bike Racing in Britain – From the mid '60s to the mid '80s (Lee)

Biographies
Chris Carter at Large – Stories from a lifetime in motorcycle racing (Carter & Skelton)
Edward Turner – The Man Behind the Motorcycles (Clew)
Driven by Desire – The Desiré Wilson Story (Wilson)
Jim Redman – 6 Times World Motorcycle Champion: The Autobiography (Redman)
'Sox' – Gary Hocking – the forgotten World Motorcycle Champion (Hughes)

General
An Incredible Journey (Falls & Reisch)
BMW Boxer Twins 1970-1995 Bible, The (Falloon)
BMW Cafe Racers (Cloesen)
BMW Custom Motorcycles – Choppers, Cruisers, Bobbers, Trikes & Quads (Cloesen)
Bonjour – Is this Italy? (Turner)

British 250cc Racing Motorcycles (Pereira)
British Café Racers (Cloesen)
British Custom Motorcycles – The Brit Chop – choppers, cruisers, bobbers & trikes (Cloesen)
BSA Bantam Bible, The (Henshaw)
BSA Motorcycles – the final evolution (Jones)
Ducati 750 Bible, The (Falloon)
Ducati 750 SS 'round-case' 1974, The Book of (Falloon)
Ducati 860, 900 and Mille Bible, The (Falloon)
Ducati Monster Bible (New Updated & Revised Edition), The (Falloon)
Ducati Story, The – 6th Edition (Falloon)
Ducati 916 (updated edition) (Falloon)
Dune Buggy, Building A – The Essential Manual (Shakespeare)
Fine Art of the Motorcycle Engine, The (Peirce)
Franklin's Indians (Sucher/Pickering/Diamond/Havelin)
From Crystal Palace to Red Square – A Hapless Biker's Road to Russia (Turner)
Funky Mopeds (Skelton)
India - The Shimmering Dream (Reisch/Falls (translator))
Italian Cafe Racers (Cloesen)
Italian Custom Motorcycles (Cloesen)
Japanese Custom Motorcycles – The Nippon Chop – Chopper, Cruiser, Bobber, Trikes and Quads (Cloesen)
Kawasaki Triples Bible, The (Walker)
Kawasaki W, H1 & Z – The Big Air-cooled Machines (Long)
Kawasaki Z1 Story, The (Sheehan)
Laverda Twins & Triples Bible 1968-1986 (Falloon)
Moto Guzzi Sport & Le Mans Bible, The (Falloon)
Moto Guzzi Story, The – 3rd Edition (Falloon)
Motorcycle Apprentice (Cakebread)
Motorcycle GP Racing in the 1960s (Pereira)
Motorcycle Racing with the Continental Circus 1920-1970 (Pereira)
Motorcycle Road & Racing Chassis Designs (Noakes)

Motorcycles and Motorcycling in the USSR from 1939 (Turbett)
Motorcycles, Mates and Memories (Snelling)
Motorcycling in the '50s (Clew)
MV Agusta Fours, The book of the classic (Falloon)
Norton Commando Bible – All models 1968 to 1978 (Henshaw)
Off-Road Giants! (Volume 1) – Heroes of 1960s Motorcycle Sport (Westlake)
Off-Road Giants! (Volume 2) – Heroes of 1960s Motorcycle Sport (Westlake)
Off-Road Giants! (Volume 3) – Heroes of 1960s Motorcycle Sport (Westlake)
Racing Classic Motorcycles (Reynolds)
Racing Line – British motorcycle racing in the golden age of the big single (Guntrip)
The Red Baron's Ultimate Ducati Desmo Manual (Cabrera Choclán)
Scooters & Microcars, The A-Z of Popular (Dan)
Scooter Lifestyle (Grainger)
Scooter Mania! – Recollections of the Isle of Man International Scooter Rally (Jackson)
Singer Story: Cars, Commercial Vehicles, Bicycles & Motorcycle (Atkinson)
Slow Burn - The growth of Superbikes & Superbike racing 1970 to 1988 (Guntrip)
Suzuki Motorcycles - The Classic Two-stroke Era (Long)
Triumph Bonneville Bible (59-83) (Henshaw)
Triumph Bonneville!, Save the – The inside story of the Meriden Workers' Co-op (Rosamond)
Triumph Motorcycles & the Meriden Factory (Hancox)
Triumph Speed Twin & Thunderbird Bible (Woolridge)
Triumph Tiger Cub Bible (Estall)
Triumph Trophy Bible (Woolridge)
TT Talking – The TT's most exciting era – As seen by Manx Radio TT's lead commentator 2004-2012 (Lambert)
Velocette Motorcycles – MSS to Thruxton – Third Edition (Burris)
Vespa – The Story of a Cult Classic in Pictures (Uhlig)
Vincent Motorcycles: The Untold Story since 1946 (Guyony & Parker)

www.veloce.co.uk

First published in April 2020. This edition published in June 2021 by Veloce Publishing Limited, Veloce House, Parkway Farm Business Park, Middle Farm Way, Poundbury, Dorchester DT1 3AR, England. Tel +44 (0)1305 260068 / Fax 01305 250479 / e-mail info@veloce.co.uk / web www.veloce.co.uk or www.velocebooks.com. ISBN: 978-1-787114-81-4; UPC: 6-36847-01481-0.

Front cover photo: Russell Lee/Sport-Pics.

RACING CLASSIC MOTORCYCLES

FIRST YOU HAVE TO FINISH

VELOCE PUBLISHING
THE PUBLISHER OF FINE AUTOMOTIVE BOOKS

INTRODUCTION

"I was just a young man caught in a dangerous occupation and needing to go on. Should you want confirmation of what it's like, ask a combat veteran from Vietnam or another conflict how they managed to go on in the face of death. And if you think there's a great difference between them and an impassioned race driver because the latter has the ability to quit at any time, you don't fully understand the pull of being impassioned."

Phil Hill (winner of the 1961 Formula One,
World Drivers' Championship)

MOTORCYCLES, AND PARTICULARLY CLASSIC RACING MOTORCYCLES, have been the love of my life, alongside my wonderfully supportive wife, Shelagh (though she might say I favoured the bikes!).

I became addicted to motorcycles, aged 16, when I rode my friend's 250cc Francis Barnet, and ultimately this led to me competing in 37 Manx Grand Prix events and two Tourist Trophy races, failing to finish in five of them, a podium finish and 100mph Senior MGP Classic lap being the highlights.

Between 1977 and 2016 I raced in classic events all over the UK and Europe, primarily on historic Grand Prix circuits, and achieved reasonable results at most of them. I won a couple of races and had some class wins to make it all worthwhile. The classic bikes I raced include Aermacchi, Manx Norton, Petty Norton, Seeley G50 and 7R, Velocette MSS and KTT, Paton BIC, Woden -JAP and BMW RS54, plus modern Honda, Yamaha and Kawasaki 400.

I spent far too much money, but had a lot of help and guidance to allow me to justify the expense.

I made and lost a lot of good friends along the way, and suffered a couple of injuries but would not change anything.

I enjoyed preparing my own bikes and am proud of their finishing record, particularly in the Isle of Man. Soon after I met him my engineer pal, Paul Duncombe, gave me a piece of advice that has stayed with me to this day: "Never be satisfied with a part until you are sure it will not fail during a race." Even now, I sometimes make an item two or three times before I am satisfied that I have met Paul's standard.

To finish first, first, you have to finish! (buy more lock-wire, cable ties and duct tape if in doubt!).

Andy Reynolds

FOREWORD

I GUESS THAT GENERALLY ALL SPORTS PEOPLE, HOWEVER successful, are passionate about their chosen sport. Inevitably, the degree of that passion depends upon the individual involved, and I have yet to meet anyone within the sport of motorcycle racing whose level of passion exceeds that of Andy Reynolds.

I first got to know Andy and his wife, Shelagh, when, after a long time away, I came back to racing via the Goodwood Revival event and the Lansdowne Classic Racing series. At that time Andy was racing his Manx Norton.

What I didn't know back then was just how committed to racing Andy had been throughout his career. Also, because he rarely spoke of his previous endeavours, it was only recently that I learned of his Manx Grand Prix exploits.

This well-written book tells the story of a devoted classic club racer who was both methodical and dedicated in his pursuit of success, particularly in the Isle of Man. It is a story that I and many motorcycle racers can relate to, as many of us have been through the highs and lows, the disappointments, elations and sometimes sadness that this wonderful but sometimes cruel sport of ours can bring.

You will read of the pinnacle of that elation when, after many years of trying, Andy's determination and meticulous machine preparation paid off, earning him a podium position in the 2009 Senior Classic Manx Grand Prix.

Andy started in 37 races at the Manx GP and two at the TT, and the fact that he suffered only five retirements bears testament to his standard of machine preparation. Out of those 34 finishes, he was rewarded with 19 MGP replicas: an achievement that many competitors would be extremely envious of.

But don't think for one moment that this book is all about the MGP. Andy, like many classic racers before and after him, raced on many of the UK's short circuits combined with trips over the channel to compete at numerous European circuits.

Andy is a popular guy and I'm pleased to report that, since his retirement from racing in 2016, he has taken on the role of machine scrutineer, so we are likely to see his ever-smiling face for many years to come.

Charlie Williams
Nine times TT winner, and winner of the
Formula 2 Class of the Formula TT World Championship

CONTENTS

It is not the critic who counts, not the one who points out how the strong man stumbled or how the doer of deeds might have done them better.

The credit belongs to the man who is actually in the arena, whose face is marred with sweat and dust and blood; who strives valiantly; who errs and comes short again and again; who knows the enthusiasms, the great devotions, and spends himself in a worthy cause; who if he wins, knows the triumph of high achievement, and who, if he fails, at least fails while daring greatly, so that his place shall never be with those cold and timid souls who know neither victory nor defeat.

Theodore Roosevelt

CHAPTER 1

FORMATIVE YEARS

I WAS BORN IN LONDON IN MARCH 1948 AND, UNTIL I WAS SEVEN, lived in Willesden, not far from Wormwood Scrubs prison. My father was a civil servant, and travelled to the city each day. Typically for the time, mum, who had worked as a secretary, looked after our small house in Buchanan Gardens after I was born, and never returned to work. I didn't see that much of Dad. I was sent to Furness Road School in Harlesden, known for being one of the London areas where the police operation, 'Trident' is particularly active against gun crime. Out-of-school hours were spent playing in the street, and occasionally fighting with the local kids who were mainly Irish: I generally lost! I remember dad making me cross the road in Harlesden to avoid going near a local pub frequented by Irish labourers. There was still sawdust on the floor, and every now and then fights would spill out onto the street. Nothing much has changed in Harlesden!

When I was seven, we moved a few miles north to a semi-detached house in Kenton, Middlesex, and around this time my younger brother, Jon (Jonathan), was born. In Kenton I went to Priestmead Junior School, and ultimately passed my eleven plus to go on to Harrow County Grammar School. I enjoyed football in the local park and cycled everywhere. I hate to admit it now, but I also spent hours collecting train and bus numbers, and travelled all over London, often with my cousin, Chris Marshall, to do so. Grammar school was a disaster and I failed miserably. My dad was mortified.

At this period of my life I was a great disappointment to my parents, and my mother described me to others as a 'difficult' child! I made few friends at school, and just couldn't absorb the numerous new subjects they tried to teach me there. I guess this was when the attention deficit issues I now know I suffer from reared their heads. Latin and chemistry were a total mystery, and I failed to gain any O'levels at all.

Aged sixteen, it was suggested that I should leave school, and try to start an engineering apprenticeship, to which my father readily agreed. He found me my first job as a toolmaker at Shipman and Co, an engineering firm in Northwood Hills, located in the basement of a block of flats, with about a dozen employees. I was the only apprentice, so became the 'dogsbody,' tasked with all of the mundane tasks, and not allowed to take on any real technical work. I did attend Harrow Technical College on day release, and over a period of five years, gained City and Guilds Engineering certificates, including a distinction for 'advanced machining,' so I *could* do it if I really applied myself. After at least one change of ownership, Shipman folded and made me redundant four years into my apprenticeship. After more hard work by my dad, the apprenticeship was transferred to Thermo Plastics in Dunstable. My dad's trade was based on furniture and wood, but he thought that plastics were the future.

As soon as I started work at sixteen, I needed my own transport, so dad loaned me the money to buy a Lambretta TV 175 scooter. This served me well and, as a couple of local friends also had scooters, we travelled reasonable distances together in some comfort. One of our crowd, Dick Findlay, had a 250cc Francis Barnett motorcycle, and as soon as I cadged a ride on that I realised that motorcycles — with their larger diameter wheels — were much nicer and safer to ride than scooters.

My girlfriend, Shelagh Walker, loved riding pillion on the scooter. We originally met at a local youth club when we were both fifteen, and enjoyed hanging out together. Our home lives were not easy: both of us suffering from parents who had other stressful issues to deal with. I thought Shelagh was a lovely girl; very pretty, and we were both always extremely happy and relaxed in each other's company: soulmates — which we still are.

The scooter had to go. I'd passed my motorcycle test at the first attempt and, for £68, I bought a 1958 500cc BSA Shooting Star from Rex Judd's shop in Edgware. It was in lovely original condition and suited me fine. The power seemed awesome; Shelagh even liked the comfy dual seat. All this happened in 1964, and the following year I passed my car test and managed to buy a red Morris Minor van for £40. It had a loose sheet of steel beneath the driver's feet to cover up a large hole in the floor, and lengths of scaffolding pipe for bumpers (this was before the MOT test). We didn't keep the Morris for very long, replacing it with a black Ford 100E van that again cost £40. Shelagh soon modified this by backing it into the Armco barrier surrounding the Dominion cinema's car park in Harrow. The 100E van had very small rear windows and, as Shelagh slowly backed it towards the barrier using the tiny offside wing mirror, she heard a clang, so stopped, went forward and had another go at it, which really bent the bumper and rear light unit. The Armco just overlapped the nearside of the van, and she couldn't see it.

I was earning about £5 a week, so I'm not sure how we afforded all of this; maybe Shelagh (who was working as a typist at Eagle Star Insurance in Harrow) helped out? Life was spent learning to drink beer (usually Ind Coope's Double Diamond or Watney's Red Barrel), going to the pictures, followed by the local chip shop, plus motorbike rides to race meetings and ice hockey and speedway events. We did visit the infamous Busy Bee and Ace cafés once or twice, and even joined the 59 Club, though were never really Rockers. We just loved the freedom of the biking life.

After wearing an ex-US army combat jacket on the scooter, I just had to have a leather jacket for the motorcycle, and bought a real Rocker-style example from Pinks of Harrow, one of our local motorcycle dealers. Jim Pink was a TT racer, and there was often a Manx Norton with a pink fairing in the shop window for us wannabe racers to gaze at. With my pale blue Levi's jeans and baseball boots, I thought I looked the business. My dad had a fit! I was the antithesis of his pinstripe suit and homburg hat.

The other local motorcycle shop was Wessells in Wealdstone, and I used to dream of owning one of the new twin-cylinder Nortons that it often had on display. A large parrot was kept in a cage behind the counter; he had quite a few choice expletives in his vocabulary.

On apprentice's wages I could only afford a rubberised 'Black Prince' two-piece oversuit, and this was the cause of my downfall as I stopped at the junction at the end of our road, en route to work in the rain on the Beeza. Unbeknown to me, the frayed bottom of the right trouser leg had caught around the footrest and, as I came to a stop, I couldn't put my foot on the ground. Over-balancing, I ended up with my leg trapped underneath the fallen bike, on the soaking wet road, but laughing like a drain at my stupidity and misfortune.

Around this time I became friendly with a tall, slim chap called Malcolm Lowe, who lived across the road from my parents. He was a few years older than me, worked in a bank, and introduced me to the Hendon Hawks motorcycle club, where I met a new crowd of enthusiasts, including Bob Biscadine, Brian Riddle, Brett Gates and his wife-to-be, Gwen, and John Walker and his wife-to-be, Linda. Bob raced a Manx Norton owned by Brian Jennings, a local shoe repairer, and took part in several Manx Grands Prix and TTs around this time. I enjoyed listening to his tales of success and failure. John and I are still close friends, and both Brian Riddle and Brett ended up living in the Isle of Man, where we are still in touch (Brett spent several years as a travelling marshal for the races). I still meet Brian Jennings at our local Vintage Motorcycle Club meetings, and talk to Malcolm via e-mail.

In 1965 Malcolm bought the third Velocette Thruxton to be sold to the public, index number ELW 12C, and I took him to collect it from Reg Orpin's shop in Shepherd's Bush, North London. We did a few rides together, and I travelled on his Thruxton's pillion for a week's visit to the Isle of Man in 1965 to watch Bob race at the Manx Grand Prix. We stayed at Tower House in Station Road, Kirkmichael. Prior to this I had been to spectate at Crystal Palace, Brands Hatch, and Mallory Park race tracks. I was really interested in road racing, though it was way beyond my financial capabilities: I had no thought of competing as an apprentice's wages were pitiful.

Shelagh and I travelled many miles on the BSA, and apart from the clutch falling off on the way home from Brighton one day, it was quite reliable. The speedo said it would just do the ton, but I think this was a little ambitious.

In January 1965, Dick Findlay and I decided to attend the Dragon Rally in North Wales, sharing my BSA. Unfortunately, the weather turned foul and we encountered ice and snow in Wales. We were ill-prepared for the cold and, in the middle of the night, decided we'd had enough. We packed up the tiny tent and summer-weight sleeping bags and rode home, agreeing we would never be that stupid again.

One dark winter's evening, I allowed Shelagh's brother John to ride the bike with me on the pillion. John was two years older than me, and an experienced motorcyclist so I trusted him. Big mistake. At the foot of Stanmore Hill he managed to overdo it, and down we went in a shower of sparks; I remember thinking that each spark represented a pound note. Fortunately, neither the bike or us hit anything solid, and we managed to ride it home with me at the controls! We were never close friends after that!

I decided to rebuild the bike in café racer trim, and fitted rear-set footrests, swept-back pipes, a central oil tank and a fibreglass fuel tank. Shelagh found a purse containing some cash outside the Granada cinema in Harrow one evening. We took it to the police but, as no one claimed it within a few months it became hers, and she donated the money to buy the fuel tank. Essentially, I ruined a perfectly good standard BSA Shooting Star, which is what happened in those days, as standard bikes looked boring to us youngsters, and we wanted them to look like racers.

Shelagh and I got engaged in 1967, much against my parents' wishes. They considered themselves middle class and Shelagh's parents working class, although, in later years, they readily admitted to being mistaken. Shelagh and I spent most of our spare time together, and I gave her the nickname of 'Tat,' because, often when I arrived early to collect her for a night out, she would still be wearing hair rollers, and I teased her by saying she looked 'tatty.' She was a very good pillion passenger, and would only complain if I knocked the heels off her boots whilst cornering too exuberantly. We rode in all weathers, getting soaked and frozen together.

The 500c BSA motor didn't last that long. A light knocking had developed in the motor, which I thought was the tappets needing adjustment. One rainy day whilst travelling home from work in Dunstable on the M1 motorway near Redbourn, I noticed that the bike had begun to weave alarmingly; looking down I realised that the rear wheel wasn't turning. I quickly de-clutched, which freed the wheel, and pulled onto the hard shoulder. By now, the bike wore a Peel Mountain Mile fairing, and in the bottom of this I found the remains of a con rod. The knocking had been the big end bolts coming loose, with the result that massive damage was caused to the engine: it was scrap. I bought a 650 Super Rocket engine in bits from a breaker in London and put that together, but it never ran as sweetly as the 500.

Having watched Chris Vincent and others drifting their outfits around Crystal Palace and Brands Hatch, I began to dream of racing a sidecar outfit, and made enquiries regarding chassis constructors. Most of the outfits raced then had their chassis welded together by the rider or passenger; they were bespoke! I had no welding knowledge, however, and would need a ready-made chassis to which I could add the commonly-used Triumph motor.

The only two chassis constructors I could identify were Mick Fiddaman and Ted Young. Mick's 'Kitten' design utilised the Triumph motor lying horizontally. I was wary of possible lubrication issues, so favoured a more traditional ETY built by Ted Young. I'd recruited my pal, John Walker, as a potential passenger. John loved a challenge, and although I had little money, I thought the dream might happen. Needless to say, it didn't. I did manage to make contact with a friend of Ted Young, who wrote to tell me that Ted didn't want to build any more outfits, so the project died there and then. Perhaps it was never going to happen anyway, but it's good to dream ...

Throughout our teenage years in the late '60s we continued to attend numerous motorcycle race meetings, and returned to spectate at the Manx Grand Prix in 1966, and the TT after that. Dick Findlay had sold the Francis Barnett, and now owned a lovely 350cc KSS Mk 2 overhead camshaft Velocette, which I coveted. Dick was a far better mechanic than me, and I tried to learn from him. We generally hung around together, and he also came with us to the TTs. On one of our trips to the island his KSS suffered a slight piston seizure as we travelled to Liverpool to catch the ferry. It was early on a very foggy morning, and we were stuck on the hard shoulder of the M1, somewhere near Watford Gap services. Dick quickly stripped the top end of the motor and used Shelagh's nail file to dress the piston, and her Ponds Cold Cream to reseal the gaskets.

Leaving the motorway, we became lost somewhere on the A5 near the Welsh border. Dick decided that he needed some more oil for his bike, and upon asking the pump attendant at a garage for some Castrol XL40, the chap said "Do you want it in the bike or on the floor with the rest of it?" Velocettes do tend to leak a little!

Over the coming years we stayed at various locations in and around Kirkmichael, and I became friendly with some of the Manx locals, particularly Ellis Lowe, who owned Michael Motors Garage at the north end of the village. His ever-smiling mechanic was a man called John Molyneux. John passengered for George Oates, a Manx sidecar racer, and an accident at Tournagrough corner at the 1977 Ulster Grand Prix on the Dundrod circuit resulted in both their deaths, sadly. John and his wife had several children, including David, who is a current, very successful TT sidecar racer: his dad would have been very proud of his achievements.

Ellis' friend, John Crowe, raced at the Manx Grand Prix several times in the early '60s, and Ellis told me many tales of their efforts with a BSA Gold Star and a Manx Norton. I was beginning to get the 'bug'!

Around this time I also got to know one of the race's flag marshals, Peter Kelly, who was stationed at Douglas Road corner in Kirkmichael. Flag marshals were located at all of the most dangerous corners around the TT circuit, playing a very important role in making racing as safe as possible. Peter had many tales to tell of past races and racers, and we often regrouped in the evening at The Mitre pub in Kirkmichael for more tales of derring-do. The local village bobby was Peter Dawson, who also used to stand at Douglas Road corner during the races and chat to us. Peter occasionally popped into The Mitre, late of an evening, to make sure that it (sometimes) shut on time! He was to have a great influence on my life in later years ... more about which to come.

The '60s was a wonderful decade in which to watch the TT races. The Japanese teams reigned supreme and, in those days, with Ellis' guidance, we found some great isolated spots to watch the Honda sixes, Yamaha and Suzuki fours, and other works bikes ridden by the best riders in the world. Shelagh and I — both Mike Hailwood fans — were lucky to witness some of his best races around the TT course. I soon realised that these riders were special, but watching those at the tail end of the field made me feel I could do a bit better; time would tell.

We would often ride around the course, where I began the long learning curve that would continue for many years. The weather always seemed to be sunny, and it felt as though we were holidaying abroad. I became pals with several of the local village lads, and we frequently travelled the fifteen miles into Douglas to find new pubs, driven there in very tired cars and vans (Austin A40s and Mini vans were very popular and cheap to maintain). At that time, vehicles registered on the island still did not require an MOT, and their reliability — and safety — left much to be desired. There was no breathalyser, either, and return trips to Kirkmichael involved driving the ancient vehicles flat-out where possible, accompanied by a drunken commentary regarding the correct racing line, and passengers instructed to lean out of open doors to assist with cornering speeds. We also occasionally detoured to the chip shop in nearby Peel, and enjoyed the fun of a lane laughingly called the 'switchback road,' the humps on which didn't do much to help keep down the local very flat beer. The well-scarred humps were also responsible for the deaths of a number of rally drivers, as the road was always included in the Manx National Rally. Incidentally, the Manx Okells or Castletown bitter was undrinkable to us Londoners, who were more used to our gassed beer. The locals drank 'pint touches,' which meant a splash of lemonade was added to the bitter. We often stuck to bottles of red or blue label Bass, and had the more severe hangovers as a result. The Mitre pub in Kirkmichael has a lot to answer for ...

Ellis would surprise us each year with a newly-constructed (bodged) scramble bike, and one year he produced a 350cc BSA B31 single, with a Bantam wheel crudely attached to the side to make a sidecar outfit. Several of us attempted to tame this beast in the fields and on the beach, and I certainly passed through at least one hedge and entered the surf a couple of times. Ultimately, I could just about handle it. The local lads had marked out a scramble course on one of the nearby hilltops, and we spent many happy hours falling off, and generally bending the bikes.

Each road junction with the TT course was cordoned off with a rope during practice and race periods, to prevent locals or spectators causing an accident by driving onto the 'live' course. This task was taken on by local barrier marshals, Kirkmichael's representative being a useful drinker called George Havercroft, or 'Haver' to his pals, who used an elderly Norton ES2 sidecar outfit to get around his patch. Rising at 5am one morning, my pal John Walker and I donned our motorcycle gear over our pyjamas, and went to watch early morning practice from Douglas Road corner, at the entry to Kirkmichael. We walked towards the end of the village, noticing that no ropes had been put in place. We rushed to the flag marshals' position, and on arrival informed them that George had failed to do his job. The marshals phoned through to race control, and first rider off — Giacomo Agostini — was asked to wait until the ropes were in place. Later in the day, George appeared at Michael Motors complaining that his Norton wouldn't run properly, causing him to be late for barrier duty that morning. Having pushed the bike into the workshop, Ellis diagnosed a sticking valve, and told George to rev the nuts off the bike whilst he gave it a good shot of Redex lubricant into the carburettor. This duly filled the whole workshop with white smoke, causing much hilarity, but did free the valve. I think George got the sack from barrier duties for that incident.

Life moved on, and in 1969, a month after I finished my apprenticeship, Shelagh and I got married. I was just 21 and Shelagh, 20. It all went swimmingly, and after a three-day honeymoon in a Tring pub we agreed to have a holiday at the TT again (had to get our priorities right!). We stayed with Ellis and his wife, Diane, in their tiny cottage in Kirkmichael. I helped Ellis in the garage and Shelagh got involved with their two small daughters. We then returned to life in our semi-detached, two-bedroom chalet bungalow in Houghton Regis in Bedfordshire — price new: £4200! I was now earning £20 a week plus overtime, and Shelagh had a job as a typist in Luton town hall.

Work at Thermo Plastics was alright, with plenty of overtime. In the summer months I played in the works cricket team in a local league, and at lunchtimes often played snooker or darts with workmates in the clubhouse. One of these, Ron the forklift driver, would often only just beat me, and commented that I must have a "cupboard full of second prizes," as I'd give anything a go, sports-wise, though excelled at nothing. I became friendly with several of the maintenance engineers, one of whom, Eric Blakely, road-raced motorcycles. He had a 125cc Bultaco that he regularly crashed, and eventually ended up with a Suzuki that met the same fate. Eric transported his bikes to race meetings in an old Citroën DS estate car, and I sometimes went along as mechanic. He eventually left Thermo Plastics and went to work at Whitbread Brewery in Luton, where he became notorious for turning up for work on a Monday after having crashed the day before whilst racing; feigning sickness or work-related injury so that he could go off sick to recover, and still be paid! Eric also had a sideline in supplying bottles of barley wine to his pals, and I frequently met him coming off shift toting a very heavily-laden rucksack destined for a 'customer.'

Eric introduced me to both Dick Upstone and Alan Wright, who also worked at the brewery. Dick had an Ariel Arrow sprint bike, and our paths sometimes crossed at sprint meetings. Alan worked in the stores, and was a Velocette fan. He managed to 'acquire' a large stock of stainless nuts and bolts in common use in the brewing industry, and most of our bikes benefited from cash purchases from him. He also owned a Velocette Venom nicknamed 'Torrey Canyon' as it leaked oil profusely. Several years later my pal, John Walker, became the lucky/unlucky owner of this well-lubricated machine. Through his brewing trade contacts, Alan also knew someone who worked nights in a chrome-plating firm; our bikes and his pocket also benefited from this contact.

I could now walk to work, but I yearned to own a motorcycle again. My Shooting Star had been sold to my cousin Francis a year earlier, and he ultimately crashed and wrecked it. Shelagh let me keep some of my overtime pay, and I bought two bikes within a short period. Around 1970, Dick Findlay sold me a Velocette MAC-framed special, and I bought and fitted a Velocette MAC motor that I fettled. The entire project cost about £30 to complete.

When I bought the bike, it came with a dismantled KSS engine that I kept with the intention of eventually building a completely standard KSS. The 'special' had direct lighting, a drip-feed to lubricate the primary chain, and a small BSA fibreglass fuel tank. I didn't understand that the gudgeon pin was fully floating in the MAC piston, so I drilled the gudgeon pin boss and fitted a tiny grub screw, using serious amounts of Loctite to secure the pin to the piston. This remained in place until I sold the bike, forgetting to tell the new owner about the grub screw. In later years I often thought of the problems he would have when trying to remove that piston!

Dick Findlay built and sprinted a KSS Velocette that had a long wheelbase and lightweight frame, and I often went to events with him. I fancied a go at cheap motorcycle sport, so when I saw an advert for a KSS sprinter owned by a chap called Laurie Nunn who lived in Cambridge, I paid him a visit and bought 'Cammilot:' a lovely, purpose-built sprint bike. It was designed to run on methanol, and was lubricated by Castrol R. Dick and I sprinted for several years and, although he usually beat me (he weighed around three stone less than me), I did win a couple of events in my 350cc class at Duxford and Bassingbourn.

Around this time Dick owned a Ford 107E van that was fitted with a Willment conversion. It also had a four-branch exhaust system, and a four-speed gearbox. It was very quick, but frequently blew cylinder head gaskets. I bought this van from Dick thinking I could fix its issues, but it proved very unreliable for me as well, so I sold it, and for £75, bought a lovely 1965 Ford Anglia 105E van as a replacement.

I did take Cammilot to the island one year, having entered the Ramsey sprint with high hopes. John Walker provided his Ford Thames van as transport, and with his wife, Linda, and Shelagh we were a happy team. I took the Velo Special along for both road use and 'circuits'! Ellis suggested that we take Cammilot up onto the back roads on Snaefell Mountain to test her, which we did. After travelling all that distance from home, the top camshaft bevels stripped. With no spares but a sprint entry, we prepared the Special for combat by fitting a huge megaphone exhaust that Ellis fabricated. We had the loudest/slowest bike competing in the event. John and I then took turns in lashing the poor bike around the 37¾ miles of TT course, both coming to the same conclusion that top speed was 'nearly' 80mph. The Special was not very special (knackered, actually) by the end of our holiday.

I entered Cammilot in an event at Santa Pod raceway and, to celebrate, bought a gallon of nitro methane from Alf Hagon, the famous grass track racer and sprinter's shop in Leytonstone, East London. The 10 per cent nitro we added to methanol really improved performance, but on one fateful run, the increased power proved too much, and the slight wheelie that the torque encouraged pulled the bottom out of the crankcase. We then added strengthened bottom frame rails, but I gradually lost interest and sold the bike. Successful sprinting involved constant engine development, and I had very little tuning knowledge.

One good decision I did make at this time was to buy a mint-condition Mk 2 KSS Velocette motor from a fellow sprinter. He had tried to supercharge the bike he owned but it never ran properly, and he ultimately gave up on the project (I think he fitted a Triumph engine). I bought the KSS motor and a large case of other spares for £100 and had a starting point for my own KSS project. I stored this lovely motor in our bedroom wardrobe for a number of years, much to my wife's anguish.

I was still looking for a 'complete' overhead camshaft Velocette, and in 1972, saw an advert in *Motor Cycle News* for a 1936 Mk 2 KTS priced at £15. The KTS was the touring version of the KSS; the only difference being smaller wheels and valanced mudguards. The advert also offered for sale a 1935 Mk 1 KTS. I called in sick at work and roared off to Leatherhead in Surrey with just 15 quid in my wallet.

To my dismay, there was already a chap waiting in the front garden. The seller's wife said her husband would soon be home from work, so we both waited in silence, with me hoping he was after the Mk 1. After a short while I broached the subject and, fortunately, he was! I was much relieved as a long queue was beginning to form. The seller was a gentleman who didn't push up the price when faced with multiple potential buyers, and I came away with an almost complete bike. A chap in the queue offered me £15 just for the petrol tank as I was leaving! Thank goodness I bought my *MCN* early that morning. The only parts missing were the headlamp, saddle, and one fuel tank knee pad.

I spent a year or so restoring the bike, and managed to source the missing knee pad from O'Neills, a Velocette and Royal Enfield spares dealer on the Edgware Road near Hendon in North London. When I called in, the motorcycle side of the business was in the process of closing down. (It was also a yacht chandler, being located very near to the Welsh Harp lake.) Very few Velocette parts were left when I got there, though there was one knee pad ... and it was the side I needed! Pre-war Velocette parts were becoming difficult to obtain by this time, and pattern spares were not yet being made.

I kept and rode this bike for 20 years, and won one or two Vintage Club concours events with it, too. In local events, frustratingly, I was often beaten by Ben French from St Albans, who owned the most beautiful 1936 500cc Rudge Ulster, and was a very skilled restorer/engineer.

Shelagh had trouble finding a job she enjoyed, and we decided the time was ripe to start a family. Unfortunately, she suffered a miscarriage early in her first pregnancy whilst we were on holiday at the 1970 TT races, and we had to stay over for an extra week whilst she recovered, well looked after in Ramsey Cottage Hospital whilst I lodged with Ellis and Diane. The boys in The Mitre bought me beer every night as I had run out of money by then, and I repaid Ellis by working the petrol pumps at his garage and being a general dogsbody on the mechanical side. I had a great time whilst Shelagh relaxed! I can still remember spending a happy afternoon in the sun assisting Ellis and his welding torch to try and straighten a very bent cattle clamp.

In 1972 we moved to a semi-detached house next to Dunstable Downs, still in Bedfordshire, and again within walking distance of work. By then we already had one daughter, Amanda, who was born in 1971, and very soon Shelagh was pregnant with our second child, who we called Julie. After her miscarriage Shelagh had been very well looked after by our GP, Doctor Twivy, who had a special interest in pregnancy. Under his expert guidance and with the drugs he prescribed, further family problems were eradicated.

Fortunately, the new house had a good-sized detached garage, where I spent many happy hours restoring the KTS and maintaining Cammilot. By this time, I had left the toolroom at Thermo Plastics to become a moulding technician on the same wages. I was never going to make a 'real' toolmaker, and I was interested in the huge moulding presses. Sarcasm and back-stabbing were rife in the toolroom, and the moulding shop seemed a much happier place to be.

In 1973, a year or so after we moved house, the three-day week was introduced due to industrial action taken across the country by the miners; all of my overtime and part of my wages disappeared. The moulding presses had to be shut down, and then restarted and brought up to temperature every three days. Life at home became very difficult, money-wise. At one stage we even took in a lodger though we only managed to scrape by even then, and couldn't afford to modify the house as we had hoped when we moved there.

Eventually, the industrial action — which concerned an overtime ban — ceased, and we returned to normal working hours. I was promoted to Technical Foreman, proving new moulds and running one of the big warehouse-sized moulding shops. We made beer and soft drink crates, and other smaller products in many different plastic materials. Management approach was frustrating as they always thought they knew better than those on the shop floor, and often tried to cut costs with disastrous results. Cheaper raw materials and increased production targets never achieved a satisfactory product, often resulting in reduced output and disillusioned workers. I sympathised with them!

My wages were adequate by now, though, and, for £600, I bought the bike of my dreams — a 1954 Series C Vincent Rapide with some

Black Shadow modifications. I convinced my wife that it was a good investment: it wouldn't be the first time that I used this ploy!

The bike was lovely to ride, but a mechanical minefield. Shelagh wasn't impressed with the lack of comfort of the pillion seat, but I loved riding the bike across Dunstable Downs in the dead of night, after a couple of pints in my new local — The Red Lion in Studham. At various times after moving to Dunstable, both Shelagh and I worked there on the odd evening, and often on Sunday lunchtimes. It added a few bob to the kitty, and we made many friends.

When I bought that lovely shiny bike it transpires I should have taken a Vincent expert with me, as I was sold a bit of a pup. The motor was tired; burnt a fair bit of oil, and the gearbox was knackered. I joined the local branch of the Vincent Owners Club, and began to discover the mistakes. I'd taken out a bank loan to buy the bike, so therefore had little or no money to fix all the issues. Ownership of my dream bike lasted about nine months, and, in 1975, I sold it for £775 to a chap who took it to Australia. I hope he had a bigger budget than I did!

Around this time, a Vintage Motorcycle Club pal of mine called Jay (Jeremy) Hall offered to sell me a 1930 500cc Royal Enfield, for which I paid him £17.50. 'Barn find' didn't come close: it was in terrible condition, although just qualified for the famous Banbury Run because it was first registered prior to 31 December, 1930. Jay told me that the bike had been found beneath a veranda, from where he had rescued it. He later told me that he had made a handsome profit when he sold it to me! I hand-painted the cycle parts using Tekaloid enamel paint, and a friend of Shelagh's from her church painted the petrol tank very professionally. I spent hours getting the valanced mudguards to look good, filling and rubbing down the rusted items before adding several layers of enamel top coat.

About a week before the Banbury Run I was ready to try and start the bike, but although it would fire initially, it wouldn't run properly. I checked everything, and eventually found that the two sprockets driving the timing chain had different numbers of teeth, so that on every rotation of the motor the ignition setting changed. The sprockets had not been fitted to the motor when I got the bike, and had come in a box with several other engine parts. I made a new sprocket blank from mild steel on a lathe at work, filing the teeth by hand. At last the bike ran properly when I re-timed it for the umpteenth time.

I rode it in the run and got a finisher's spoon, but going up the famous Sunrising Hill the clutch slipped badly. The last straw was when a spectator at Banbury informed me that my precious, painstakingly-restored mudguards were incorrect, and originated from a 1930s BSA

Around this time Roy Richardson was advertising to buy bikes for the new National Motorcycle Museum, and he bought the Enfield from me for a little over £300. I just about got back the money I had spent restoring it and said good riddance. I saw the bike on display there a few years ago: with the correct mudguards and leather tool boxes fitted; it looked lovely. Best place for it! Compared with a vintage Velocette, it was a very poorly-engineered bike.

Many things were about to change: my career and hobby were on 'the up!'

CHAPTER 2

ROAD RACING AT LAST ...
PLUS A NEW CAREER

DURING 1975 I BECAME VERY DISILLUSIONED WITH WORK IN THE factory, so I decided to follow my heart and try to join the police. As a boy I had watched *Dixon of Dock Green* on the TV, and held a secret wish to be his Station Sergeant. My father thought I'd gone mad, and did everything he could to make me change my mind. Shelagh was fully on board, as we wanted to completely change our lifestyle and move to the Isle of Man as well.

I took the police entrance examination in London and passed well: the Manx Constabulary had one of the highest pass mark requirements and I achieved this level. My application had been submitted some while ago, and there was another long wait after I passed the exam. Eventually, I was told that there was no likelihood of a vacancy, and it was suggested I try another force. To say we were upset is an understatement, but I was determined and applied to the Derbyshire force. Dick Findlay had by now moved there, so we knew the county well and loved its rural areas. My exam results were adequate and I had to travel up for an interview, which went well, but a couple of weeks afterwards, this force also wrote to advise that it had no vacancies ...

By this point I was even more determined to become a police officer, and, in desperation, applied to the Metropolitan Police. I went to London for an interview but, after a lengthy session, I was informed that I had failed this. I believe it was felt that I wouldn't want to work and live with my young family in inner London after residing in the home counties. Much family discussion took place, but I wouldn't be persuaded to give up and promptly sent in an application to the Hertfordshire force.

I also knew that I just had to have a go at road racing and bought a 350cc 1969 Aermacchi Ala D'Oro for £600, after seeing an advert in *Motorcycle News*. At this time, the single cylinder racing class was popular, and I really wanted to own and race a thoroughbred Grand Prix bike. I travelled to Northampton where the vendor, Rod Dawe, lived. The bike appeared to be in good condition, and looked very original. It was in the colours of the famous tuner Francis Beart — Ludlow Green — and I promptly paid the asking price. Rod gave me loads of advice regarding starting and maintaining the bike, but warned me that they were fickle things!

Rod was the second racing owner of the machine, the original being Theo Louwes from Holland. Theo had ordered it new from Sid Lawton, the Aermacchi concessionaire in Southampton, and had commissioned Beart to tune and prepare the bike. He rode the bike to second place in the Dutch 350cc Championship and was a top-level racer. Rod subsequently bought the bike, and raced it at a number of British circuits, achieving some good results, particularly in the wet. He had maintained the relationship with Francis Beart, and I decided to do the same. I contacted Beart and he agreed to maintain the bike for me.

Soon after my purchase I was invited to Hertfordshire Constabulary's HQ at Welwyn Garden City for an interview. At this point I should own up to the fact that I had numerous points on my driving licence due to misdemeanours on my BSA. I had owned the bike for only a few months when a speed cop, on his Triumph Speed Twin, pulled me up on my way home from work in Northwood. Three points and a good telling off for doing 45mph in a 30mph limit was the result. About a year later, I was riding home with Shelagh on the pillion when I got nicked again. I had been working on the bike, and suddenly remembered I had promised to collect Shelagh from her home in Wealdstone. Unfortunately, I hadn't got around to refitting the fairing. As we raced along a local road, helmetless, at well over the 30mph limit, I heard a tinkling sound, and had a quick check around the bike before glancing behind and realising that the sound came from the chrome bell mounted on the front bumper of a police Daimler Dart that was chasing after us. I pulled up quickly as soon as I realised, and the heavy old Daimler skidded past us, its wheels locking up and squealing. The driver emerged and, with handlebar moustache bristling, spluttered "Maniacs like you should be off the road!" More points for speeding, no horn (it was fixed to the missing fairing), and dangerous vehicle condition as I'd decided that my bike didn't really need a rear chain guard. For some reason the charge of 'no front index plate' (also on the missing fairing) was dropped.

My third conviction occurred whilst I was travelling to Dunstable one Saturday morning, on my way to work from my home in Kenton. I was enjoying the traffic-free pleasures of the sweeping bends on the A5 Roman Road as I approached Radlett, whilst also appreciating the lovely barking sound emitting from the twin Gold Star straight through silencers I had recently fitted. There was no speed limit on that stretch of road then, and I was going well: so well that I failed to brake sufficiently for the 30mph limit signs as I entered Radlett village itself, whereupon a police motorcyclist flagged me down just after the signs and booked me for speeding and excessive noise. I went to court and pleaded guilty to speeding in a 30mph limit, but not guilty regarding the excessive noise, claiming that, as standard BSA silencers were fitted, they must have been efficient. The traffic bobby had done his homework though, and had documentation that proved they were pattern items. Even more points, and I had to use the solicitor that Shelagh now worked for to keep my licence, as I needed it to enable me to get to work. I was still an apprentice, and I think the whole deal landed me with a £25 fine that was to be paid at £2 a week.

The interview at the Herts police HQ was lengthy, and I was cautioned regarding my driving record and told that motorcycling would have to stop if I joined the constabulary. Of course, I promised to refrain forever, and I was accepted for initial probationer training to start that year, in October 1976. I breathed a sigh of relief and we put our house on the market, just as Shelagh announced she was pregnant again — oops!

Although the road racing season was almost finished for the year, I wanted to at least try out the Aermacchi, and so, with dad as mechanic and pusher, entered a midweek practice day at Brands Hatch.

My father had retired early, aged 62, and I found out quite recently that he had suffered a slight nervous breakdown. His last years at work were very pressurised, and he often brought the problems home. Until he retired we got on okay, but I had a rather distant relationship with him, and he and my mother spent all of their free time playing flat green bowls to county level. I guess it took his mind off work, and in his later life we got on well. Bit too late by then, though. Throughout their lives my parents implored me to take up bowls and give up motorcycles. They were both risk-averse like many of their age group who had been through the Second World War. Anyway, the practice day went alright with me circulating at the same time as Mick Grant and some other locally-based 'stars.' I felt my way around whilst they ducked and dived around me. It was the first and last time dad ever saw me on a road racing bike.

The police provided us with a cold and soulless house in Rickmansworth, where I would be stationed after completing my initial three months training at Eynsham Hall Police Training College. The house was on a flood plain next to Rickmansworth Aquadrome, and was very damp, so when we moved in, the pristine Aermacchi went to live in the front sitting room, at least for the winter months.

The three months passed quickly for me, and slowly for Shelagh. I missed the family terribly, but was fully occupied with the theory and practical lessons. Eynsham had a small, subsidised bar, and I quickly learnt to like the local Hook Norton bitter, and made some very good friends from Hertfordshire and other county forces. One of them, Alun Thomas, who was with Bedfordshire police at the time, encouraged me to write this book; we're still great pals.

Our family car was a 1967 1500c VW Beetle, and I used this to travel home every two weeks for weekend leave. It snowed heavily that winter (our passing out parade was cancelled), and the rear-engined Beetle was 'fun' to drive on slippery surfaces: 'useless' would be a better description!

The teenage probationers were very homesick and I tried to support them, in return for which they helped me with the theory homework, and allowed me to be goal keeper during our sports periods. My penalty was to go and get the tea at half-time, as I was expendable during the game. I was 28 when I joined the police and they called me 'Grandad.' I struggled with the required swimming qualifications, but with much encouragement and extra tuition from the younger lads, I just managed to recover the brick from the deep end without drowning. I still loathe swimming. The end-of-course long distance run saw me finish twentieth from the eighty lads on our course intake. Many of them just gave up when it hurt, but I plodded on. My pain tolerance is quite high, as you'll discover later!

I did pass out from Eynsham near the end of December, and started work on foot patrol in Rickmansworth on night shift over Christmas. The little woman was not impressed! I had a good shift to work with, and was encouraged by one of the experienced area car drivers, Derek Shine, to learn to two-finger type as I'd have plenty of it to do, so it was no use avoiding the issue. This has stood me in good stead ever since.

I did only one week of foot patrol, and then became an observer in one of the double-crewed panda cars. After about six months I undertook a basic driving course and, as I was over 21, also qualified to drive Transit vans. I soon learned about and joined Hertfordshire Constabulary Motor Club, and went along to the meetings. Fortunately, there were few competing members and, as the club received a grant each year from the Police Central Sports and Social fund, this was to be my benefactor for many years, helping towards some of my travel costs and entry fees. I could fill another book with police tales, and I spent many happy years driving fast cars and riding police motorcycles for a living.

Katherine was born on May 3, 1977, and my first race was the day after Shelagh came home with the baby. My priorities never seem to have agreed with hers! I entered a number of race meetings at Brands Hatch during the year, and a couple of other circuits including Snetterton and Waterbeach, which was a military camp in Cambridgeshire. This meeting was run by the Newmarket Club and, although simple in format, I quite enjoyed the open spaces. Many of the meetings I entered were run by the British Motorcycle Racing Club (Bemsee) and the Southern 67 Racing Club. All the races involved bump starts, and the technique was not easy to acquire. Carburetion had to be spot-on, and throttle control delicate: no flapping of the twist grip. It was a long learning curve but I began to finish nearer to the midfield than the back, and the bike proved a delight to ride and also reliable. I transported it on a three-bike trailer which also carried a large coffin-like container that my dad made from plywood with aluminium corner trims. A Volkswagen Beetle has little boot space ...

My competitors at that time included some names well known in classic racing circles today. Malcolm Wheeler, who, until recently, owned Mortons Media Group; motorcycle racing journalist Alan Cathcart; Aermacchi spares guru Dick Linton, and Reg Arnold were all fast riders on their own immaculate Aermacchis. I was in good company. I also made friends with experienced racer Roger Imberg during an early meeting at Brands Hatch when we set up in the same part of the paddock. At that time he was campaigning a 750cc Triumph Metisse that seemed to gently self-destruct at most meetings we went to. It vibrated alarmingly, and much time was spent effecting Heath Robinson-style repairs between races to try and keep it together. It was fast, though. He and his wife, Pam, became lifelong family friends, and our young children played together at the circuits. Roger had been road racing for a number of years, and ultimately became a Classic Racing Motorcycle Club champion. He provided me with much valuable advice and guidance as I tried to improve; these days we exchange memories more than advice.

My first season proved a steep learning curve. I fell off early in the 1977 season whilst racing at Brands Hatch when I ran out of bottle around what was then called 'Bottom Bend' (now named

Graham Hill Bend). I floated out onto the grass on the outside of the corner, skidded out of control on the kerbing, and the bike and I slid to a stop alongside a marshal's post in a heap of damaged fibreglass and hurt pride. No injuries but no more racing that day. A couple of meetings later, Alan Cathcart and I were on our 'out lap' for a practice session when, approaching Clearways and on the main straight, we were overtaken by a novice on a Kawasaki who was clearly out of control. Just after the apex of the bend, the novice threw the bike down the road directly in front of us and, with bike and rider spinning down the track, neither Alan or I managed to avoid the debris, ultimately joining the carnage! Fortunately, there were no injuries, and Alan leapt to his fee, calling the unfortunate novice all sorts of unkind names. I was just glad to be unhurt with a bike that was only slightly damaged and still raceable.

Later in the year, my first visit to the Thruxton circuit was a disaster. I felt out of my depth; it rained heavily; in my only race water got into the ignition, then I collected a rear wheel puncture and had to retire. We had no van or awning, so it was pretty miserable, and I began to wonder whether I would ever be a competent racer. Self-doubt is part of my make-up and I often question my own decisions, relying on friends and family for reassurance.

The bike was fast enough, but my skills needed honing. Everyone used Dunlop triangular tyres at this time, and throwing the bike over onto the flat side of the tyre took nerve. We used five star petrol such as ESSO Golden or Shell Super. The Castrol R vegetable-based oil that many of us used smelled wonderful, and we warmed it on primus stoves prior to putting it into our precious motors: everyone owned a special grubby saucepan for this very reason. The modern equivalent just doesn't have the same delicious aroma.

All races began with a push-start, and much time was spent in the paddock prior to racing, practising the starting technique. The Aermacchi routine was critical as the carburettor was mounted horizontally and had a remote float chamber. The slightest flapping of the twist grip guaranteed a stall, the bike would have to be pulled back on compression, and it would all have to be done again. I was far from expert at starting, however, and poor starts were not uncommon, due to my nervousness mixed with excitement.

The 1977 season passed quickly: Shelagh had produced Katherine Charlotte (Charlie) our third daughter, and Julie joined her elder sister at the junior school in Rickmansworth. Our eldest,

Amanda, distinguished herself at this time by using the 'eff' word to one of the dinner ladies, and Shelagh was called to the headmistress' office to explain. Honestly, I have no idea where she might have learned that word! Work was fine and I managed to get enough weekends off to put together a reasonable racing programme. The Beetle race transport was swapped for an air-cooled VW van, but serious engine problems soon put me off it, and it was replaced by a Vauxhall Viva estate car. The trailer was still employed and I now had some boot space. Our local police recovery garage was a friendly place, and the owner kindly agreed to respray the Aermacchi's paintwork for me. I chose a lovely dark blue colour but this alienated most of the traditional 'Macchi owners — red or Beart green being the only official choices. I also reduced the size of the Police Motor Club decal on the fairing. Previously displayed in large print, I found that some riders chose to keep me at arm's length when they discovered who my employer was! This issue has accompanied me throughout my racing career, although most competitors mellow when they get to know me better.

Our police house in Rickmansworth was so damp that we had toads in the garden, and after we left the section of the road near our house suffered flooding. In the winter we had ice inside the Critall (steel-framed) windows, and the garage in a block of five at the rear of the houses was so damp it was only any use as a car shelter. I did manage to service the 'Macchi during the winter, and looked forward to the new 1978 season.

I again entered a number of race meetings at Brands Hatch, Snetterton, and Cadwell Park. Results improved and, in most of these races, I managed to finish in the first half of the entry, gaining points towards a national licence that would allow me to enter more prestigious events. To be fair, many of our races were a combination of 250 and 350 singles classes, and my Aermacchi was one of the better machines: ninth and tenth places were typical for me. Opposition usually consisted of Ducatis, AJS 7Rs, and two-stroke singles such as Cottons and Montesas. If I entered four-stroke races for 250/500cc machines they were usually won by Dick Cutts or Richard Ruth, and they both rode 500cc Seeley Matchless machines owned by Dick Cutts. Alan Cathcart would often be the best 350. I frequently diced with a Ducati rider called Bob Field. The 'Macchi remained reliable but did have an appetite for the chrome plating on its cam followers, probably due to me occasionally missing gears and exceeding the normal rev limit. Dick Linton made a small fortune from me in replacements!

At the end of a Brands meeting in June, Alan Cathcart asked me if I was going to enter the Manx Grand Prix the following September. I hadn't really thought about it but Alan said "You must have enough points on your licence by now, I've got a spare entry form if you want it." I had finished in the first half of race finishers again so went to get my licence signed at the race office: sure enough, I just qualified. Shelagh and I had a heart-to-heart, and I persuaded her that I just had to try and get an entry. Reading the entry form we realised that entries closed the following day, so rushed home to complete the form.

Early the next morning I drove to Heathrow and rushed to the departure gate that travellers to the Isle of Man and Ireland passed through. I planned to ask someone going to the Isle of Man if they would deliver my entry by hand to the race office in Douglas: it was the only way I could get it there in time. The first person I asked was going to Ireland, but I struck lucky with the second: a middle-aged chap who said he would love to help a rider, and would ensure he got it to the race office in time. He succeeded in this and I was accepted as the last entry in the 1978 Newcomers' Race!

I did another couple of meetings after that, and then visited Francis Beart at his lovely cottage in Sussex to ask him to prepare my motor for the island. Francis was rather elderly but still maintaining motors for existing customers. I remember that he criticised me because the throttle cable attached to my carburettor was slightly kinked. He completed the work quite quickly and I carefully prepared my bike for the mountain course. I had left it rather late to arrange digs and garage facilities on the island but Derek Chittenden, a friend and brilliant engineer who made the Hejeira racing motorcycles, kindly offered me some of his garage space in Union Mills, where he and his family stayed. His landlady agreed that my little family could set up camp in the loft of the garage that Derek was using in her rear garden. It was going to be an adventure!

We loaded all of my kit and the Aermacchi onto the trailer and, with three kids, piles of nappies, and a lot of apprehension, set off in our Viva estate, which made it to Liverpool, and was the last vehicle squeezed onto the ferry for the four-hour crossing. Being last aboard we were actually parked on the deck and, with inclement weather looming, Shelagh and our three daughters were directed to a 'ladies only' cabin, whilst I elected to doze in the car, correctly deducing that the soft Vauxhall suspension might absorb some of the ship's movement. A little later, as the old boat lifted and dropped in the heavy swell, I was woken by four very green-faced girls who thought they would feel less sick and be more comfortable in the car. That was the end of my kip!

On our arrival with Derek, he allocated me a corner of the garage and I settled down to check over my bike. I enjoyed watching and listening to Derek's preparation of the Hejeira, trying to learn more about my chosen hobby. I received lots of valuable advice from Derek and his mechanic pal as they worked on the bike that their rider would soon be thrashing round the course. Practice was a steep learning curve and I loved the ride up to the pits for the 6.00am morning sessions. All went well until during one evening session later in the week, when I noticed oil seeping from behind the cover of the outside flywheel, and dripping onto my left boot. I sought help from the Bladon brothers, Paul and Chris, who were regarded as Aermacchi experts, and were on the island supporting riders of bikes they had prepared. I needed a threaded puller to remove the flywheel and they kindly lent me one. Once the flywheel was off I could see that the screws retaining the driveside main bearing cover had come loose because they'd not been wire-locked during the engine rebuild.

Riding flat out at over a hundred miles an hour through Kirkmichael and other villages on the TT course just after dawn was a unique experience that is no longer available to modern riders. I'm convinced that on some mornings there were very few marshals up on the mountain, but health and safety made itself known in the late '90s when practice was not allowed until enough marshals were available. Silencers were not required, either, and the Aermacchi rattled the windows of houses with its sharp exhaust crackle. I concentrated on my racing lines, and tried to keep tucked in under the low fairing screen. No amount of short circuit racing prepares you for a lap of just under 30 minutes' length, and we were scheduled to do four of them during the race. One mistake and death — or, at the very least, serious injury — would be the result; best not think about that, eh? Just concentrate. As Michelle Duff says in *The Mike Duff Story: Make Haste, Slowly*, that's very good advice.

By this point I had completed many laps of the course on open roads, and Ellis and the boys at the pub had given me much advice, but finding the correct lines on closed roads is an altogether different thing. Dick Linton had kindly agreed to do a tutorial lap with me in my car, and this proved an eye-opener. I had no hope of remembering everything he told me but I gleaned lots of useful information, and hoped I could at least remember some of it. Many of the bends are blind, and it takes time to form a picture in the back of your mind that will allow you to keep the throttle pinned, and aim for the late apex that takes you safely round the corner and on your way to the next challenge, be it another bend, a jump, or hard braking for a hairpin. It's addictive and I'm a confirmed junkie!

Race day arrived far too quickly and the weather was not kind. The start was delayed, which made us newcomers even more nervous, and the organisers decided not to run the race scheduled to follow ours later in the day, but did let us start several hours after the allotted time. The race distance was reduced to three laps, and most of the course remained wet or damp. The mountain was hooded with Mona's Cloak (or thick mist as we know it). At one point in the pits Shelagh heard the commentator from The Bungalow, high on Snaefell mountain, say that he could hear the bikes but not see them. The race was tricky and miserable. I realised that my course knowledge was inadequate in the mist; I simply couldn't remember the exact sequences of bends for the eight or so miles of mountain road. There are few solid roadside features up there, and one kink looks just like another; often, my only choice was to follow the white line as visibility was down to about 50 yards in places. My bike didn't enjoy the rain and ran poorly as moisture crept into the carburettor. I did finish 19th out of 26 finishers, and the third Aermacchi from the six that finished, the rest of the bikes that completed being Yamahas, but I felt cheated out of a good race. The postponed second race was run the next day in perfect conditions just to add to my frustration. My feeling was that the organisers had gone ahead with our race to reduce a possible log jam if the following scheduled races suffered similar delays. Were we 'newcomers' so dispensable ...?

CHAPTER 3

A FLIRTATION WITH GRASS TRACK RACING, AND OTHER PAINFUL EXPERIENCES

THE 1978 MANX GRAND PRIX WAS THE AERMACCHI'S SWAN SONG, and Shelagh and I decided that the purchase of a house should be our priority. House prices were rocketing, and we were rapidly losing out on the property ladder. We never recovered from the financial losses incurred during our two years in the police house, and this cost us any chance of buying a larger house in subsequent years. We needed a deposit, and one of my bikes had to go.

Single cylinder road racing was losing popularity and the Aermacchi was worth more than my Velocette KTS, so it was sold via *Motorcycle News* to a club racer, Graham Godward, for £995. We bought a reasonably modern but quite spacious ex-housing association terraced house in Hemel Hempstead, and settled down to family life.

After two years in the police I was accepted into the traffic department, and enjoyed several years of driving large fast cars and motorcycles for a living. Police advanced drivers are graded according to their capabilities under test, and I gained a grade one in cars but only a two on the bikes. I was regarded as fast but slightly 'scruffy' on the bikes … harsh but true. A couple of years later my car grade was downgraded to a two after a refresher course. On test day whilst driving a V8 Rover I was exiting the A1 motorway and, travelling quickly in the middle lane in rain, I slowed slightly to allow a motorcyclist in the nearside lane to clear the exit before I roared up the slip road. My examiner later told me that my grade one lay at that junction on the A1, as I should have exited in front of the biker. I disagreed as I would have covered the biker in spray, but it did me no good. It hurt my pride as I had made an informed decision, but it made no difference to the vehicles I was allowed to drive, and I just had to deal with it.

One of the more memorable arrests I was involved in whilst with the traffic department involved a local known troublemaker. I was driving a Range Rover on night shift when our vehicle was assigned to assist in a chase, following this man trying to elude the police and in possession of a large knife. My partner was already occupied at the police station with the paperwork concerning a suspected drink driver that we had arrested a few minutes previously, so I was on my own. I roared out of the station yard single-crewed, and listened carefully to the radio. The chase went off towards Watford from my location in Hemel Hempstead, and I realised I would never catch up in the heavy vehicle I had, so I parked up near the M1 motorway hoping that the Ford Transit the man was driving would come my way. Well, it did, but the man used the back road from Watford and not the motorway. I accelerated away towards a junction with this back road and, as I arrived, I was met by a string of blue lights in the distance coming towards me. I stopped at the junction, and waited patiently whilst the offender's van approached my position and came to a stop a little way from my position. We had a stand off! He then accelerated as fast as he could to try and get past the front of me, but I drove into the front offside wing of his van, and pushed it sideways using my V8 four-wheel drive power. The van made contact with the end of a substantial wall, and I kept my foot on the accelerator, pinning it there. The driver refused to get out of the van, even after a police dog handler politely asked him to, so a large German Shepherd was allowed to jump into the van, dutifully and gleefully biting the driver until he surrendered.

After all the excitement I had a look at the Range Rover, which appeared virtually undamaged. My Sergeant had to deal with it as it was a 'police vehicle accident,' and after he had made a sketch of the scene, he asked me to reverse away from the van. I shoved the gear lever of the Range Rover into reverse, and as I moved backward, there was a loud metallic noise. I quickly stopped, but not before realising I had pulled off my vehicle's front bumper as it had been tucked inside the front wing of the Transit. Bother, it had all gone so well up until then.

Another incident of interest concerned our new BMW R80 police motorcycles. Several riders complained of steering-shake at high speed, and this began to cause great concern. I offered to try and establish the cause, and soon found a suitable downhill bend on a stretch of dual carriageway to test this. Our police bikes had a heavy set of radio equipment on the rear carrier, and I discovered that, if travelling at high speed and moving backward on the ample single seat, the steering did indeed feel vague. If I moved my weight forward and pushed, instead of pulling on the handlebars all was well. However, these bikes were also fitted with panniers, and if these were also heavily-loaded the problem became worse. I think the aerodynamics of the large police fairings didn't help either, but at least we now understood the problem, and could take measures to prevent a disaster by adapting our riding style.

Being a member of the Police Motor Club kept me connected nationally to police motor sport, and early in 1981 I was approached to see if I wanted to take part in a competitive motorcycle road rally in the Pyrenees as part of a British team. I jumped at the chance of course, and was soon asked to go and collect a brand new 350cc LC Yamaha from Yamaha's headquarters. Yamaha had agreed to sponsor the British police in the event, and loaned the team two 350 LCs and a 250. I ran in the bike and soon began to love it.

I thoroughly enjoyed the event itself, which occurred in early summer, and I finished in the middle of the overall results, winning a gaudy plastic trophy for first in class. Some years later I retraced the route with Shelagh, and the scenery in summer, with snow on the high peaks, was stunning. I hadn't taken it all in during the event as I was concentrating on thrashing the LC.

After the event Yamaha offered the bikes to us at trade prices. I couldn't resist and bought mine. I did many road miles on it, sometimes with my nine-year-old daughter, Julie, as pillion. She often nodded off behind me: I knew when this happened as her helmet began to nudge me in the middle of my back. I did road race just once on the Yamaha, at a Cadwell Park club meeting in 1982, with mixed results in both production races and high speed trials.

I should add that, during 1979/80, my friend, Jay Hall, had offered me the chance to own a Mk 1 KSS Velocette. He owned two of these bikes, stored in bits in his large garage for years, and he said that if I built him one using the best parts, I could have the second one as payment. Finding parts for these 1935, four-speed Velocettes was difficult but, using contacts I had forged over the previous years, I managed to build quite a respectable bike for Jay, and mine also looked good, though tired mechanically. It took about a year or so to complete both bikes. As, cosmetically, mine looked great, I decided to sell it whilst in newly-rebuilt condition to fund my other motorcycling activities. I advertised it in 'the comic,' *Motorcycle News,* and found a buyer for £1495. Four-speed Mk 1s are not common as they were manufactured in 1934/5 only. They are so much lighter than the Mk 2 version, and very pleasant to ride. I sometimes regret parting with it so easily. Jay kept his for some years but ultimately sold it.

At the end of 1979 whilst all this was going on, I had decided on a possible change of direction, and bought myself a 500cc Ansel-JAP grass track racing bike. I still had the racing bug, and thought this might be a cheap alternative to road racing. It still involved single cylinder engines, which I loved, and although I never had the bottle to tackle speedway, I thought I might be able to give grass track a reasonable go. In our teens Shelagh and I had been fans of Wembley Lions, and often went to watch speedway at Wembley Stadium. Any crash usually involved a hard smack into the fence and a visit to hospital. At least in grass track the fences were only rope and the bikes had brakes, plus rear suspension.

Had to be easier and less painful ... didn't it?

The Ansel had a 4B JAP motor, an AMC two-speed gearbox, and DULA forks. I stripped the motor and found that the bottom end was in poor shape. George Greenwood Motorcycles in Kilburn repaired the flywheel assembly for me, and I bought new valves for £7 each, and new needle rollers for the rockers as a precaution. The whole job cost about £200, which brought the total cost of the bike to £500: not too bad.

Now, grass track racing looks relatively easy, but going round bends is not simple! I had spent two years learning to stick my knee out at Brands Hatch, and now I had to learn to stick my left foot out, and use it as a form of support. I fell into a sort of lean into the corners; leg trailing-style. This is okay if you have perfect balance and don't fall off — which, unfortunately, I did, occasionally. The Ansel had a sand racer-style frame, and a 19in rear wheel rim when I bought it, so I changed it for a 22in one in the hope that my left leg would naturally fall forward more. This did help, so the next step was to get the rear wheel sliding, keep the throttle open, and steer the front wheel into the skid. I was convinced that I was brave enough to do this, but it turns out I wasn't, as I thought I'd fall off. If the rear wheel slides on the road you shut the throttle ...

I gradually improved during 1980; more so if the track was reasonably smooth and not just a ploughed field. At least the bike was reliable and, by now, I had made friends with Paul Duncombe and Trevor Latimer who ran DULA Engineering in Kings Langley. They manufactured speedway and grass track bikes that were used by Simon and Julian Wigg, Trevor Banks, and other top racers at that time. I got to know these lads and did eventually improve my style, but all of them agreed that a 500 JAP is a bit of a fiery beast to learn on and that I would be better off with a Weslake motor. I just could not stretch our finances that far, though, and decided to buy a 350 JAP and sell the 500. A pal of Paul Duncombe had a DULA chassis for sale that was in good nick, so a deal was done for that, and I then bought a rather worn 350cc 4B JAP motor to complete things.

Les Kempster and his right-hand man, Tony Baker, at LGK Racing Motorcycles in East Wembley rebuilt the motor for me. I spent £225 on the chassis which was in good order; £100 on buying the motor, and another £140 rebuilding it. It sounds so cheap now, but I still didn't earn a lot in those days. It was cheaper than road racing, though. I put the bike together in Paul's workshop and, with his and Simon Wigg's advice and help, it was soon completed. Simon started the completed bike by pulling the rear wheel around with his hand. I was amazed as it had a 14:1 compression ratio, but Simon set up the carburettor carefully and she just sat there ticking over. I was chuffed.

The 1981 season started off wet, and several meetings were cancelled as a result. I sold the 500 for £325, and ultimately found the 350 much easier to control. I was in charge; not the bike. I still attracted a few comments from Paul's dad, an ex-speedway rider, regarding my road racing style, but results improved, and I did win a couple of heats at one Barnet Club meeting, held in a large park in Brixton. I found that moving my body forward when cornering helped a lot, and allowed the rear wheel to move around without disturbing the front of the bike so much. An ex-road racing friend who came to watch me at a Vampire Club meeting in Ware declared that he thought I was a different bloke, my style had changed so much. He'd seen me ride the previous year, and had told me to forget it and take up trials riding.

I enjoyed the 1981 season far more than 1980, but grass track was on the decline in our area and organising clubs were closing down. Then, in the autumn of that year, out of the blue, I got the offer to race a Velocette in vintage road racing that signalled the end of my grass track activities. Two Velocette Owners Club pals, Pete Clements and Ron Clowes, had collected enough parts to build the basics of a 500cc racing bike, and said that if I wanted to put the lot together I could compete on it. This sounded like a good proposition so the Dula-JAP was sold on and I planned a winter in my shed.

By now I knew Velocettes quite well and, during the winter of 1983, the chassis began to take shape. With Paul Duncombe's advice, and use of his factory machinery, I lightened many of the parts, and made others out of aluminium instead of standard steel. Pete and Ron were very experienced Velocette lads and they'd squirrelled away some really good items. They produced a gearbox that was in excellent condition and had close ratio gears. Pete knew of a local chap who had a mint front hub for sale, which we bought, and another pal in the Velocette Owners' Club supplied a lightweight 'cotton reel' rear item. Both brake drums were in good nick, and I soon got alloy rims fitted by our local wheel builder, Dick Waldron. A nice Amal GP racing carb and a top-spec BTH competition magneto added to the quality selection. I raided my KSS parts for a rear-set gear lever, and Thruxton Velocette fork dampers were fitted to a set of reconditioned fork legs. A decent pair of rear shock absorbers and a chronometric rev counter completed the basic list. In the meantime, Pete and I built up a nice 500cc Venom/MSS motor, and tuned it to the best of our knowledge, but it was relatively standard.

Our bike was never going to be pretty but it was functional, and I removed anything that wasn't necessary in the way of frame lugs and small fittings.

I had got to know Brian Barrow and Larry Swann. Larry was the brother of a very successful road racer called Ray Swann. Brian and Larry were both highly skilled fabricators, and worked in a farm-based unit in Studham, a few miles from where I lived. For a reasonable price they produced a lovely high level exhaust system and a 'trick' oil tank to allow the exhaust pipe to pass very close to it: together with a clever combined fork brace/front mudguard bracket, this completed the essential parts of our racer.

I used to find excuses to visit Brian and Larry, often to collect parts they had made for me, whilst I was on motorcycle patrol during my Traffic Police years. One day, I was approaching the farm when a chap road testing a Reliant Scimitar car he was thinking of buying pulled out of a side turning in front of me. I reacted quickly and tried to squeeze past him using the offside grass bank and almost made it, but just clipped a concrete post-based pillar box that was in the bank, that sent me and the police BMW bike spinning down the road. The bike slid to a halt on its side and I lay in the road wondering how I was going to explain this to my superiors. The farm was just over the county border in Bedfordshire, and I had no logical reason to be patrolling that area.

I was unhurt, and the BMW suffered only a few scratches, so I used the bike's radio to call my traffic base and asked for a Supervisory Officer to attend as required in all police vehicle accidents. Fortunately, my own shift Sergeant, Dick Catton, who I'd known for some years, was soon on the scene asking me what the hell I was doing there. I told him the truth and he decided that I had used a legitimate short-cut to an area in Hertfordshire requiring speeding patrols. This cost me a few drinks in the police station bar that I was happy to pay for. The car driver was never prosecuted, and I think Dick managed to get it all written off as 'no police action': probably the best result for all concerned.

Around this time I was on the bike squad at the traffic base. Watford FC was in the first division, and we provided escorts for the visiting teams' coaches and their fans. Sometimes these fans could be a trifle aggressive, so we used the oldest bikes for these duties in case they got damaged. For general duties we had BMW R75s and R80s, but there were still a few Norton Commandos in our garage, and these were wheeled out for 'footie' duty.

Naturally, because they had old-fashioned electrical systems, they were unreliable when it came to using the electric starters. The police radios drained the batteries, and when the bikes were left unused for a week, invariably, these were flat. Their charging systems would just not take the extra loading. As I was used to bump-starting my race bikes I was often volunteered to try and start the Nortons, some of which had a right-side, four-speed gear change and some a five-speed version: one up and four or five down. The BMWs had left-sided gear changes with five ratios, and were one down and five up. I often agreed to ride a Norton as I was confident I could restart one if it stalled or the battery gave up.

Our traffic base was located on a dual carriageway. To get to Vicarage Road and the football ground in Watford, we had to ride across the dual carriageway, utilising a crossover point outside the base. One Saturday morning, three of us left the base on bikes and, having crossed the road, in turn we accelerated towards Watford. One of the squad was leading on a BMW, and I was running second on a Norton, with another officer, Dave Melvin, on a BMW behind me. As I exited the crossover point I gave the Norton full throttle, intending to race after my pal on his BMW (nothing if not still competitive). Unfortunately, I was on a five-speed Norton, and had pulled away in second gear, having forgotten that the gear change worked the opposite way to the BMW that I rode daily on normal patrol duties. At maximum revs, I mistakenly hooked the gear lever up from second to first gear, and promptly locked the rear wheel. Dave was not far behind, and the only warning he got of my error was a puff of tyre smoke and a lurch from my bike. I looked around to see him flash past, fist waving and very justified expletives coming my way. He later said he had no idea how he missed seriously shunting me. Another fine mess only just avoided: my riding style was more cautious for the rest of that shift.

Ron Clowes, one of the Velocette racer partners, ran a small motorcycle business in Potton End called RIP Motorcycles (RIP stood for Ron, Ivan, and Pete). Ivan had dropped out of the business by this time, however, and Pete was a sleeping partner, mainly earning his living as a bailiff. I used to call in for a drink sometimes, and one autumn day Ron showed me a nice but cheap 250cc Montesa two stroke trials bike he'd taken in part-exchange. For the price he was asking I thought I might have a go as the trials scene was quite active in Hertfordshire at this time, and the winter needed filling with something.

I duly bought the bike, prepared it for action and, with my daughter, Julie, acting as faithful mechanic, entered a closed to club trial at Dews Farm near Uxbridge. I was so far out of my depth, and fell off numerous times, even though I was riding the novice course. Eventually, I gave up before the last few sections; knackered. Julie asked me very firmly never to do a trial again as she was so embarrassed, and I had to agree that it was not my forté. I knew nothing about two strokes, and the Montesa did need a tune-up as it would not run cleanly at low revs. I was also unfit, however, and this was clearly demonstrated to me. I sold the Montesa for a small loss and walked away from trials for good.

The racer was completed in time to compete at a couple of meetings at the end of 1984, and more improvements in the form of a full race specification motor were agreed for the 1985 season, for which we planned to race the bike in the 1985 Manx Grand Prix. Through our road bike experiences, Pete and I had become friends with the Velocette dealer Geoff Dodkin, who, with a little persuasion, agreed to rebuild our motor for us. Geoff's chief mechanic and Velocette racer, Nick Payton, would do most of the work, and he and I ultimately became good friends. Geoff had a lot of experience from preparing racing Velocettes, and often used a couple of pet phrases that I will never forget. He promised that they would do their 'incapable best' to give us a good motor, and that he would get Nick to do a 'lovely' on our crankshaft to ensure it revved freely. Visits to his shop were always fun.

At last the call came from Doddy's (as we called Geoff Dodkin's shop) that our motor was finished. Pete and I drove into Putney to collect it, and, as was our habit when visiting Geoff, enjoyed a liquid lunch of a couple of pints of Young's wonderful bitter in a pub near to his shop. We made any excuse to visit Dodkin's emporium, and always learnt something. Geoff would stress the importance of having adequate clearances on plain bearings such as the gearbox sleeve gear (especially for racing), and complained that the pattern spares available to him were often not within tolerance, so fettling would usually be required to achieve an adequate engineering fit. Nothing has changed, has it? When Geoff closed his shop for good, a few years later, he told me that he spent so much time modifying and correcting pattern parts to fit customers' bikes that it was no longer viable.

The bill for the motor was hefty but fair at just over £1000, and we set to fitting it into the rolling chassis.

Fortunately, we had picked up some valuable sponsorship from our Velo Club pal, Alan Wright, who supported our efforts for several years whilst he ran EWP Auto Parts, a pirate Porsche spares outlet that he set up after closure of the brewery. I got the feeling that when Alan ever did a good cash deal we received a little part of it! Porsche eventually forced Alan to close, as he was seriously under-cutting its prices, but by then he'd established a very successful and profitable business, helping many Porsche owners keep their cars on the road at reasonable cost. We are still close pals although he now lives, with his wife, Annie, in a lovely part of rural France. I believe he still has a good stock of stainless nuts and bolts, and I know that he still enjoys a few pints of 'fizzy' bitter. None of your real ales or posh wine for an ex-Whitbread employee! (I was told a lax attitude to alcohol consumption at Whitbreads existed at that time, and the lads I knew who worked there certainly took full advantage. I think there was even a free bar they could visit after their shifts. I sometimes wonder whether Alan and his pals contributed in some way to Whitbread's sad demise ...)

Many of Whitbread's stainless fittings found their way onto a Velocette Venom Clubman Mk 2 that I bought from our Woburn Centre Velo Club chairman, Danny Wilson. Danny told me that the motor had been 'breathed on' by Chick Parr, a well known Velocette tuner from the Luton area. Well, he didn't do a very good job on my Venom as the motor never ceased to vibrate horribly, no matter what I tried. The riding position was also very uncomfortable as it had rear-set footrests but straight, Vincent-type handlebars. Over any distance I got neck ache, so the bike didn't last long. I took it along to a Vintage Club Banbury Run, and left a 'for sale' sign on it. A butcher from Kings Langley paid me the asking price, and I never saw it again — thank goodness! (Danny retired to France years ago, and lives not too far from Alan Wright — small world, eh?).

Around this time we chose to move house again as Shelagh had returned to part-time working and our finances had improved accordingly. One of my first tasks was to get a fabricated concrete garage/workshop installed at the foot of the rear garden as, although the house came with a detached garage, this was in a block nearby, which meant it was no use as a workshop. The workshop soon took shape and, with electricity installed and a wooden work bench, plus a second-hand hydraulic bike ramp, I was soon ready to get back to work on our racer.

In June 1985 I raced — with some success — our Dodkin-tuned bike at Brands Hatch, and again at the end of July at the Velocette Owners Club annual race meeting at Cadwell Park. I finished fifth in the Vintage race and second in the Velocette-only race. In this latter race I was beaten by Dave Fox, and had the pleasure of finishing in front of my pals, Richard Adams and Tony Wright. Looking at the results, arch rival Nick Payton appears to have been absent.

One of my main opponents at this time was Martin Greenland, who also lived in Dunstable. Martin's dad, Ralph, was a wonderful engineer and Velocette enthusiast. Ralph owned several Velos, one of which was a Chick Parr, 350cc Velocette race bike. It had a highly modified, KTT engine and a special frame made by Chick, with the oil tank located beneath the motor. Ralph and Martin spent many happy hours trying to get this bike to perform properly — and occasionally it did!

We then began plotting in earnest our Manx Grand Prix adventure. Another friendly visit to Geoff Dodkin's produced a box of spare parts that we could take to 'the island' on a sale or return basis, and he also lent us a genuine Smiths conical rev counter, plus a set of TT ultra close ratio gears that we had been unable to source ourselves. Pete provided his large capacity Velocette Thruxton petrol tank, his bolt-up primary chain case as we had only a skeleton alloy one fitted for short circuits, and removed his motor and clutch so that we could carry that as a spare complete unit. I managed to get some sponsorship from Keith Collow of Shell Oils, and this provided some vegetable racing oil at a very discounted price. The Police Motor Club agreed to assist with some financial backing, and I also received similar help from The Federation of British Police Motor Clubs. Every little helped then, and both of these clubs have sponsored me to some degree ever since. We tested the racer in island trim along the runway at nearby Radlett Aerodrome: with a little tweaking she ran well.

In late August we overloaded my poor Astra estate car and trailer and travelled to the Isle of Man, having found lodgings in Hutchinson Square in Douglas for our fortnight's visit. It had been a tight fit with Shelagh, myself and three kids, plus luggage, full racing kit (including spares), and the Velocette aboard. Pete and other Velo Club pals were to join us on the island for race week.

Luckily, we had been promised the use of a garage near to our guest house for 'fettling' although it was actually only half of this as the other half was full of unused spare furniture; neither did the garage have electricity. We arrived in the rain on the Saturday prior to practice week, and the rain continued into Sunday. I signed on at the pits and went to the Battery Pier to buy some Avgas. 'Not open until Monday at 10.00am,' read the notice, so off we went to Ronaldsway Airport to try and blag some, as I wanted to do the early morning practice session on Monday. Telling innumerable lies, I eventually acquired some, having done the deal for pound notes behind a hangar. I did wonder if Manx Petroleum ever got its cut?

I had decided to go on the coach provided by the organisers to give newcomers advice on how to race the mountain circuit. Although I had raced there once before, you can never have enough advice about racing lines and tricky features. Unfortunately, it continued to pour with rain, and the very humorous commentary from an experienced rider made all aboard laugh like drains until the windows steamed up. None of us saw much of the course, as a result, but all thoroughly enjoyed the experience, and did acquire the odd smidgeon of knowledge, too.

We got to the pits for 5am the next morning, passed through scrutineering, and I was away from the start, down Bray Hill, just after six. I stopped at Ballacraine to adjust the clutch as it was slipping slightly, and carried on to Ballaugh Bridge where I stopped again as I had noticed oil on my left boot. An overfilled oil tank had caused the problem, and a quick wipe resolved this for now. Just through Ballaugh village I came across a fallen rider lying on the pavement alongside a very bent Suzuki RG 500. The flag marshal at Ballaugh Bridge was obviously not aware, so I stopped again at Quarry bends to let the flag marshal there know. The fallen rider was Graham King, one of the pre-race favourites, and he sustained a badly-broken leg.

Our Velo completed the lap and seemed okay so I went sight-seeing with the family in the afternoon.

The weather for evening practice was dry but with blustery winds. I completed two laps: the second in a time of 29 minutes 30 seconds, with qualifying time being 29 minutes. On the third lap clutch slip occurred again and, at Sulby crossroads, I stopped to adjust it and noticed a small amount of smoke coming from the chain case. I waited for things to cool down before proceeding, but thought I heard a slight knocking from the motor so decided to retire at Ramsey in Parliament Square.

I informed the marshal there that I didn't intend to proceed, and asked him to inform my wife and ask her to collect me. This she did after an hour or so, and I had good reason to thank the young lady who bought me a bag of chips from the nearby chippy, as I was getting cold by then. It rained again on Tuesday morning so I slept in, then stripped the motor to the crankcase, finding little wrong apart from the tappets having closed, probably due to new gaskets settling down. Tuesday evening practice didn't last long for me as the clutch slipped again as soon as I applied full throttle, and I retired at Ballacraine with a burnt-out clutch. Shelagh brought the trailer again; this time with my pal, Paul Rose, for company as he had arrived on the island that afternoon.

Wednesday morning was wet so we spent it fitting Pete's clutch instead of the failed one, and then phoned Geoff Dodkin to ask if he could possibly send us another complete clutch in case we needed it. Kindly, Geoff despatched one immediately, complete with a typically humorous note.

Another incident concerning our digs has remained in our family anecdotes. The young couple we were staying with were not very experienced in running a guest house, and one morning, after breakfast the hostess apologised if our sausages had tasted strange. She had cooked them whilst still wrapped in cling film ... none of us had noticed!

Wednesday evening practice went well and I qualified with a second lap of 28 minutes 5 seconds. It had been misty coming down the mountain, which had possibly cost me about 30 seconds so I was well pleased. I thought that the bike's performance had tailed off towards the end of that second lap, and so on Thursday morning the cylinder head came off and I found that the inlet valve seat was damaged slightly, probably caused by a piece of gravel getting inside. A trip to Jurby Airfield for testing proved that performance was again 100 per cent, and we decided to miss the damp and misty Thursday afternoon session, grateful to Geoff Dodkin for his advice to try and qualify as soon as possible.

Pete and several other Velo Club lads had by now arrived, and we all got up early for Friday's morning practice session. Giving a racing bike full throttle from the start line down Bray Hill, just after dawn on a lovely late summer morning, is a wonderful experience that only a few privileged people have had. I distinctly remember thinking "no one in their right mind would think this is sensible," as I tucked in, and gave the bike full stick towards the flat out, blind left-hand bend that followed St Ninian's crossroads, before the steep drop down Bray! Many of us had ridden to the pits from our garages, spread all over Douglas, for scrutineering, and the sound of a big single cylinder race engine firing up and then burbling along on an open megga, at 4.00am in the dark is the most marvellously surreal way to start the day. Most riders would go back to bed for an hour or two after practice, but if there was important work to be done on the bike it was very hard to go back to sleep. The low sun soon after dawn could be very hazardous, and over the years several riders fell victim to this, losing their sense of direction when dazzled rounding a bend on the course and crashing badly. I certainly had my share of low sun problems, and great caution was necessary at certain locations. Yet another thing that was unique to Isle of Man racing, and part of the steep learning curve.

During this practice session the bike ran well along the lowlands, but would not pull cleanly climbing up the mountain, so another visit to Jurby was undertaken, where Derek Cheesman, my regular mechanic, proved himself a carburation wizard. Pete had his first quick run on the bike down the runway, and declared it the best Velo he'd ever ridden. Evening practice proved him wrong though, as the bike still would not run very cleanly when held on full throttle. I was worried by now, and decided to lift the head again and replace both valves, as I thought the inlet valve may have been slightly bent. This required a late-night session, and we had to resort to a lead light stretched across the adjoining lane to allow us to complete the task. Our workmanship required testing, so we all got up for Saturday's early practice, and in pouring rain I went as far as Ballacraine, where, with help from two of the lads, Paul and Terry Chalk, I changed the main jet for one that was 10cc larger, then continued as far as Kirkmichael where the lads again met me with the trailer, and we headed for the garage before I caught pneumonia. Only a handful of riders had turned up for practice on that filthy morning.

Everything now seemed to be okay, and we could do no more other than to clean the bike, with the three-lap race due to start at 5.00pm.

The bike didn't want to start after scrutineering — probably due to nerves on my part — but, once going, sounded fine. It was a dry evening though the wind was strong and blustery. I got a good bump-start though others didn't fare as well: as I waited for my turn to go I watched Alan Cathcart push his lovely Paton almost the length of the pits before he got away, and Ken Inwood almost toppled off his Manx Norton when it did eventually fire.

The bike ran well all the way through the lowland section to Ramsey, but the headwind up the mountain prevented me from using top gear. It would, however, pull 6200 revs, the factory approved maximum, along the Sulby Straight, proving that the motor was now in good order, and we had selected the right gearing.

I envied the Aermacchi riders with their five-speed gearboxes, and even with our close ratios the gap between third and fourth was too large when climbing uphill. My final lap was my best at 28 minutes 11 seconds, and I finished in 20th position out of thirty finishers in the 500 class at an average speed of 79.968mph. A good result, really, for only our third meeting of the year, and against some thoroughbred racing bikes on what was essentially a road bike.

Neil Tuxworth, now a Honda race team manager, won the race at 96.010mph average speed on a Cowles Matchless, John Goodall, also on a G50 Matchless, was second. Pete and the boys were well pleased, the bike had finished in good, oil-tight condition, and I had done enough laps to improve my course knowledge for future use. Drink was taken!

A couple of weeks after the Manx we took the Velo to Snetterton, confident that it would perform well, considering how it had gone on the island. In the first race of the day, somewhere near the end of the back straight and at maximum revs in top gear, there was a loud graunching sound and a sudden loss of power. I rolled to a stop and waited for the recovery truck, fearing the worst … and I was not disappointed. As we removed the exhaust pipe to investigate, a valve head dropped out, and it was well-hammered. That did not bode well for the cylinder head and piston, did it? Sure enough, the hemisphere in the head and the top of the piston were deeply peppered and seriously damaged. It was the end of our road racing for 1985.

Pete and I fancied sampling some more Young's bitter and took the motor, in pieces, to Doddy's. We hoped his 'no quibble' guarantee would sort things out, but some hope. The lovely motor that had been so carefully built was in a sad state, and we discussed the way forward with Geoff and Nick.

After cruelly taking the mickey out of us they floated the idea that we should utilise a Velocette Viper 350cc head, and build a squish-type motor. They had successfully machined other Viper heads to this specification, and Pete and I had a spare Viper head, so the decision was easy to make. Geoff supplied a new piston and, during those winter months, a fresh motor was created. We had high hopes for it and spent the winter working on other folks' bikes to earn enough to pay the bill.

I think it was around this time that I was asked by Ray Thurston, a Velocette Owners Club pal, to create for him a Velocette racer similar to our own. He was to supply the parts, though where he found them remains a mystery. All came from different bikes, and it was quite a task to make everything fit together. I managed it eventually, though cheerfully cursed him for some time afterwards, and often tapped him for a pint in compensation. I saw the bike at race meetings for years after this, so I couldn't have done too bad a job, and Ray and I are still good friends.

In spring 1986, after a few early season tuning sessions at Mallory Park practice days, we did get the new motor to perform reasonably, but it never felt quite as sweet as the original Doddy creation. I had some success with the bike at a Brands Hatch meeting, winning my first road race after a great dice with Graham Rhodes, who, to be fair, was on the Rhodes family's beautiful vintage 350cc KTT Velocette. At the Velocette Owners Club meeting at Cadwell Park I finished third in the Vintage race, with Nick Payton back in seventh place. I think he must have had mechanical issues for once. I secured another trophy in the feature race, beaten again by Dave Fox, but this time also by Nick. I enjoyed thrashing the Velo and it did remain in one piece, despite my best efforts to over-rev it.

Over the next couple of years we had more good results, but I never managed to beat either Dave Fox or Nick in a straight fight. They were both talented racers with quick bikes that they knew how to prepare. However, at one Cadwell Park meeting, I did have the pleasure of witnessing Dave Fox crash a 1000cc Egli Vincent so well that he broke the forks off it. Must have cost a fortune to fix that mess. Fortunately, Dave suffered a broken arm only, and could still grin as he relayed his excuses for crashing … it's never our own fault, is it?!

My last race of the season was scheduled for Brands Hatch and I was up for it. Practice went well, but during the second race of the day, disaster struck. I had just overtaken Mike Colin riding a Manx Norton on the approach to Paddock Bend. Negotiating the downhill bend, I squirted the Velo on down the hill through the dip, and was aiming for the inside line at Druids Hairpin, when Mike Colin squeezed past me on the offside, then moved slightly to his left before he was fully past me … which removed my front wheel from the equation. The collision caused my bike to fall over onto its right-hand side and I hit the track, but my right foot became trapped between the rear wheel and the swinging arm, and I was dragged along the track still entangled with the bike. After what seemed like an eternity, my boot came off, allowing me to slide to a halt. Poor Shelagh had seen the whole thing, and ran towards the scene of the crash, angry that I had been knocked off.

The medical crew of two Territorial Army lads stationed at the hairpin came to my aid and assisted me off the track whilst the marshals removed the Velo. By this time I was in a great deal of pain, and as they examined my right foot, I heard one of them say "Wow! That looks bad!" There was a lot of blood, and I was quickly conveyed to the medical centre where my foot was bandaged, and I was bundled into another ambulance and taken to Sidcup Hospital. Doctors there quickly established that the heel was so badly injured that the bone was exposed and scraped, and there was a lot of soft tissue damage. I had to keep the foot raised, and the pain was excruciating if I lowered it at all.

I was in hospital for three days after an operation to stitch it all up, and the Traffic Police boys brought Shelagh to visit me when shifts allowed; they were brilliant. I had to have several weeks off work on crutches, and it was a long time before I could put my foot to the floor. I hadn't broken any bones, but the nerve damage caused still gives me gyp.

Several witnesses approached Shelagh to say they were sorry I had been knocked off, but Mike Colin denied any liability, and blamed me for the crash. A racing 'incident,' I guess?

Maybe high speed exploits on four wheels would be safer than on two — perhaps I should give it a try ...

CHAPTER 4

THE LOTUS ELAN AND BUILDING THE SEELEY MATCHLESS

DURING MY RECOVERY FROM THE INJURED FOOT, AT THE END OF 1986 I had thoughts of abandoning motorcycle racing, and, with Shelagh's eager support, we bought a 1972 Lotus Elan Sprint. I had sold her on the idea that we could travel in comfort together, far and wide, to classic car events instead of me clearing off to bike race meetings with my pals. Although Shelagh never failed to support me, she worried terribly about the dangers involved in my racing and riding motorcycles on the road. In my Traffic Police role I often had to deal with the aftermath of serious and fatal road accidents involving motorcyclists, and, of course, I related the gory details to her at the end of my shifts.

We had received a small inheritance from an uncle, and I sold my road bike, a Mk 1 Velocette Venom Clubman, to fund the car's purchase. The way I sold the Venom was a stroke of genius: I cleaned and polished the bike, then rode it to a vintage run event in Banbury, parking it near the organisers' site with a 'for sale' sign stuck to it. A potential buyer spotted it, and I ultimately sold it for £1500, I think, to a chip shop owner from Kings Langley, about five miles from our home.

I then did some research and discovered an expert car restorer who lived in Suffolk, by the name of Mick Miller. I visited Mick's emporium at his house in Saxmundham, and he gave me much advice on which model to look for. He could not have been more helpful.

I began scouring the advertisements in classic car magazines, and soon spotted a 1972 Lotus Elan Sprint for sale in Thirsk in Yorkshire. It was a long way from home, but it sounded as if the car was in good original condition, and the price was reasonable. I negotiated on the phone with the owner, and we struck a deal conditional on it being as good as it sounded. I then called Mick and asked if he would come with me to vet the car if I paid his expenses. Mick kindly agreed, but then had a heart attack a few days later!

Alone, I took the train to Thirsk and checked over the car to the best of my limited knowledge. A price of £4500 was agreed, cash was handed over, and I drove home in a thunderstorm.

I drove the car a few times the following spring, and, after he had recovered, took it up to Mick's place in Suffolk for him to inspect. It was not all good news, unfortunately. The car was correct for its year, but the chassis had rotten suspension posts, needing replacement. This meant that the body had to come off, and a new chassis bought and fitted with all the running gear prior to re-installation under the body. This wasn't in the plan, either practically or financially, and it took twelve months to complete the work, aided by a bank loan.

After much discussion it was decided that a Spyder tubular space frame chassis would be the best option. The replacement galvanised sheet steel chassis available from Lotus had a reputation for distorting, and there was no difference in the value of an Elan fitted with either chassis type. The Spyder chassis offered the opportunity to have splined driveshafts instead of the short-lived and difficult to fit rubber doughnut types. It also allowed more adjustment of the wishbones.

I liked these options, so duly collected a new red powder-coated chassis from Mick Miller. I enlisted the help of a few of my neighbours, and after removing all of the fixing bolts, with some difficulty we lifted the body off the chassis and stored it on our patio. The rolling chassis went into my garage workshop, and I spent many happy hours removing anything that could be used in the rebuild.

The motor and gearbox were now easily accessible and quickly removed. The brakes and suspension parts were exposed, and I saved anything serviceable, but scrapped badly-worn or rusty parts.

Fortunately, Lotus had utilised many components from other British manufacturers, and I ordered a lot of small parts from specialist dealers at reasonable prices. I lifted the cylinder head from the motor and had it fettled by a specialist in Oxford. This was quite costly, but all of the car's performance comes from the head, and the rest of the motor seemed in good order.

The gearbox had a non-standard alloy competition bell housing fitted, so I sold that to a Lotus racer and sourced a standard item, making a few bob in the process. I fitted stainless steel braided brake lines, and got Paul Duncombe to turn up some stainless disc brake pistons, as rusting of the standard items was a common problem. I bought a reconditioning kit for the Weber twin-choke carbs and carefully rebuilt them. I also bought a full stainless steel exhaust system and a nut-and-bolt kit for refitting the bodywork and other major parts.

Numerous other bits and pieces were obtained, and the chassis was eventually ready to receive the body. More help from the neighbours to lift it on, and then final jobs were done.

I decided to partially rewire some of the car with the help of another good pal, Pete Rust: a fully-trained forklift truck engineer and car enthusiast, and very experienced with electrics. Pete guided me through it all, one lunchtime leaving me to finalise the wiring to the vanity lights on the door pillars. I was instructed to buy some double barrel connectors, and did this while Pete went for his lunch. I didn't realise that there are two types of double barrel connectors — some are paired independently and some are joined together — and bought the joined type. In Pete's absence I fitted these, and then tested my workmanship, shorting the wiring loom back to the dashboard in the process. I just managed to rip apart a wiring joint before the entire dashboard wiring went up in smoke.

Since that day, Pete has banned me from any serious electrical work — probably a good thing: stick to what you know best.

The Elan proved a nice car to drive on 'certain' days. The Weber carburettors were finicky, dependent on weather conditions. One day they'd be perfect and the next, if it was slightly warm, everything went rich and she ran like a dog, particularly at low speed. I fiddled endlessly but soon learned to tune them on a moderate weather day, and then leave well alone.

The brakes would still stick a little when the weather was wet, and the tiny mechanical disc brake pads for the handbrake were useless, and had to be keenly adjusted prior to the annual MOT test. The clutch, which had a very heavy pedal pressure, would insist on sticking when the car was parked for any length of time during the winter, so I then had to get Shelagh to tow it at low speed with our family car whilst I dropped the Elan into first gear to free the clutch. The door seals, although new, were never a perfect fit because the door mouldings were distorted ... and the car was draughty in winter. Wearing its original plastic-covered seat covers meant the car was not much fun to spend time in during very hot weather, either.

If I drove it quickly Shelagh became a nervous passenger as we were so close to the ground, and the HGVs looming over us appeared enormous. I saw 120mph once or twice — it was a fast, very light car, and had acceleration to match. Cornering at speed was exhilarating, and she stuck like glue to a selected line, but we did feel vulnerable in the little fibreglass cabin. Unfortunately, my plan to get away from bikes failed because the Elan was not that much fun to drive, and you could go as fast and in more comfort in a VW Golf GTI!

After several years of low mileage ownership, its value had dropped dramatically from a high of approaching £20,000 to a low of £8000. This was because collectors now only wanted original specification cars, and the new original design galvanised chassis available were of a much improved quality: I had devalued our car by fitting the Spyder space frame, even though it was technically an improvement. £8000 was about what it owed me so I sold it to an agent who exported it to Japan, and moved on. Back to racing motorcycles!

Pete Clements and I still enjoyed our pub sessions, both of us still harbouring ambitions to own and race a 'proper' classic racing bike. We expressed our plans to Geoff Dodkin on one of our visits, and floated the idea of putting together a Seeley Weslake twin. Geoff was totally against the idea, and warned us that the early production Weslake engines available then were unreliable and suffered from vibration issues. He told us to be patient and try to build a big single.

At this time in 1988/9, full replica Manx Norton and Matchless G50 motors were being planned for production by enthusiastic engineers, but none was available as yet, or ready for sale. Some replica frames and chassis parts were, however, already on the market.

Pete and I decided that our best bet was to build a Seeley Matchless and, although our budget wouldn't stretch to that then, we made plans to fundraise and go ahead as soon as possible. The key to this decision was that a contact of mine, Mick Taberer, a butcher by trade and classic racing sponsor from Hinckley, promised he would soon have available enough new parts to construct a complete Matchless G50 motor

We quickly sold the Velo racer to a Velo Club member, plus all of our spare parts that were bought by the sponsor of another Velocette racing pal, Tim Johnson. The day after we sold the spares the sponsor phoned and said he thought he had paid too much for the parts, and wanted either his money back or a price reduction. Pete and I discussed this and concluded that our price had been fair, so we stuck to our guns. Some months later I bumped into the sponsor, and nothing more was said about the deal, thankfully, but it left a sour taste for all involved.

Pete and I then rebuilt and sold a couple more road bikes — a Velocette Venom and a Matchless G9 — boosting our profits by selling the registration numbers. Shelagh regained ful use of her wardrobe after I managed to sell my precious spare Velocette KSS motor for £1000, and I also got several hundred pounds for most of the spare parts that had come with it in the original deal. I had run this motor in my own KTS for a while, whilst I rebuilt the original, so it was now surplus to requirements.

Pete put in some money from his savings and I put in the rest of my spare cash, plus a small bank loan (most of which Shelagh repaid), and we eventually had enough budget available to start building the bike. Pete had never doubted that we would succeed and worked tirelessly to raise money by any means.

Our plan was to race the bike in the 1990 season, and at the Classic Manx Grand Prix that year. We began ordering components in October 1989 and, over the winter, the stash gradually grew.

I had known Richard Cutts from my Aermacchi racing days: a prominent classic racer with his well-prepared, fast Seeley G50, and winner of many championships. I contacted Richard and explained our 'cunning plan,' and also asked for his advice and any useful contacts. He was very encouraging, and kindly provided an A4 list of recommended suppliers. He advised us to use a Roger Titchmarsh chassis, Dick Hunt forks and wheels, and John Pearson for oil and fuel tanks.

There was little choice regarding gearboxes, and we had to opt for a Quaife six-speed item with primary drive via a Bob Newby belt drive and clutch system. Drum brakes were not obligatory for short circuit events, so we chose a more easy to maintain front disc brake, with the disc and hub again coming from Dick Hunt. Mick Hemmings supplied the caliper and reservoir.

Geoff Tunstall— another quick Seeley G50 rider — was using a BSA conical brake drum in the rear wheel of his bike, and generously provided me with information on how to modify it to fit a Seeley swinging arm. I quickly sourced a new rear brake drum and brake plate from a classic BSA/Triumph spares dealer in nearby Watford, for a very good price (£70, I believe).

Using Richard's contact list I spoke to Nick Paravani from Racing Fabrications near Snetterton in Norfolk, who agreed to manufacture a high level exhaust system for us once the engine was in the rolling chassis; Speedway Services supplied a new PAL magneto for ignition. Original conical Smiths rev counters were too expensive for us so we bought an electronic Krober unit from Phil Pick who ran Triple Cycles, the Triumph Trident specialist. My racing friend Ken Inwood sold us a seat and a rear chain via his paddock services van, and the late Graham Boothby from TGA Classic Spares provided suitable fibreglass items.

I can't thank enough some of these chaps: they prevented us from making basic errors, and saved us money because we bought the right parts from the beginning. Richard Cutts, Geoff Tunstall, Dick Hunt, Roger Titchmarsh, and Ken Inwood couldn't have helped us more, especially considering we were the 'new' opposition. It's not always like that in motorcycle racing.

A beautiful Seeley Mk 2 frame, plus swinging arm complete with fairing brackets, arrived quite quickly, and we soon had the forks and yokes to fit to it. Another Velocette Club pal, Terry Chalk, had bought the RIP Spares business from Ron Clowes by this time, and offered sponsorship by way of a pair of Marzocchi rear shock absorbers and some racing sparkplugs — every little bit helped.

Pete and I enjoyed a trip to Hinckley to collect the motor parts from Mick Taberer, and swiftly delivered them, on the return journey, to a well known racer and engine builder who had agreed to build us a race motor in a state of tune suitable for the Manx Grand Prix. A price and delivery date had been agreed, and we trusted him to provide us with a reliable engine. The engine builder came recommended by several other riders, and his own bike was certainly swift and regularly finished at the front of the field.

We worked away putting together the various chassis parts; again, with much help from Paul Duncombe, who provided various brackets and small fixings at knock-down prices. Both front and rear hubs were delivered to our wheelbuilder, Dick Waldron, and he quickly laced a pair of alloy rims to them, after which I fitted a pair of Avon racing tyres, sourced from Sones Tyres, which gave us racers a small discounts.

Towards the end of the build we also bought a new Suzuki 750cc 'Kettle' front drum brake from the Bladon brothers, for future use at planned continental meetings where drum brakes were obligatory, though it would be a little while before this would be needed. The Bladons, Chris and Paul, were engineers and Aermacchi specialists who had an immaculate basement workshop in Hemel Hempstead, where I lived.

Once the rolling chassis was complete with the motor installed, I took it up to Nick Pavarani, who finalised the fitting of the exhaust system — complete with a double-skinned, silenced megga — whilst I waited. I remember that acquiring the front brake hydraulic hose of the correct size was a pain, and I spent many happy hours using a lathe at Paul Duncombe's factory to tune numerous spacers and washers to make the whole thing look as professional as possible. We wanted to be proud of our creation.

Total cost for the complete bike came to £10,675. Pete and I had £285 left from our original fund, and the Suzuki brake was purchased from that for £150.

Whilst the final creation was taking place I had been busy trying to find sponsors to bolster our finances enough to finish the project. My neighbour and friend, Dave Whitby, gave us some cash via his garage business, and three other motorcycling pals — Roger Brown, Alan Wright and Eddie Faulkner, all of whom ran small companies — chipped in. A Silkolene Oils rep, John Cartwright-Howell, lived locally, and he sponsored us by providing a quantity of R40 vegetable oil for free, adding more at a discounted price. We would soon be ready for testing.

Would our new race bike take us into the 'big league' of classic racing? We would soon find out!

CHAPTER 5

THE START OF THE SEELEY YEARS, AND PETE

BY THE SPRING OF 1990 MY ELDEST DAUGHTER AMANDA HAD LEFT home, permanently, as it happens, to become a student nurse in Southampton. Julie was now 17 and had just left school to start work. At this time she was what my mum would have described as a difficult child (like father like daughter?). She had not been particularly studious and was often very quiet and not easy to communicate with. I persevered though, kept talking to her, never allowing it to become too frustrating, and we are still close. It's just her way of dealing with life. Katherine Charlotte (or 'Charlie' as she's known) was 13 and working hard at school; her issues were yet to surface. Shelagh was now a legal secretary, working full time, not far from where we lived near the centre of Hemel Hempstead. I was commuting to Stevenage where I had secured a post as a Scenes of Crime Officer. I had always been fascinated by forensics, and I learnt that the SOCO Sergeant often had a drink in the Police headquarters bar at lunchtimes. When I was on a suitable shift I offered to take the daily Traffic Base dispatches to HQ and managed to buy him the odd drink, if I timed it correctly. When I ultimately went for my job interview this may just have paid off!

We took the Seeley to Mallory Park in March and I completed a number of laps without drama. Pete was delighted with the whole project and we both looked forward to many enjoyable years as racing partners. Pete had a very laid back character and we never ever argued, he was easy to deal with, generous and very popular with everyone. I raced the bike several times that summer, finishing in the second half of the field which was full of very experienced classic racers. I was determined to develop my craft but avoid crashing if possible as we had very little in the way of financial reserves. We suffered a couple of minor oil leaks and the carburetion was difficult to get spot on. At Mallory Park in May I finished 16th and then 18th from about 30 entries, and in June finished 20th from 31 on the Brands Hatch GP circuit. During a June meeting on the Brands Hatch Indy circuit, I lapped around the minute mark and felt that the bike and I were getting to know each other better!

There was another Brands Hatch meeting in July, and that was scheduled to be our last prior to the Manx Grand Prix, for which our entry had been accepted. The motor had never seemed particularly quick, but I assumed that the performance was acceptable for a new build motor. During a lull in proceedings, I decided to check the tappet clearances, and on removing the covers I discovered that the roller cam followers had severe chatter marks across their surfaces. The person who built the motor was also competing at the meeting and I asked him to have a look when he had a minute. He was not best pleased at being disturbed and after looking at the followers he said something to the effect that he had four motors to build before the Manx GP, and that I should leave it alone as it would be alright if I fitted new rollers. He made it clear that he had no time to investigate why it had happened in the first place. I had to bite the bullet and the following Monday phoned Mick Taberer to order some new roller followers and the needle roller bearings that they ran on. Mick was confused as to why I needed replacement parts so soon, but quickly posted them to me, as requested.

I fitted the rollers and went through the whole bike prior to leaving for the Isle of Man. Experienced racer from the classic period, Charlie Sanby, used to attend our Velocette Owners Club meetings at Woburn and sometimes I would pick him up from his home and we would enjoy the evening together. He had a dry sense of humour and could be funny and good company. Charlie had also built himself a MK 3 Seeley replica chassis using an original Matchless G50 motor. My frame was a MK 2 version, which had frame rails under the motor similar to a featherbed Norton. Charlie's was lighter and utilised removable front down tubes with the engine hanging from those and the top frame rails. As we planned our Manx GPs together we agreed that we would travel in Charlie's Ford Transit van and also stay in the same guest house in Hutchinson Square in Douglas. I was responsible for booking the ferry and Charlie arranged for us to use a workshop in Douglas owned by a friend of his. I think he had sponsored Charlie some time previously in his Isle of Man TT racing.

All went according to plan, and Shelagh, daughter Charlie, aged 13, and I were collected by Charlie and travelled north in plenty of time to catch the midnight sailing from Liverpool. Ha-bloomin'-ha!

We adults travelled in the front and poor Charlie had to sit on a drum of fuel padded with a cushion, behind the driver's seat! The journey soon passed with plenty of amicable conversation until we arrived, on time, at a deserted quayside in the Albert Dock next to the Mersey. I was baffled. On questioning the only ferry employee still there, it transpired that the ferry going to the island at that time of night went from Heysham, at least another hour's journey north. I was not popular, I'd never travelled from Heysham and had presumed that we would go from Liverpool as in previous years. A quick ticket-check, that I'd booked more than six months previously, showed my mistake. I drove the van flat out in thick mist up the M6, but by the time we arrived at Heysham, the ferry had gone and we found another deserted quay. The next ferry was due to leave from Liverpool around 7.00am the next morning and a very subdued group travelled back down the M6 hoping that we would be allowed on that one.

After an uncomfortable night parked on the dockside in Liverpool we were allowed on the ferry. Upon arrival at our chosen guest house in Douglas I duly apologised to our landlady for our late arrival. My poor daughter had been very patient and never complained — at least not until some time later. Once we had unloaded our bikes and tools at the garage, Charlie clearly spelled it out to me that he would be doing his 'own thing' and that he would only help me if time allowed as he would be concentrating on his own purposes. I was a little disappointed as I had hoped for some coaching and assistance as neither of us had a mechanic with us. Charlie's long time mechanic, Wally Maisey, would be arriving for the race week and I had Pete and some Velo Club lads arriving at the end of practice week, but for now I was on my own. Charlie did concede to take me on a training lap of the course in his van prior to practice and he shared a number of course 'secrets' with me for which I was very grateful.

Our landlady was a dry, middle-aged Geordie character called Joyce and her plumber husband Ian was another, but more cheerful, Geordie. They had a small bar in the rear lounge, and with Ian acting as 'mine host' evening debriefs were to be a delight, full of banter and tales of derring do!

We signed on, filled in numerous forms, attended a lengthy briefing, got the bikes and our riding kit scrutineered and prepared for the first practice session on the Saturday evening. The weather was clear and dry and I completed two laps, pitting in between to check for anything amiss with the bike. My first lap was completed in 27 minutes 51 seconds and the second one in 27 minutes 36 seconds. To qualify for the race we had to complete a total of five practice laps with at least one being under 28 minutes, so all seemed ok at this stage. I did notice some unusual vibration through the left handlebar but thought that perhaps the carburetion settings were slightly rich. I had also been peppered by gravel at Quarter Bridge, from recent road repairs, and this prompted the fitting of small fairing extensions to protect my exposed fingers plus the addition of duct tape to the front of the fork legs to prevent damage to the polished alloy. I also increased the setting on my hydraulic steering damper as the bike had shaken its head a bit when the front end became light over the various jumps around the course. This was a problem that never occurred on short circuits.

Derek Cheesman, a Velo Club pal and trained motorcycle mechanic had travelled over for the races and willingly accepted the role of mechanic. He was to fill this role faithfully for many years and we are still the best of pals, although he does now live in Portugal. We cleaned the bike ready for early morning practice on Monday and socialised on the Sunday. Leaving the start line at dawn on Monday, I again planned to do two laps, and the bike ran well for most of the first lap, but I felt that horrible vibration again as I descended the mountain section, so pulled in at the pits to check things out. There seemed to be a faint knock coming from the bottom end of the motor, and I decided against another lap. We glumly returned to the garage and removed the magnetic sump plug to check for debris in the oil. To our dismay there was a veritable 'Christmas tree' of steel filings all over the magnet. This spelled serious trouble.

Without a doubt the big end was shot! Now I began to panic and rushed back to the paddock to ask everyone I knew if there was anyone on the island who would take on a big end replacement job for us. Mick Rutter, another racer, offered to rebuild the flywheel assembly as he had a special jig with him, but he didn't have a spare big end that would fit our motor and hadn't the facilities to rebuild the complete motor. The only name suggested was a very experienced and quick rider called John Goodall, and I hurried off to his garage workshop near the top of Bray Hill to try and beg him to do the job for us.

I eventually found his garage, with him working away on his two race bikes. He dryly said that he did have a spare big end assembly that we could have, and if we stripped and cleaned all the engine parts he would reassemble it for us, but only if his bikes didn't require all of his spare time. We had little choice but to gamble on this solution, so set to stripping the motor and cleaning every small part to remove any particles of damaged big end. We delivered all the parts to John on the Tuesday morning after practice, and went away to twiddle our thumbs whilst he did his magic for us. John was as good as his word, and on Thursday we visited his garage and were relieved to see our motor in one piece and ready for some punishment. John charged me £200 for his work and Mick Rutter £30. Frankly I didn't care what it cost, I just wanted to get back to racing the TT course. John said that the motor had been built carelessly and at a later date he gave me a long list of faults that he'd corrected. I asked if he would service the motor for me in the future and he agreed to, but warned me that it would take at least three years before I would see the best from it. He said that the cylinder head and some of the other motor parts needed a lot of refining, and that the hours required for this work and other tasks would be costly, time consuming, and consequently would be spaced over the three years. He said he wouldn't have time;

and I wouldn't have the money to have it all completed in one go. As an engineer, I could appreciate what he was saying and gratefully paid up and left, noting his serious caution to give it a 'soft' lap before using sustained full throttle.

We practised the following day, Friday, completing two laps and I rode cautiously, running the motor in and trying to concentrate on learning some smooth, safe lines — and we had qualified. All went well with our pre-race preparation, but on the Wednesday race day the weather closed in, and heavy rain meant a race postponement until the following day. Pete and the boys couldn't change their ferry bookings and had to return to work anyway, so they would miss the race. There was much sadness amongst everyone. On race day, there were high winds, but it remained dry. I had a problem with the bike occasionally jumping out of fifth gear and I found the rear shock settings to be too hard. Gearbox problems were to be an issue with different makes of gearboxes for many years to come. Sometimes it was the fault of the gearbox and sometimes I was concentrating so much on my lines that I didn't hit the pedal firmly enough. Seriously missed gears and consequential screaming revs often bent valves, and I was to have my share of these.

There were a large number of mechanical retirements in the race and I remember that as I passed each stationary bike, leaning against a wall or hedge, I smiled to myself and thought 'that's another one beaten'. I finished the four laps in 35th place at an average speed of 84.04mph. The last lap had been very tiring, but I had retained my concentration and stayed safe. The race was won by Bob Heath at an average speed of 99.68 mph. Bob narrowly beat the experienced USA rider Dave Roper by three seconds and John Goodall was fifth just in front of Richard Cutts. Charlie finished a commendable and stylish seventh. I had a lot to learn but was delighted that our preparation had paid off. Much Okell's Manx bitter was consumed at the prize-giving ceremony and Pete and I had a tearful phone conversation, we were so happy to have finished safely after all the trials and tribulations! Plans were made for 1991 and lists of modifications and future purchases concocted. More sponsorship and fund raising would have to take place and the coming winter's pub sessions would be used to finalise our 'cunning plan'! The Manx Grand Prix signalled the end of our racing for 1990, as Pete and I were broke. In late September I drove to South Wales and delivered the G50 motor to John Goodall and returned the gearbox to the manufacturers for rectification. The gearbox was quickly returned with the assurance that the selector mechanism had been adjusted and all would now be well.

What would the future hold for us? We would soon find out — and it wouldn't all be good.

CHAPTER 6

MUCH SADNESS, AND SOME GOOD RACING

PETE AND I AGREED THAT THE ALLOY-CASED QUAIFE GEARBOX wasn't as good as we'd hoped, and, after rebuilding another couple of bikes, we ordered a PGT five-speed 'box from Summerfield Engineering. We had heard good things about this company's gearboxes, and I had become friends with the three Summerfield brothers — Mike, Roger, and Jerry — who ran a huge engineering business in Derbyshire, and rode and sponsored riders on their Petty-framed Manx Nortons for many seasons with great success. John Goodall finished our motor in January 1991 and I drove down the M4, 240 miles deep into rural South Wales to collect it. He gave me a detailed description of the faults he had corrected and the improvements he had made. I also qualified for a tour of his comprehensive machine shop and the small ex-bedroom that served as his race engine building room. John seemed confident that his efforts would be an improvement over the original build, which proved to be the case. This was the beginning of a long racing relationship and friendship with John and his lovely wife, Rose, that continued until his untimely death in the 2008 Manx Grand Prix.

John knew that Pete and I were not wealthy, and that I, at 43 years old, was unlikely to set the classic racing world alight. Accordingly, from the start he concentrated on making our motors reliable and rideable so that I could finish races, and concentrate on improving my riding skills. John's policy was to make the moving parts of the motor as friction-free as possible, with a very true and accurately balanced crankshaft to allow it to rev freely. He would lighten and polish parts where possible, but not to the point of risking breakage, as our target was always to finish in the Manx Grand Prix races. Compression ratios were set with the Manx circuit in mind, which meant that we were not top of the performance figures compared to most other riders when competing on short circuits. We could only afford one motor rebuild per season, and John scheduled a new piston, crank pin and big end every three years, barring disasters! He told us to more regularly check tappet clearances as any sudden changes could mean potential mechanical issues. The only engine oil filtration on standard Seeleys was the oil tank mesh filter, so we usually changed the three or four pints of oil after each meeting. The quantity of oil used varied according to length of circuit.

John was slightly old school, favouring standard iron cylinder liners and not advocating our use of chrome or other ceramic finishes, which did away with the weight of the liner. He knew the close tolerances that could be utilised with these plated bores did provide improved performance, but they also made carburetion setting critical, as even a slight mixture weakness could cause piston seizure and consequential damage to the piston and bore. Riding a different bike in later years I was to become a victim of this particular problem, and watched many frontrunners suffer the same. Re-plating the cylinder and purchasing a new piston were expensive costs mid-season, and if any debris from piston seizure got into the nooks and crannies of the motor, repairs also entailed a full engine stripdown.

In the Manx races in the years that followed I would ask John for his recommendation for our main jet size on the morning of the race. He would have checked out the barometer in the hall of his guest house after breakfast, and calculated the best size for both his and my motors. I often found that after the race the inside of my exhaust megaphone had black carbon deposits, and that the carburetion had been set slightly rich, but I'm pretty sure he did this to ensure that I finished the race. John was a hard racer but not a risk-taker. Estimating the correct jet sizes for both the coastal lowland part of the circuit and the section over Snaefell mountain was a fine skill, and John took it all very seriously; usually getting it about right. Many other racers — especially the two-stroke riders — regretted under-jetting in the hope of extra performance: piston seizure and a possible high speed crash frequently resulted from this.

We commenced our season at Brands Hatch in early March. I finished tenth from 18 entries in the first race of the day, but retired from the second race with a sticking throttle. We were still using the six-speed gearbox as the new PGT box was not yet ready. I had a slight panic when we initially went to start the bike before practice, as the oil took ages to return to the oil tank, and I quickly killed the motor to prevent any damage due to under-lubrication. Chris McGahan, who also raced a Seeley, saw that I was flapping, and came to help. He advised me always to reverse prime the motor before trying to fire it. This meant using a pump-type oil can to fill the main oil feed pipe that connected the oil tank to the oil pump, and then, with the sparkplug removed, spinning the rear wheel forward and backward to remove any air locks in the feed pipe; continuing to spin the wheel forward until the oil returned to the oil tank before firing the motor. Thanks, Chris. I remembered this kind advice for the rest of my racing years, and always did this, especially for a newly-built motor.

At lunchtime racing stopped and we all grabbed a bite to eat. I remember Pete sitting on the race bike, resting his sandwiches on the Seeley's fuel tank, laughingly commenting that he was having his grub on a £10,000 dinner table!

The new PGT gearbox was delivered to us shortly after this race meeting, and at the end of the month we took ourselves off to Cadwell Park in Lincolnshire for a second outing. I rode poorly on a cold damp day, and finished the first two races towards the back of the field. My third race was an improvement but I decided to miss out the last, very wet, race and we headed home. Cadwell has remained one of my least favourite circuits.

Noise checks were now common at race meetings and I bought another silenced megaphone while we were at Cadwell. My carburetion settings didn't like the dampness and the bike wouldn't accelerate cleanly from low revs around the slower parts of the Woodland section of the circuit. Derek had travelled with us and did his best to adjust the big Amal GP carb but, like the Webers on my Lotus Elan, large bore GP carbs are very sensitive to changes in the weather, and it often proved difficult to find and maintain good settings.

In May and June I raced at Snetterton in the damp, and Brands Hatch and Mallory Park in damp or wet conditions with very average (poor) results. The bike ran okay but the grids were strong, and I was a cautious rider in wet conditions. The new PGT gearbox seemed fine and I had no serious carburetion issues.

One sunny day during early June Pete and a couple of the Velo Club lads went for one of their regular Sunday lunchtime rideouts to a pub for a couple of pints, and to enjoy a bit of bend-swinging on their Velocettes. On their return journey, riding along the Leighton Buzzard Road near the National Trust parkland called Ashridge, they approached a crossroads known locally as Four Ways crossroads. They were on the major road and, by Pete's own admission, were going well, though not exceeding the 60mph speed limit.

The road to their left at the crossroads flowed downhill from Studham, and visibility to the right from the mouth of this junction is poor; anyone pulling out, therefore, should take great care. As the boys approached the crossroads a lady driver decided to pull out to join the Leighton Buzzard Road traffic. What happened next is disputed, but she hit Pete and his Velocette Thruxton. Pete said he had no warning whatsoever until she pulled out and hit him a glancing blow on the left side of his bike, that sent him and the bike crashing into a garage forecourt just opposite the Studham Road.

Pete suffered several fractured bones, and his lovely bike was well scuffed and bent. Police and ambulance crews attended, and the first I knew of it was when someone phoned and told me Pete was now resident in the local hospital, bashed about, but with no internal or head injuries.

I visited Pete, and he was in his usual good humour. He had a broken wrist and pelvis, and a shattered knee, which the doctors had assured him was fixable, but he would take time to recover fully. Pete joked that, as his leather jacket and trousers were insured, he would make a claim and I could then have a new set of racing leathers!

Pete had his wrist operated on and his pelvis was kept stable in traction. Several days after he was admitted they arranged to operate on his knee, and it was during this operation that things went seriously wrong. (I learnt about these problems a few weeks after they happened.) Prior to the operation commencing the anaesthetist appears to have inserted a breathing tube into Pete's mouth, but the tube was incorrectly placed in the entry to Pete's stomach rather than his airway. After a short time Pete showed signs of oxygen deprivation, and a theatre assistant pointed this out to the anaesthetist, but this was ignored and the assistant reiterated his concerns. Again, the anaesthetist did nothing so the assistant tried to bring his concern to the attention of other nursing staff, by which time the anaesthetist at last noticed that all was not well, and repositioned the tube. This was too late for Pete, however, as his brain had been oxygen-starved for too long, and he suffered a cardiac arrest.

The operation was abandoned, but Pete did not regain consciousness. Pete's wife, Gladys, and his daughter, Tracey, visited the apparently peacefully-sleeping Pete every day, and Shelagh and I paid regular visits, but there were no signs of recovery, or of him regaining consciousness. Sometime soon after Pete's failed operation we had been told by a nurse that they wouldn't know how he was until the brain swelling had reduced. This confused us as we had previously been told he had suffered a cardiac arrest, with no mention of brain swelling. Obviously, any cover-up had already begun by that point. Sadly, Pete died in late July, six weeks after the accident, aged 63.

My police role as a SOCO meant I worked closely with CID officers. One day, a little while after Pete's death, one of them quietly informed me that his wife, who worked in another hospital, had heard on the grapevine that an anaesthetist had made a serious error during an operation, and that she thought this related to Pete. I asked my pal's wife to try and firm up the story, and a day or two later she confirmed that Pete was the victim. I then asked to speak with the consultant responsible for Pete's care, though didn't say what about. I asked him to explain what had happened with Pete's operation.

The consultant began explaining the technicalities of the operation, saying that, unfortunately, Pete had suffered a cardiac arrest during the procedure and resultant serious brain damage, from which he could not recover. I told him that, through my police connections, I had received reliable information that an error by the anaesthetist had been the cause of Pete's problems, and that this was widely known amongst nursing staff. The consultant went quiet, then agreed that there had been an error, but that he "hadn't told me that!" He asked me to discuss this further with the hospital manager, so I arranged to meet him. After I presented the information I had, and without mentioning my conversation with the consultant, the manager confirmed that the hospital would admit liability, and Gladys would receive compensation. He also said that the matter was now with NHS solicitors.

Shelagh was still working at a local law firm, and with the help of one of its solicitors, negotiations began regarding compensation. As soon as the NHS solicitors were formally contacted, they denied liability, and it took a further three years of bitter arguing and discussion before Gladys received anything in compensation, by which time she was extremely bitter about the whole business and never fully got over it.

Some months later at the inquest the anaesthetist declined to speak, as was his right. No one accepted responsibility. I learned that the anaesthetist had been moved to another hospital, still allowed to practise. Sometimes, there is no justice.

Life had to go on, but the sadness stayed with me: it would never be the same without Pete. I didn't race in July, and prepared the bike for the forthcoming Manx Grand Prix, compiling a comprehensive list of spares and tools to take with me, and strengthening the fibreglass around the fairing mounts as cracks had begun to appear. I managed to arrange to borrow a Transit van from Hemel Self-Drive, and felt that I was as prepared as possible before we left.

Shelagh and I travelled to the Isle of Man for the Manx Grand Prix, hoping that, mechanically, things would be smoother. For the first time our bikes were noise-tested: a bad omen, perhaps? We happily settled in at our guest house, and found a better garage with Manx friends David ('Bush' cos he had a beard), and Pat Kerruish, which we used for the next 15 years. I first met Bush in the Mitre pub in Kirkmichael during my early visits in the '60s, and we had remained good friends.

Practice went smoothly, and the jetting and gearing I had noted the previous year worked well. I enjoyed an early morning instructional car lap with ex-TT ace and Manx GP winner Selwyn Griffiths, who was nursing a terrific hangover when I picked him up. The lap was hilarious: his language was colourful when describing every difficult bend or feature, and all with tremendous humour. I learnt a huge amount, and he willingly showed me where to use unnatural lines that avoided adverse cambers or nasty bumps in the road surface. No wonder he could lap so much faster than me!

Prior to agreeing to tutor me we had been talking in the paddock whilst I admired his genuine Arter Matchless G50, after an evening practice session. He had very short clip-ons fitted to the bike, and obviously stayed tucked into the bike for the entire lap, unlike us more modern, climb all over the bike riders. Proper 'old style.'

John's engine rebuild had provided me with exactly what I wanted: a reliable, oil-tight, smooth-running motor. I regularly lapped at just under 90mph (my average race speed was 89.72mph), and had a good race, finishing 29th from 52 finishers with a best lap of 25.06 minutes and just over 90mph. 92 riders started the race from over 100 entries. The attrition rate usually equated to about 50 per cent.

I left the island feeling satisfied with my efforts, but very sad that Pete could not have been there with us. I decided there and then to sell my KTS Velocette to finance the purchase of an AJS 7R motor, so that I could also enter the Junior Classic race at the 1992 MGP. I contacted Geoff Dodkin on my return from the Isle of Man, and he found a buyer for my bike who lived in Holland. This chap paid £5250 for my Velo — a good price at that time: thanks, Geoff — and I again contacted Mick Taberer to order the 7R motor.

Whilst waiting for this I realised that if I could afford to buy another frame kit I had a lot of the parts required to build a second Seeley: the spare Quaife gearbox, a front brake, tacho, fuel tank, various exhaust parts, and several other items that could be utilised. That winter's project began taking shape.

John Goodall conceded that lighter magnesium crankcases would be strong enough for a 350 motor, and Mick Taberer confirmed he could provide them. I duly collected the full motor 'kit' from Mick and delivered it to John so that he could build the motor. To help finance this second racer I sold all the spare Velocette parts I had collected over the years, as I now no longer owned any Velocettes. Some of these items were quite valuable, and included three TT carbs and some more KSS engine parts.

Pete's funeral had taken place in August prior to the Manx, at which I had reluctantly and foolishly agreed to speak. What a difficult task: no one in the family felt capable of doing it, but they and I felt that someone near to Pete should say something. To this day I have no idea how I managed to get through it all, I was so emotional. We chatted at the next

Velo Club meeting and agreed that we should have a collection amongst club members and Pete's friends and family to create a memorial to Pete, who had been a very active and popular past chairman of our section. I suggested that we try and have a memorial seat placed somewhere on the TT course, and this was universally agreed.

We began collecting donations, and I contacted the Manx Grand Prix organisers to see if it was feasible. They readily agreed, and were very helpful in sourcing a supplier. We soon collected just over £600 to pay for a lovely hardwood seat with a carved inscription that would be placed near Guthrie's Memorial, on a bend overlooking the picturesque Ramsey Bay. The seat is still in lovely condition as I write this, and is stored indoors through the winter months, returning to beside the memorial for the use of marshals and members of the public during the TT and Manx Grand Prix races. A few years ago I gave it another coat of lacquer: fortunately, no one has carved their initials on it. I'm sure Pete would have approved of the seat, still able to enjoy the view from one of his favourite Isle of Man locations.

Life without Pete would be difficult. He would have loved to be there, without doubt: exciting times were to follow!

CHAPTER 7

SEELEY RACING, AND IMPROVEMENT

WITH THE NEW 350 CHASSIS TAKING SHAPE, ON A COLD AND damp Mallory Park practice day in mid-April 1992 I completed 20 laps on the 500. All seemed okay, with some adjustments to the 38mm Amal Mk 2 smooth bore carb. I was running the bike on 60 per cent super unleaded petrol with 40 per cent 100 low lead avgas. The top runners used pure race fuel, but this was unobtainable in the Isle of Man, and also very expensive. I thought it best that we ran the same fuel all season, so never contemplated using race fuel; John Goodall agreed with this policy. I had a couple of sources for avgas, including a work pal, John Smith, who did part-time work at Duxford War Museum, and I enjoyed several tours of the workshops there whilst collecting fuel. Over the years various tales circulated regarding the quality of the super unleaded petrol and avgas available on the island, and we usually took our own supply, hidden away in the depths of the van. I used to put the 20 litre avgas jerrycan inside an old suitcase in case port authorities decided on a more thorough search. They never found our supply.

In early 1992 I raced at Snetterton, Cadwell Park, and Brands Hatch and moved up the field so that I achieved midfield results. The bike proved reliable and handled beautifully, and at a sunny meeting in mid-July I even managed to lap the Brands Hatch short circuit in 58.58 seconds: I was well-pleased with that.

I collected the 7R motor from John Goodall in late July, just in time to get it into the chassis and tested prior to the Manx Grand Prix. It had a compression ratio of 12.04:1, and John advised me not to buzz it over 7800rpm.

I took the completed bike to a midweek Mallory Park test day and completed 30 laps with no obvious problems. It was not easy to keep the revs within the power band, which was narrower than that of the G50. If I let the revs drop below 5500 megaphonitis set in, the bike lost power dramatically, and would not accelerate cleanly. Good old Derek sorted this by advising me to ride the bike on the rev

counter, and if the revs dropped to 6000 just kick it down a gear ...
I did have six of them, after all! This technique took a bit of practice
but soon became the norm. The G50 never required this treatment
as it had power down to about 4000 revs.

Around this time I had been chatting to Robin Packham,
who manufactured and marketed the Falcon shock absorbers
for motocross, grass track and trials use. I had used his shocks
during my grass tracking episode, and he was a good friend of Paul
Duncombe, my engineer pal. I told him that there was a good market
for classic road racing shocks, and he produced some for me to try.
I soon had them fitted to both bikes and they were very good. I did
question whether they were strong enough to stand the impact
of bottoming at the foot of Bray Hill, and landing after jumping at
Ballaugh Bridge on the TT circuit. Robin laughed and said his motor
cross shocks withstood very high jumps, and he was sure they would
survive all I could throw at them. He was soon selling them as part
of his product range, and they are still popular amongst classic
racers.

We took ourselves off to the Manx GP in late August. My long-
time pal, Pete Rust, travelled with me; his wife, Lyn, joining us for
race week, along with Shelagh. Although not a motorcyclist Pete was
an excellent car mechanic and rally fan, and he and Lyn wanted to
see the scenery and action on the Isle of Man.

Soon after our arrival we drove the van to Guthrie's Memorial,
and were delighted to see the lovely seat, dedicated to Pete
Clements, that the organisers had, as promised, placed there. As
often happens, the first practice on the Saturday evening after our
arrival was cancelled due to rain and poor visibility. To us racers
this was a disaster, as we were full of adrenalin, and desperate to
reacquaint ourselves with the course, let alone check out the bike
after its thorough race preparation.

John Goodall contacted us and offered to swap the 7R's valve
springs, as he had heard of problems with the type he had just
fitted to our new motor. Obviously, we agreed because broken valve
springs can cause serious engine damage, and delivered the bike
to John's rented garage in Douglas the following day. I practised on
each of the following five days, although the Friday morning session
was wet. Various adjustments were made to gearings and carb
settings, and we prepared for both races in a good frame of mind.

The Senior race went well in dry but windy conditions, and I
thoroughly enjoyed it, finishing 26th from 55 finishers with a race
average speed of 90.53mph: gradual improvement. The Junior race

was not as much fun, and it rained at various times at different locations. Riders never knew what they would meet around the next corner, so caution was necessary. I had a steady ride in a race that was reduced from four to three laps, and finished 23rd. Keeping the 7R on the mega was tricky in the wet, and I probably rode too cautiously. Great preparation by us, though, and two finisher's medals to show for it.

It had not been the same without Pete Clements, but Pete Rust had been a great helper, although at one stage he said to the girls "Do they ever stop talking about racing bikes?" Sorry, Pete but "No!"

I rode once more in 1992 at Cadwell Park in mid-September on the 350. The meeting was run on the shorter circuit without the Woodland section, and I had two races, finishing sixth and seventh: a good way to end the season.

I worked hard to raise racing funds during the following winter months, and rebuilt an Indian Velocette for my Velo Club pal, Ray Thurston. The bike was essentially complete so it was not back to the 'basketcase' problems. These Indian Velos, with frames commissioned by Floyd Clymer in America, had been built towards the end of Velocette production, using Thruxton and Venom motors, and were a really poorly-engineered item compared with a genuine Velocette chassis. Just over a hundred were produced. I made a good job of the restoration but got little pleasure from the finished product. Nothing lined up properly, and everything had been done on the cheap. Ray paid me promptly, and sold the bike for good money at a later date: we were both happy I've restored a number of bikes for Ray subsequently. Nobody said racing was cheap and, to keep going, I had to spend every winter trying to raise sponsorship, and rebuilding bikes.

1993 followed the previous year's pattern and I duly collected my rebuilt motors from John Goodall. The G50 had to have new flywheels from Mick Taberer as the tapers had stretched in the old ones, and John could not get them to align and balance correctly. It also received new valves based on race mileage. The 7R was thoroughly checked over and had new piston rings fitted.

I had spent some time over the winter drilling lightening holes in some of the heavier chassis parts, generally trying to reduce weight where possible but staying on the side of safety as everything took a real hammering around the TT course. I had inherited a small Myford ML10 lathe when Shelagh's uncle died, and I made good use of this, manufacturing alloy spacers and washers, plus reducing the size of some other components.

On April Fools' Day we went to Mallory Park to run-in both motors. Everything seemed fine, and I completed a total of 32 laps, allowing us to go home happy, looking forward to another season's competition. I raced the 350 at Cadwell Park later that month, and came away with a seventh place in the first race, though didn't get a second ride as the race was called off due to heavy flooding on the circuit in places.

In mid-May I took both bikes to the TTS dyno at Silverstone, and found that the G50 produced 40bhp at the rear wheel and the 7R 32.5bhp. Nothing to write home about, and well below some of the short circuit competition, but I was confident that John could improve these figures in time, which was the case. I was advised to keep to my 60/40 fuel mix, and to use longer carburettor bellmouths on both bikes, as testing various sizes of Amal bellmouths showed a slight improvement in acceleration, with the longer versions available for the Mk 2 smoothbores.

For the first and only time I raced at West Raynham Airfield in mid-May. No spectators apart from race crews were allowed because the army was still in occupation. Canvas toilet tents over earth trenches didn't impress our womenfolk, and a huge dropped joint in the middle of a turn onto the main concrete runway section of the course rattled riders' teeth somewhat. I finished fourth in the first race and fifth in the second, and the bike ran well after having snapped a throttle cable towards the end of practice. Fortunately, I always carried spare cables.

In mid-June I paid my first visit to the Dundrod course in Northern Ireland, not far from Belfast, for the Dundrod 150 race meeting. I immediately loved the fast-flowing, undulating 7.4-mile course with an excellent road surface. We had just one race in which the G50 ran well on perfect gearing recommended to me by friendly local riders. I finished 19th from the 36 entries, and was well-pleased.

We soon got to know Billy Patterson, a local beef farmer involved in the organisation, and in later years would stay with his family in nearby Crumlin. The atmosphere there was wonderfully casual, as is the Irish way. The course is virtually unchanged from the '50s, and is challenging as it's so fast: almost everyone racing there declares it their favourite circuit. I vowed to return, and planned to compete in future events on any of the historic Irish courses still in use.

The long drive to and from Stranraer was a nightmare. On our way home after the races we caught a late evening ferry, then, in darkness, endured HGVs racing each other along the single carriageway A75 as we travelled east across Scotland towards the A1 and home.

I competed in a couple of other race meetings prior to setting off for our annual pilgrimage to the island, and, on the 350, managed a couple of top ten results. I liked riding the 7R, which was quite competitive against the Aermacchis and Ducatis. Power delivery was softer than the G50's, and this gave me the confidence to open the throttle wider and for longer. As usual, I took a month off to prepare the bikes, and enjoyed the quiet workshop time, culminating in two fully-sorted bikes. My Velo club pals Dave Carter and Derek Cheesman joined me as mechanics for our Manx sojourn, as Pete Rust claimed he had heard enough about racing bikes around the Isle of Man to last him a lifetime, and declined to join us!

Practice week went well although I had to ask John Goodall if he would look at our PGT gearbox as I had trouble selecting gears cleanly. John diagnosed the problem as the selector mechanism needing adjustment, and sorted this for me.

One evening we went for a drink in the Douglas pubs. On the way back to our digs we came across none other than Joey Dunlop wandering along the promenade. He was what the Irish call 'in drink,' just meandering along in no great hurry. I approached him and asked how his bike was going as he was riding a very special lightweight 250cc Aermacchi in the lightweight classic class. He managed to mumble "effing slow," then wandered off on his way home. It transpired that the little 'Macchi couldn't tolerate his quick riding style, and called a halt during the race, so it didn't matter how slow it was!

The weather was fine for our Senior Classic race, and Shelagh opted to spectate and use our newly-acquired video camera at Creg-ny-baa, the right-hand bend on the descent down from the mountain section. She went off with our friends, John and Linda Walker, leaving me to start the race on a sunny day aided by Derek and Dave.

I enjoyed a good first lap but, towards the end, as I rounded Kate's Cottage, the bend above Creg-ny-baa, I saw smoke drifting across the fields. Dave Saville, a well-known and successful sidecar racer, had decided to enter the Classic Senior race on a Manx Norton, whose fairing design was similar to mine. Shelagh was following the bikes through the bend using the viewfinder of the black-and-white format video camera, and, as Dave approached her, she initially thought it was me, and followed the bike through the bend. Having watched the film she took, it appears to me that Dave changed down very viciously as he approached the corner, and as he sped into the bend the rear wheel lost traction and he fell from the bike, which hit the straw bales and the resulting spilt fuel caught fire.

Shelagh filmed all this in panic, thinking it was me; deciding at some stage to look over the top of the camera and realising that it wasn't. She then looked up the road and recognised me approaching. By then the fire had been extinguished, but I had to ride slowly through the smoke and past the marshals who were waving yellow caution flags. Poor Dave was paralysed following this crash. The police asked for witnesses to the accident, and we supplied our video film.

I had a good race, placing 32nd from 65 finishers at an average speed of 91.15mph. Two days later I again enjoyed my race on the 350 machine, finishing 24th. I reflected on another good season with improved lap times around the TT course. Must still try harder, though!

I delivered both motors to John Goodall for a thorough service and, after collecting them a few months later, ran them in at Mallory Park in early 1994, ready for the first race meeting around the club circuit at Silverstone. My best results were tenth in one 350 race and 11th in a 500 race: not a bad start to the new season.

In June Dave Carter and I returned to Dundrod with the 350 Seeley, hoping to move further up the results on a bike I loved to ride on road circuits. Another racing pal, David Whitehouse, came with us, along with his 350 Aermacchi, which helped with travel costs. Practice went well for me but David found some broken spokes in his rear wheel. Being very superstitious, he decided that this was a bad omen and he should not race. I managed to convince him that he hadn't travelled all that way only to spectate, and duly found a local wheel builder who could fix his problem.

The next morning after a great 'Ulster fry' breakfast, cooked at our digs by Billy Patterson's wife, Marjorie, we made our way to the circuit and unloaded the van whilst the first event of the day got under way. I climbed into my leathers and, knowing our one and only race would soon be called, Dave dutifully helped me to bump-start the bike across the gravelled paddock. No sooner had we begun warming up the motor than they told us to shut down as there had been an incident in the previous race. I stopped the bike, pulled it back on compression, and motioned to Dave to reinsert the bath plug in the carb as loose gravel was being flung up by passing bikes (I protected the motor from ingesting debris or stones by keeping a rubber bath plug in the carburetor bellmouth when the motor was not running). Dave obliged but, within a couple of minutes, we were told to quickly start up and make our way onto the track for the warm-up lap.

By now, both Dave and I were nervous, and anxious to get going, so I selected second gear and Dave pushed me to bump the bike into life. As I made my way around the lap, however, the bike would not pull anything over half-throttle. I flapped the throttle and changed down several gears but nothing helped. On my return to the startline I found my place on the grid and shouted at Dave, who was watching nearby behind the armco barrier, to help me change the sparkplug as I believed it may have whiskered across the points. This had occasionally happened at other meetings, causing a loss of power, so Dave usually carried a spare plug and plug spanner in his pocket. We accomplished this just in time for me to start the race with the other riders, but the bike was no better and I retired after another slow lap.

As you will no doubt have guessed by now, in rushing, we had forgotten all about the bath plug: as I returned to the paddock I looked down to see the plug still in place; it had rotated through 90 degrees, allowing the motor to start and run, albeit slightly restricting air flow. Bother!

David Whitehouse had a great race and was euphoric, forgetting all about his earlier spoke issues.

We had a very quiet drive home via ferry and motorway as neither Dave or I wanted to discuss our disaster, and David sensed it best to stay quiet. I wasted a lot of money that weekend, and never again used a bath plug for this purpose!.

The travel bug had bitten, though, and foreign circuits drew my attention. A winter's planning and plotting was about to take place ...

Me outside Shelagh's house with 'Laddie,' a neighbour's dog. 1965.

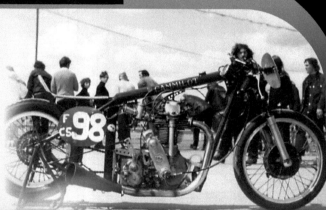

'Cammilot' — my Velocette KSS sprinter at Santa Pod Raceway, 1971.

My Vincent Rapide and Velocette KTS, 1975.

My Lotus Elan Sprint.

Pete Clements on his Velocette Thruxton, 1980.

Grass tracking at High Cross, Herts, on my 500cc Ansel-JAP, number 28, 1980. (Courtesy CH Melhuish)

Left: The Velocette MSS at Brands Hatch, 1985.
(Courtesy Peter Wileman Photography)

The Triumph Triple at rest, 1996.

Schleiz, 1998. Warming up Cleve Brightman's (in green shirt) Aermacchi. (Pete Sharples in green striped shirt).

Skerries, 1998; Shelagh and Dave Carter relaxing in the grass 'Paddock'!

Below: Warming up the Seeley G50 at the Nürburgring, 2000.

Above: Derek Cheesman advising Dave Whitehouse at Mettet, 1995.

Jurby airfield, IOM, John Goodall testing my rear shocks, 1998.

Skerries, 1998 a (very) rare autograph request.

With John Walker and Dave Carter at the 1998 MGP.

At speed (120mph plus?) over the Ballacry jump on the Seeley-G50 in the Senior MGP, 1998.

Stuart Jukes and me,
Le Mans, 2002.

Shelagh and me at
the 1998 MGP.

Checking my 'blue
book' notes, Assen
1999.

Snetterton; me taking
advice on push-
starting from Dan
Shorey, 2000.

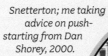

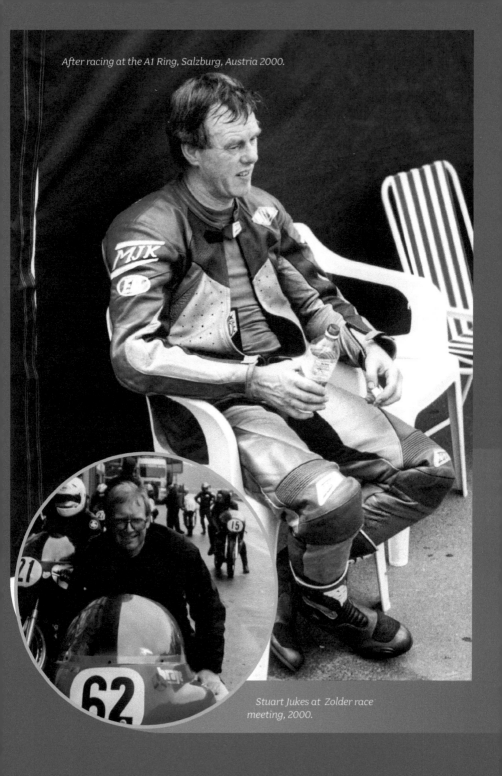

After racing at the A1 Ring, Salzburg, Austria 2000.

Stuart Jukes at Zolder race meeting, 2000.

'Spannering' the Norton at Le Mans.

Above: Brian Richards, Pete Edwards, Stuart and me stripping the bike to a bare frame, Le Mans.
Above right: Roger and Pam Imberg, MGP scrutineering, 2002.

On Honda VFR 400, 2003 TT, Ballacraine. (Courtesy Keig's Photography)

TT 2003 pit stop, Honda VFR with Stuart Jukes and Bob Johnson.

*Riding Don Williamson's Petty
Norton, MGP, 2004.
(Courtesy Russell Lee/Sport-Pics)*

Testing Bob's 400cc Honda VFR at Brands Hatch, 2003.

CHAPTER 8

CREDIBILITY ... AND THE DOWNSIDE

I COMPETED AT MALLORY PARK AND BRANDS HATCH AFTER OUR abortive trip to Dundrod, where my results were not too bad, and included a second and third in my class at Brands. I then committed myself to preparing for the island, and both John Walker and Dave Carter agreed to come along as 'spanners'; we made a very happy team.

We settled in with Joyce and Ian at the Allerton guest house, and then helped Bush clear out our garage workshop so that we had enough space to work in. Manx folk are very laidback, and the disruption we caused every August never seemed to faze them.

This year we did get to practice on the Saturday after arriving, and all went well with the 500, though the 350 felt 'woolly.' The exhaust system had a new silencer, which may have been the reason for this. Silencers were obligatory for all bikes competing at the Manx Grand Prix from this year. I don't think any specifications were enforced, but an effort to reduce bike noise had to be seen being made.

I took out the 350 again for early morning practice on the Monday, with just a padded megaphone, and, although the course was wet in places, the bike ran better. I used the 350 for practice that evening but stopped at the Bungalow on my second lap because I thought I could feel a light knock in the motor. Subsequent inspection found a broken timing chain tensioner spring, so it was not the big end disaster I had initially feared.

After the first practice session there was much discussion amongst the riders regarding the new rules about the use of silencers on their classic machines, and the marshals commented that they couldn't hear the bikes coming towards them as a result. Chris East, a long-time friend of John Goodall, rode a very original specification G50 Matchless with, of course, a large, unsilenced open mega. When this was noticed by the scrutineers they refused him permission to practice or race the bike in this form, so Chris threw his teddy out the pram and went home. Many of us sympathised with Chris as his bike was so much in the spirit of the classic races, but the new regulations, circulated to all riders prior to the event, were very clear. He must have known that not having a silencer on his bike was bound to cause problems.

Further ructions regarding this issue occurred when a podium finisher in one of the classic races was alleged not to have had a silencer on his bike during the race, although his result was allowed to stand. Sensibly ,the silencer regulation was permanently dropped for classic machines in future years, and Chris East returned to race again.

Practice week weather held, and after John Goodall had replaced the broken spring, both the 350 and the 500 ran well for the remaining sessions. During the Thursday afternoon session I lapped at over 93mph, which cheered up all of us.

We spent the Saturday preparing both bikes for the end of the week race, and luckily found a nail lodged in the rear tyre of the 500. No puncture but if the nail had not been spotted it could have been another DNF (Did Not Finish). Dave wrote in my notes that the QB (Quarter Bridge Hotel) interrupted play so we must have lunched there: Okells bitter for Dave, of course, and Diet Coke for me.

The Senior race on Monday was run in lovely conditions, and I finished 21st, having lapped at 94.61mph on one lap, and averaging 93.86mph for the four-lap race. On draining the engine oil after the race we found a tooth from an idler gear on the sump magnet; again, it seems that Lady Luck had been on our side. The Junior race was also run in good weather conditions, and I finished 14th with an average speed of 88.47mph. I was still a little short of replica times in both classes but I was improving. At one stage in the middle of the Junior race I remember charging around the Glen Helen section of the TT course in the sunshine, grinning to myself because I was having so much fun. This part of the course is bordered by near vertical rock faces, and has a number of very tricky, dangerous bends that have witnessed numerous accidents, yet I loved pushing the 350 to its limit through there. It didn't have enough power to allow me to embarrass myself, yet had just enough to make it challenging. I had to concentrate fully to remain on the correct racing line, and never had time to consider the consequences of crashing.

Since staying at the Allerton we had made friends with a couple of other racers who lodged there. Paul Marks and Scott Richardson raced in the Manx Grand Prix but used modern machinery. They were both real road racing enthusiasts and, during race week, would volunteer to marshal alongside Paul's sister, Denise, if they were not competing.

On the Monday of my Classic Senior race, they were marshalling towards the end of the tricky Quarry Bends section near to a council depot. Unfortunately, one of the leading riders, Cliff Gobell, crashed right in front of them, and they had to deal with the aftermath. Cliff had passed another competitor as he approached the bends, and this overtake appears to have forced him slightly off-line, clipping a kerb which threw him from his machine into a wooded area. Cliff suffered severe injuries, and died in the accident, which Paul, Scott and Denise witnessed. I had considered marshalling following conversations with Paul, but am glad I never did. I was well aware of the dangers but had to put them to the back of my mind, otherwise I would never have taken the risks necessary to compete.

1995 was a big year for me, with some exciting new circuits and the Manx GP. I spent another winter saving money, and, by the spring, had enough to pay John for the motor rebuilds *and* buy a new PGT six-speed gearbox (selling the original Quaife box helped to fund this purchase). I tested the bikes at Mallory Park, and prepared the 350 for a meeting at Mettet in Belgium.

The original Mettet road circuit was basically a triangle with a couple of cambered corners, and one chicane near the end of the lap. The first right-hand corner was at a major crossroads, near the paddock, and on the inside of the course was a petrol station and bar that we often frequented. I liked the circuit's very long straights that encouraged slip-streaming, and although the roads were damp, I had a good second race, finishing eighth.

A month later we were off to Mallory Park, and I had my first class win with the 350, finishing tenth and 12th in the 500 races. By this time, both bikes were well sorted and running properly, I was still a bit weak at braking but loved fast bends, so one often cancelled out the other. I guess you can't be good at everything!

In June we returned to Dundrod and I had a very enjoyable ride to fifth place on the 350. The weather put paid to practice on the Friday, but we had completed a few laps in the van, and I now knew my way round. Shelagh travelled with me and Dave Carter, and, during one of our laps in the van, we were stopped by troops wielding semi-automatic rifles. The 'troubles' were in full swing at that time, and, en route to the circuit from the ferry we had got ourselves lost in the Falls Road area of Belfast, where the political flags on lamp posts and images painted on house walls certainly made us feel uncomfortable. We got out of the area as soon as we could find our correct route.

Later that day we went to Crumlin for a meal in a pub. We had just settled in and ordered a pint when, out of the window, I saw troops checking out underneath my van, the rear windows of which I had covered with black dustbin bags to conceal our tools and bikes. It was dusk by now, and I realised that the van might look suspicious because of this. I rushed outside, removed the bags, and showed them the contents of the van, which calmed them but shook us up.

Home from Ireland, I immediately prepared the two bikes for our first trip to Assen in Holland. IHRO (International Historic Racing Organisation) had managed to get the organisers to include two classic races as part of the Dutch TT programme, and I was eager to try out the famous 4.5-mile circuit. I had also managed to get an entry for a meeting at the partly-banked track at Montlhéry in France the same weekend, so we were going to take that in on our way home.

Pete Stockdale lived quite near to me, and I arranged to borrow his Ford Transit, whilst Dave Carter agreed to come with us. Pete had been a passenger for the famous sidecar racer George O'Dell. Some years earlier George had heavily crashed his outfit at Greeba Bridge during a TT race, and poor Pete suffered serious injuries to both feet. Pete said that George never bothered about him after the accident, and simply found another passenger for the upcoming race, leaving Pete to his own devices.

It took an entire, very long day to get to Assen, during which I suffered a small disaster. Riding in the passenger seat of our van, we travelled in convoy with another van being used by my racing pal, David Whitehouse. I wound down the passenger window and looked back to check that David was still with us, and my new, quite expensive sunglasses were whipped off my face by the wind, whereupon Dave's van ran straight over them! I've never bothered with 'good' sunglasses since then.

We eventually made it to the Assen circuit and set up camp in one of the secondary paddocks on the outside of the track. The roadways were all block-paved, and the toilet/shower block was immaculate. I completed two dry races and finished midfield in each, so no disgrace there. Our races followed the 'professionals' practice' on the Thursday evening, and it was quite an experience to be passed by three-cylinder MV Augustas and Benelli fours all on open exhausts — deafening! There was a terrific classic entry with numerous exotic bikes being ridden very quickly. We felt like stars performing in front of a really good crowd that had stayed on to watch us.

Dutch TT races were all held on the Saturday, and the Friday evening party in Assen town centre was something to behold. The entire area is pedestrianised, and there was a fairground ride plus a bandstand in each of five interlinked squares. Tented bars were spread out along the route, and locals and racegoers spent the evening moving from square to square, listening to the various types of musical entertainment and sampling the excellent Dutch lager. There was a certain amount of drunkenness but all in good humour. Okay: almost everyone had too much to drink and really enjoyed themselves!

We left Assen and travelled south to Montlhéry for another new experience. We were to use part of the pre-war banked track, which was so steep that we had trouble climbing it on all-fours during our pedestrian pre-practice course inspection. The weather was sunny but cool, and my 350 ran well in a meeting that mixed car and bike races. My guessed gearing was adequate and I finished second in my class of the 350 race that was run at 8.30am, receiving a nice trophy and a bottle of bubbly for my efforts (the latter didn't last long).

We arrived home safely, and I enjoyed returning to work and reliving our adventures with my colleagues.

A week later, I enjoyed a race meeting on the GP circuit at Brands Hatch, dicing with classic period GP ace John Blanchard, and then set to preparing the bikes for the Manx GP the following month. Dave Carter and John Walker travelled over with me, to be joined by Derek Cheesman. After Saturday evening's practice session I was well-pleased, deciding that the 500 bike was a 'beast'! For the Monday evening session Dennis Trollope, who ran a spares outlet van in the race paddock, asked me and Steve Ruth (both of us regular customers and friends of Dennis) to test some new chain that Renolds had supplied to him. Renolds had produced a limited amount of the race specification chain with a view to putting it into production. We both completed two laps but the chain had already developed tight spots, and I don't think Reynolds produced any other classic race chain after that failure. Steve and I reverted to Regina's reliable heavyweight chain.

Tuesday's session went well but, after checking the bike in the garage, we found that the 500 motor had lost some compression. I hadn't missed any gears, so spoke to John Goodall about it. He suggested we remove the cylinder head and he would check out the valve gear. We set to on this, and subsequently found that the inlet valve seat had distorted, so John re-cut the seat and ground in new valves. After replacing the head, compression was found to be back to normal.

The Senior race went wonderfully: run in dry conditions but quite windy up on the mountain. I finished tenth with a best lap of 96.30mph. A replica trophy at last and a top ten finish. At this time, replicas were awarded to any rider who finished the race within $^{11}/_{10}$ of the winner's time: a serious achievement in our racing world. I now had the credibility I so wanted; a '96mph man,' as riders were graded.

The Wednesday morning's 350 race was an anti-climax as the motor went silent on the second lap as I negotiated the fast and dangerous left-hand bend at the Black Hut, up on the mountain. The timing chain had broken, though fortunately did not damage or lock up the motor. Someone was looking after me that day. Before the afternoon race the course car completed a lap to check conditions, and I was 'lucky' enough to be picked up by the driver, so didn't have to wait up on the mountain until after the following race to get back to my team. I found the rear seat of the car already occupied by another couple of unfortunate riders, and together we endured the trip back to the pits at breakneck speed in the brand-new Volvo T4 RR driven by David Mylchreest, a garage owner and sponsor of the races. He was also a very experienced rally driver, and we were speechless as he braked at the very last minute from over 100mph for Creg-ny-baa corner, on the way down the mountain. None of us believed the car would or could slow enough to make the tight bend ... but it did!

At the prize-giving I went down on my knees to receive my replica trophy from the Mayor of Douglas, in front of the Manx GP committee who, in those days, were seated on the stage, all dressed in dinner suits and posh frocks. I was handed the compere's microphone to say a few words, so commented that the tiny trophy had probably cost me £40,000, but it was worth every penny! The other riders and their friends in the audience laughed at my antics ... drink was again taken.

My confidence was improving, but would it prove to be my downfall when I was offered a ride on a classic superbike?

CHAPTER 9

GOOD RACING BUT WITH SOME PAIN!

SAME OLD, SAME OLD WAS THE WAY THAT 1996 STARTED WITH A running-in session at Mallory Park followed by a pleasant meeting at Silverstone, then off to Dundrod (but without bath plug). Ninth in the 500 race and a really good ride to fourth in the 350 class sealed a great trip.

The trek to Assen was repeated, and my course knowledge improved to the point that I finished eighth in the 350 class and 15th in the 500. Back home, I took both bikes to the TTS dyno at Silverstone, and was rewarded with figures of 34bhp for the 350 and 45bhp for the 500. John had certainly kept his promise: performance was much-improved from our earlier check. Both of these bhp figures were good (though not exceptional) for standard AMC Matchless and AJS engines.

Now that I had competitive bikes to ride I just had to keep improving my riding skills.

Late August we returned to the island for the MGP. Saturday's practice session went smoothly, with the usual fettling taking place. Each year, during that first weekend, if the weather was kind we took ourselves off to Jurby Airfield to test the bikes prior to mid-week practice sessions, and John Goodall was often there with us, testing his own machinery. The runway was quite long, which allowed us to adjust the bikes' carburetion and do numerous high speed runs to bed-in new brake linings and tyres.

John was a good friend of Jack Gow, the Scottish classic racing champion, and a very experienced racer. I had just begun to chat with Jack, and found him generous with his advice and a really nice man.

We all turned out on a crisp Monday morning for early practice, and I completed one satisfactory lap on my 500. As I walked around the paddock afterwards, I bumped into John, who said that he thought Jack had suffered a 'big one' at the 32nd Milestone bend, coming down the mountain near the end of the lap. The 32nd was a tricky, triple apex left-hand corner with a blind approach, that could be taken at very high speed on a classic bike if the rider was very confident, and exactly on the right racing line. I certainly rolled off the throttle slightly when I negotiated it on a 500, and could just about do it flat out in fifth gear on my 350.

Later, I was told that Jack had wanted to put in a 'firm' lap to show the opposition he was a contender, but that, unbeknown to him, there was a damp area on the track around that fateful bend, probably due to early morning dew. Jack's tyres lost traction as he kept the throttle wide open the way he had many times before, and he lost control of the bike. Jack succumbed to his injuries a short while after his arrival at Nobles Hospital in Douglas. Later that week, I attended a memorial service for Jack at St Ninian's church, near the paddock, and this upset me so terribly that I did not go to another memorial during subsequent Grand Prix weeks. Naturally, John was very upset when he heard the news of Jack's death.

I finished 13th in both Manx races and qualified for replicas in each. I have never been superstitious, and achieved a race average of 96.22mph in the 500 race with a fastest lap over 97mph. Track conditions had varied, with some damp patches, but the bike ran beautifully and I was on good form, finishing just behind Manxman Danny Shimmin, and in front of Franz Glauser, a Swiss racing pal. The 350 race was run in good weather and I averaged 91.48mph: a considerable improvement on previous years.

Shortly after I arrived home from the island — and probably as a result of my Manx GP results, I received a phone call from a Metropolitan police officer, offering me a ride on a Triumph 750cc triple classic race bike that he and his wife sponsored through her bearings distribution company. A satisfactory practice session at Mallory Park followed, and I agreed to race their bike at a Mallory race meeting a couple of weeks later. The Triumph felt powerful but very heavy compared to a Seeley single, and I was wedged between the seat and fuel tank whereas, on a Seeley, I could move around a bit. The owners put no pressure on me, though, so it all seemed worth a try. Much better to wear out someone else's machinery, eh?

On race day my eldest daughter, Amanda, and her husband, Ian, came along to support me, with Shelagh completing our team. Practice went well, and we cleaned the bike ready for the first race.

My start from the middle of the grid was average, but when I reached the first long right-hand bend at Gerrards, probably travelling at around 70 or 80mph, I found that the bike simply did not want to turn right in the way I was used to. The rear end slipped out slightly and I ended up heading for a tyre barrier on the outside of the bend. I ditched a lot of speed crossing a gravel trap, but when I reached the grass in front of the barrier the bike gained impetus and I hit the tyres head-on, still on the bike and with the front brake pulled on as hard as possible. I was probably travelling at only 30mph or so, but the impact threw me over the side of the bike and I ended up very winded, though okay, I thought.

A marshal joined me and asked if I could climb over the tyre wall, though offering no assistance to do so. I stood up and attempted to climb ... ouch — that bloomin' hurt! I got over the tyres with his help, but realised that something was amiss with my right shoulder. I sat there, feeling faint, until the race ended, then walked back to the paddock, met up with my 'team,' and went to the medical centre.

The doctor there took one look at me and asked Shelagh if I was always that colour: apparently, I was very pale and really struggling not to pass out. I was hugging my right arm close to my chest, and didn't want anyone to touch or move it. The doctor had to do his job, though, and after a prod around suggested I might have broken my shoulder blade, despatching me to Leicester Infirmary in the circuit ambulance to get his diagnosis confirmed. After the usual wait, a doctor at the hospital grasped my wrist and gently lifted my arm above my head, causing me to gasp with the acute pain, although, once in the air, this subsided. I had broken my shoulder, he told me, and the bad news was that I now had to lower my arm, which was *really* going to hurt ... and, wow, did it! My arm was placed in a sling, and X-rays revealed several cracks across the shoulder blade, including one into the joint. Painkillers and physiotherapy was the only available treatment, and that was me knackered for several weeks. End of season.

Some months later I was approached by another rider who had taken my place racing the Triumph. He said that when they had been repairing the bike after my crash they found that the rear wheel bearings had collapsed, which may well have caused my loss of control. Considering that the owner's company that had sponsored the bike sold bearings, this was rather ironic.

I endured a quiet autumn and plotted for 1997. I made a list of the areas of the TT course I believed I was weak in, and began to watch 'on-bike' videos, so that I could correct and memorise my lines, braking and peel-off points. Initially, I used a Joey Dunlop film, but then found a couple of others that were nearer to classic lap speeds. It passed the winter evenings and, together with regular gym visits, I consoled myself with the thought that at least I was working to improve my performance capability before the new season. I had recognised that, on the last lap of a Manx race, I tended to get tired, and to back off slightly to ensure that I finished. I now had that precious replica, so finishing became less of an issue compared with improving my lap times and finishing position.

From now on I intended that my last lap be my fastest: whilst my opponents flagged, I would make a real effort.

My pal Paul Marks had lost any chance of winning his first replica, after several years of trying, when, during a Senior Manx GP fuel stop, he was alleged to have crossed the 'stop box' white line by a fraction. Penalised ten seconds for failing to stop within the marked area put him outside of replica time by a couple of seconds. When you are approaching that stop box after travelling for many miles in excess of over 100mph, it is very difficult to gauge the stopping distance needed to hit the stop box area precisely. I felt very sorry for Paul, especially as our classic bikes didn't need to stop for fuel, so any problems with that dreaded stop box were avoided. A year or two earlier I twice had to bump-start my bike at the beginning of one of my earlier Manx GP races, and the time I lost was equivalent to the time by which I failed to win a replica award. Every second counts, and I resolved to put all my efforts into avoiding these issues in future, so the gym and the videos became vital.

The 1997 season began at Snetterton, where a few small problems reared their heads, though midfield results were okay for that stage of the season. A month later I raced at Mallory Park where both bikes ran well. I was relieved to find that, after my crash there the previous autumn I didn't seem to have lost my nerve around that hectic short circuit. I actually enjoyed 'Gerrards,' the never-ending right-hand bend that had seen my demise.

Always up for a challenge, I decided to have a go at the Skerries road circuit in Southern Ireland. I wanted to ride on as many of the original road circuits as possible and, having enjoyed Dundrod, I was encouraged by my Irish pals to visit Skerries, and also Tandragee. Dave Carter agreed to come with Shelagh and me, and so in early July we travelled to Fishguard for the long ferry journey to Dun Laoghaire.

Navigating our way to the circuit, we found that the 'paddock' was a field only recently vacated by a flock of sheep! Locating a patch of reasonably flat grass next to Manx racer Danny Shimmin, we set up camp.

A trip to a pub in Skerries that evening proved amusing. Still with the bikes in the van, I parked directly outside a pub recommended to us by local racing lads. We'd arrived at about 9pm to a quiet pub, and nothing much happened until about ten when there was an influx of locals and racers.

By now it was getting dark, and the pub's curtains were drawn. At one stage I peeked out to check that our van was secure, and the chap sitting next to Shelagh said "Shut the effing curtain!" I asked him what the problem was, and was quietly informed that local police tended to ignore late-night drinking providing it was not obvious as they passed by. Shelagh asked him what time the pub shut and he replied "September!" Only the Irish.

Next day I spent some time chatting to Danny Shimmin, who gave me a few tips regarding the circuit, and then set about preparing the bikes for practice. All went according to plan and, although I finished well down the field in both races, I enjoyed the circuit, even if it did have some loose gravel and manhole covers on a couple of the off-camber corners to add extra interest. The next morning we left at the crack of dawn to catch an early ferry, but became slightly lost in a remote village. Fortunately, an local elderly chap was walking his dog, so I stopped to ask directions. He pointed to the white line in the centre of the road, and told us to follow that for so many miles, then take a turning off it. We left him, slightly bemused but better informed; it turned out his directions were correct.

Safely home it was time to begin preparations for the Manx Grand Prix. 1997 was to be a big year. Classic Racer magazine asked me to keep a diary throughout the fortnight and I faithfully complied. We arrived back on the island, set up the garage, and completed Saturday's dry practice session with both bikes appearing fine. After returning to the pits I was informed that Danny Shimmin had crashed at Greeba Castle, his bike was reported to be a mess, and it looked serious. Not a good start to the racing.

Sunday passed with a little bike maintenance and relaxation, but Monday morning brought the sad news that Danny Shimmin had died. We should have been up early practising but the morning's session had been cancelled as all five intensive care beds in Nobles Hospital were in use. I had enjoyed Danny's company at the Skerries, and his passing saddened me greatly. This racing lark certainly has its ups and downs ... Practice week passed quickly, with changeable weather mixed with interludes of spannering.

On the Tuesday my faithful mechanic, Dave Carter, disgraced himself by allowing the G50 to fall over in the grass area of the paddock, slightly damaging the fibreglass fairing. More repairs; easy to fix, though. Thursday's afternoon session was very wet so I opted out and worked on the bikes.

Friday was spent waiting for the evening session, and I managed to persuade Bill Swallow to take me around the course in an effort to improve my racing lines. He showed me different approach lines into Handley's, Kerromoar, and Ballagh Bridge. I wasn't brave enough to use his recommendation at Hadley's; at Kerromoar I worked on his line, and in the evening session I tried his line at Ballagh Bridge, succeeding in jumping further than I ever had previously, though wobbled like mad on landing, deciding I'd have to rethink that one. Evening practice went well and, on returning to the paddock, I handed the G50 to Dave, asking him if he wanted the stand or would he prefer to throw it on the ground? He looked at me a bit strangely!

I again decided against practising on the Saturday evening as it was generally wet all round the course, and both the bikes seemed fine. After much persuasion from Graham Rhodes I joined the MGP Riders Association Committee, and enjoyed my first meeting with the other members. Graham told me how lucky he had been after crashing at the 11th Milestone, which is a really fast bend. He had a lot of bike damage to repair before Wednesday's Junior race. I was reasonably happy with our practice week: I could have done with more track time, but both bikes seemed okay, and my qualifying times were an improvement on the previous year.

On Monday, Senior race day, we took the G50 up to the pits, were scrutineered, and I went for a physio session to ease some tension I often suffered in my shoulders. We watched the Newcomers race from the bottom of Bray Hill, noting some unorthodox lines. On our way back to the paddock a black cat sauntered across the road in front of us. A good omen, perhaps?

My race started on time at 1.00pm, and the weather was brilliant: hot and sunny. I made a good start and the bike seemed to be flying; revving freely. I had started at number 26, and already passed a couple of riders by the time I exited Quarry Bends. Tucking in for the Sulby Straight everything seemed fine as I carried maximum revs in top gear past the Sulby Hotel. Just after this I felt a slight vibration through the handlebars that hadn't been there previously. I eased off the throttle then reapplied it, but the vibration increased and I knew my race was already over.

I pulled over at Sulby Bridge, pushed the bike into a side road and killed the motor. I couldn't see anything amiss so decided to restart the motor with a quick push aided by Colin Wilkins, a Velo Club pal who happened to be spectating there. The bike fired but sounded and felt awful. If I was eight-years-old I would have cried. What a waste of all that dieting, training, hours of preparation, discussion, planning and so on. Shelagh collected me in the van before the end of the race, and when we checked the magnetic sump plug back in the garage, it was covered in metal debris. The crank pin had broken. John Goodall later told me that, on close inspection, he found the pin had been incorrectly machined, and we were lucky it had lasted as long as it had. John didn't have a good race, either, so we were in good company.

The Junior race was a bit of an anti-climax. Delayed due to heavy rain, when we eventually did get off there were damp patches everywhere, and I rode cautiously to finish 18th, but well off replica time. Not a Manx Grand Prix to remember, but it made good copy for the magazine. All my pals posted their fastest race and lap times in the lovely weather, and I missed out.

I ended the year with meetings at Scarborough and Snetterton. I liked the challenge of Scarborough's narrow parkland circuit, but if it's at all wet it becomes a dangerous place with its three hairpin bends and tree-lined spectator areas. In damp, misty conditions I finished about two-thirds down the field, but sort of enjoyed the experience.

Snetterton was better and I finished the weekend with sixth and seventh places, so the racing year did end with a smiley face on the rider. As a guide to costs, John Goodall's bill to rebuild my motors during the following winter was £1000, and I had to pay Mick Taberer £750 for replacement engine components that included a new flywheel assembly for the G50. I also bought a new 1½in Amal GP carb from Tony Harris for £390, and my pal, Alan Wright, lent me a 1⅜in Amal GP carb for my 7R motor. Up until this point I had used Amal Mk 2 smoothbore carbs, but John advocated GPs, and I was looking for any power gains I could find.

I needed to move up a step to join the front end of the grid: improvements would have to be made in all areas.

CHAPTER 10

ADVENTURES IN EUROPE, AND OTHER PAINFUL EXPERIENCES

OVER THE NEXT COUPLE OF SEASONS I CONTINUED TO RACE AS often as financially possible; the sponsorship I received from the Hertfordshire Constabulary Motor Club and The Federation of British Police Motor Clubs assisting with entry fees. My pal, Robin Packham at Falcon Shock Absorbers, looked after my suspension units, and I continued to rebuild friends' classic bikes to raise race funds. Via work I got to know David Speed, the boss of a company that developed automatic number plate reading systems, and he bunged some money in the pot for a couple of seasons (in hindsight, through my job as a Crime Prevention Officer I did maybe manage to help him secure a lucrative contract with the police ...). My mates say I would have made a good salesman but that's not a career that I've ever fancied, though I do work hard at networking, which has paid off over the years as I have received valuable support from a number of businessmen and small companies. Every little bit helps, and I have remained friends with most of them.

During the late '90s I approached the Classic Racing Motorcycle Club and requested it add an extra championship to promote the use of more genuine or non-modified classic race bikes. The Club eventually gave in to my nagging and, for a couple of years, ran The Hailwood Championship for more original bikes within the normal race programme event. I entered my Seeley 7R but, although I won my class a couple of times, the Championship failed to attract the genuine bikes that languished in their owners' workshops, gathering dust and rarity value. I had hoped that a few genuine Seeleys, Manx Nortons and Matchless G50s would reappear but few ever did. The class was open to full replicas but most of these were developed lightweight versions and not eligible. The Club did allow a lightweight 350cc Ducati to enter, though, and it became uncatchable. I protested to the Club's eligibility officer but he said that there were so few entries for the class he felt obliged to allow marginal bikes to compete. I even protested to the bike's owner but he just shrugged and said "As long as they let me in I'll enter it." This went against the purpose of the Championship and it soon failed to exist. At least I tried. Pot hunters will always bend the rules to gain any advantage, I guess, but what is the value of a trophy won by cheating?

New circuits were added to my 'done' list including Croft, Rockingham, and Lydden. I really enjoyed travelling to foreign circuits and, during this period, enjoyed trips to Le Mans, Mettet, Chimay, Assen, Schleiz, Nürburgring, Zolder, the A1 Ring in Austria, and even Tandragee in Northern Ireland. I could usually finish midfield, and in the top dozen on the odd occasion, amongst some of the top classic racers in Europe.

Mettet and Chimay in Belgium became firm favourites. I loved the downhill section at Chimay, and spent ages trying to take the last esses section at full throttle in top gear. After a couple of years I could just do it, but a number of my pals crashed in this section of the track, and Tony Myers' race career ended when he crashed after he touched a tyre wall on the exit of the esses. He damaged the nerves in his arm and they never recovered properly: a great shame as Tony was a very quick, experienced racer, and a good friend. He's recently taken to parading a Ducati with a specially-adapted clutch mechanism, and the old smile has returned to his face. Good on you, Tony.

One year my youngest daughter, Katherine (Charlie), came with us and, with Simon, her husband-to-be, we camped in a large, six-berth tent. At around six o'clock on the Friday practice morning we were awoken by the sound of Led Zeppelin's *Stairway to heaven* being played at full volume over the tannoy system. We thought we'd died and gone to heaven: brilliant!

My first trip to Schleiz in the former East Germany seemed to take forever. As soon as we reached the old border from west to east the roads changed from perfect autobahns to two-lane knackered concrete roads. It took us two days to reach the most perfect road course next to the village. I loved it and rode reasonably for a first-timer. The weather was blazing hot and the food cooked in the paddock for visiting fans was incredible. Huge frying pans heated by large gas rings contained lovely goulash, and cheap beer and white wine pleased everyone.

The track, as it was then in 1999, cut through open fields, then meandered through woodlands, passing the verandah of our hotel, before breaking out onto the main road. Such a variation and good quality tarmac. It was worth the long journey just to experience life in that part of the world. Lots of different bikes to look at and race against: foreign race meetings are a must for keen classic racers, in my opinion.

I returned there a couple of years later to race one of Cleve Brightman's Aermacchis. Unfortunately, I was third in the list for bikes, and the machine I was allocated leaked oil and kept losing the exhaust pipe attachment. Poor Cleve tried so hard to repair it, but had to give up in the end. I practised but never raced, so enjoyed spectating and socialising instead. For a couple of years there was no racing there, but then a shorter version of the track was introduced, although I never had the opportunity to return.

Tandragee was a humbling experience. The track is narrow, contained by high hedgerows, and the only year I went it was damp to add to my problems. The locals knew the track like the back of their hand, and I felt lost. I wandered round near the back of the field, and went home a wiser racer. I should have travelled over a few days earlier and learnt the circuit better. I did get some tips from very experienced racer Dennis Gallagher, but failed to utilise them to any degree! Never mind: the paddock banter at an Irish race meeting is worth the trip alone. I did fancy a ride at the Temple 100 road races but my Irish mentor, Billy Patterson, the father of GP rider Alan Patterson, advised against — or rather forbade me — from competing there. He regarded it as too dangerous with its very narrow confines and numerous vicious jumps, and not at all suitable for my Seeley. I did listen to Billy, and probably saved myself even more embarrassment.

When racing in Northern Ireland I often lodged with Billy and his wife, Marjorie, and we became good friends with his family. He was a mine of information on Irish road racing and its characters, and had been deeply involved in organising race meetings in his area for some years. He introduced me to many of the local riders, and one evening took me to their local bar, which was actually in the front lounge of a local cottage. Shelagh was advised to stay at home with Marjorie: this bar was not a place for our women! There were some rough-looking characters amongst the local farming community, but they loved talking about the racing, and could manage a Guinness or three.

Rain and wet tracks are not my favourite but my only trip to Le Mans with IHRO (International Historic Racing Organisation) turned out okay in some ways. We were there with the Moto GP and enjoyed watching the stars perform, though failed to get much sleep as our classic paddock was next to the fans' campsite, who enjoyed exploding Honda Fireblade engines, fixed to pallets, at two in the morning by putting them on the rev limiter and, whilst being encouraged by drunken pals, revving them to death. I went with my pals, Pete Edwards and Stuart Jukes, and enjoyed the worry of Stuart collapsing in a diabetic coma one evening. Fortunately, I had been briefed by his wife, Jan, that Stuart was bad at regulating his diet, and she advised me what to do if he collapsed. He soon came round after I force-fed him a Mars bar, with no recollection of the panic he had caused Pete and me.

We had only one race on the Saturday of the weekend, and it poured with rain. A number of aces fell off but I steadily gained confidence and finished 11th. Unfortunately, I then found a crack in the frame and, as the next scheduled race meeting was the Manx GP, we quickly stripped the bike in the Le Mans paddock so that Brian Richards could take the frame home with him, and deliver it for repair to Keith Stephenson, the frame builder, who lived near him in the far north of England. My thread locking and wire locking slowed the process considerably, and Brian frequently cursed me as he was worried about missing his ferry (Brian had sold the Petty Manx Norton that I was riding at this particular meeting to my new sponsor, Don Williamson,).

At the Nürburgring in 2000, this time with INCA (International Classic Association, formed and run by George Beale, a classic racing enthusiast and long-time sponsor at GP level), at a race meeting combined with a truck race event, we endured numerous mosquito bites after camping overnight in a paddock garage. The trucks laid down a huge amount of tyre rubber debris, and the slippery track didn't encourage hard riding. A shame, really, as the circuit was to Grand Prix standard and enjoyable — if you could stay on the bike, which several riders didn't! Midfield result again for me.

The A1 Ring was another slippery sucker, with a very long drive to get there, but taking a look around Salzburg was compensation. A dry practice day was followed by a lot of rain, and I was glad I slept in the van, and not in the tent. Fortunately, Stuart had rigged the ground sheet correctly in our awning/tent, and he also stayed dry whilst many around us didn't.

The A1 Ring was very boring to race on: a series of right-angle bends and hard-braking areas. Not my favourite but a good experience, and located near the Alps in a most picturesque part of Austria. I rode within my capabilities again, finishing midfield on a damp track; mindful that we had a very long drive home, which my old Renault Traffic van managed, thank goodness.

I really enjoyed riding on these famous and historic race tracks. Results were important but the experience and social life were my priorities; good results just made things better. My bikes gained a reputation for being reliable and well-prepared, and this was appreciated by the organisers. I often managed to squeeze in a late entry or get a slightly reduced entry fee. They knew that I was not wealthy or fully sponsored like many of the riders, and I couldn't afford to travel to all of the championship rounds. Not quite shoestring racing, but close ...

Around this time Stuart and I took ourselves off to Zolder in Belgium, again with INCA and the bloomin' trucks. As is often the case in Belgium it rained. The track at Zolder is armco-lined so not a place to take risks. The track itself is quite enjoyable but we got very little practice, and I thought we were shortchanged a little. It was a long journey for us, and one wet race wasn't really a worthwhile exercise — but the Belgian beer is very tasty, as are the frites!

Mettet, on the Seeley G50, caused me a few headaches. The original postwar Mettet road course, competed on by many famous car and bike racing stars, was almost a figure of eight, covering a similar distance to the later 8.3 kilometre course we raced on (now replaced by a modern, self-contained race track complex). This later version was essentially a triangle, with a bus stop chicane added just prior to the finish line to slow riders approaching a downhill hairpin bend around a café/garage that led onto a very long downhill straight. Two further long straights took you back towards the finish line. It was in the flat, rural countryside near to the pretty town of Mettet, and one year during practice I watched a large deer saunter across the track as I approached at over 100mph. The animal was oblivious to me but certainly drew my attention. Gearing was similar or even taller to the TT course, so you'll gather that it was a fast course, generally.

I was in the middle of a race on the Sunday of race weekend when, braking and changing down the gears for the café corner, my Seeley G50 began to weave slightly. I gripped the bars tightly and kept braking but the weave increased, and eventually the bike dumped me on my ear quite firmly. I realised later that I had been sliding forward on the bike under the very hard braking required for that particular corner, and, as I did so, my left foot pressed harder on the rear brake pedal, inadvertently locking the rear wheel. Too stupid to realise what was happening at the time, I was simply trying to reduce my braking distance for that corner.

The bike was slightly damaged — as was my pride — and we packed up and headed for home. As I drove through Belgian villages I realised that my concentration was wandering: something was not right inside my head. I also felt hot and slightly faint so let mechanic Dave Carter drive, ultimately arriving home battered but safe. This was my first and only experience of concussion which I would rather not repeat!

The Circuit Van Drenthe near Assen in Holland is everyone's favourite circuit. In the form that we raced on in the '90s it flowed wonderfully, with very little heavy braking, and the emphasis on the perfect line for the combination corners, which suited my riding style perfectly. The track is quite narrow and is cambered nicely, which aids corner speed. I raced there six times and our IHRO events were part of the Dutch TT Grand Prix meeting. One year our 500cc race took place straight after Mick Doohan had won on his works NSR Honda. Around half of the 100,000-plus crowd stayed on to watch us, and it was the thrill of a lifetime to be part of that event. Another year I finished seventh in the 350cc event after a great tussle with Terry Shepherd on his Aermacchi: my best result there, from a full grid of 40 bikes.

For race weekend the town of Assen parties like nowhere else. There were also Orangeboom stalls all around the circuit perimeter service road, and it was normal for fans to leave their viewing spots and relieve themselves against the wire fence next to the track whilst racing was taking place. The Dutch are not shy folk.

At this time the Rockingham race track in Northamptonshire was created, and the CRMC decided to sample its delights. It's a large oval designed for American stock car racing, with a modern in-field for smaller machines. The crash barriers were rather intimidating, especially at the entry to the first corner, but the weekend was dry, fortunately, and there were few incidents. We pulled tokens from a cloth bag to select grid positions, and I drew the front row for all the races. I wasn't bad at the push-starts used then, and got away well, but after the first race I realised that I was a moving road block for the faster riders, all of whom were anxious to get past me once they had got going. I got bombed by all the quick chaps at the second corner.

I approached my friend and very quick rider Phill Sharp, and expressed my concerns. He replied "You're not a problem, Andy. Being a road racer you're always on the traditional line, and we know where you're going to be on the track. Just ride the way you usually do and all will be fine." Phill was absolutely right. I had spent a lot of time perfecting my racing on true road courses, and these demanded accuracy on every tree- or wall-lined bend, if you wanted to stay alive. I wasn't and would never be a scratcher, and would always achieve better results on the road than any short circuit.

In the late '90s my Manx Grand Prix exploits continued to dominate each year's race programme and machine development. John Goodall continued to service and improve my motors; the G50 benefiting from an electronic ignition system. I purchased a set of lightweight magnesium fork parts, gave Dick Hunt a large amount of money for a lightweight front wheel with a disc brake assembly, and bought new disc-braked rear wheels for both bikes. I ordered and eventually received two new fuel tanks, and also bought new, more enclosing-type fairings for each machine.

These fairing were a real pain to fit, but did enclose my hands and theoretically were more streamlined. It took a while to get used to riding within them, but it taught me to tuck in more and move around less on fast bends.

As a guide to the competition my notes refer to a conversation with Vernon Glashier, a top classic race winner during this period. Vernon told me that his 500cc Tickle Norton was producing 55bhp at the rear wheel (my G50 produced only 45bhp). He knew I was no competition to him, and asked me to keep that information to myself. No wonder he flew past me on occasion, though, to be fair, he was also a brilliant and very brave rider.

My Manx GP results gradually improved and, if all went well, I could now finish within replica award time in both Junior and Senior Classic races. You need a certain amount of luck to finish as consistently as I did, plus good preparation, of course. One year, whilst polishing the lightweight front wheel of the Seeley 7R after a Manx practice, Stuart Jukes asked me to look closely at the dimples in the wheel rim: he had spotted hairline cracks appearing between six of these dimples. I had been jumping the bike quite firmly at Ballagh Bridge, and probably the landings caused the cracks. Stuart has a long history of fastidious machine preparation on his own championship-winning grasstrack racing sidecar outfits, and I was most grateful for his attention to detail and, of course his good eyesight. We consequently used the heavier front wheel for both races as we couldn't source a new rim on the island.

My best result on the G50 was tenth in 1995, and I was lucky that year as so many fast riders failed to finish. My best lap time on the G50 was just over 97.29mph in the 1996 Senior race, and 92mph on the 7R in the Junior race in 2002. Weather conditions played a large part in lap times. High winds and damp patches meant that new records would not be set by anyone some years. As an example, I finished 13th in both races in 1996, and 16th in both in 2000. Around half of the starters failed to finish most years, but this happened to me only twice on the Seeleys: in 1997 when the G50 crank pin broke, and when the timing chain broke on the 7R in 1995. John built me very reliable motors, and I did my bit, chassis-wise.

Failing to finish meant one of two things: a mechanical breakdown or a crash. Some years were worse than others for this, although I did lose a number of racing pals in the MGP races and practices. Rob Wingrave and I had become friends and, during the first practice sessions at the 1998 MGP, we agreed that at the last race meeting of the year at Snetterton, we would swap bikes and I could try his Manx Norton, whilst he had a go on one of my Seeleys. This was not to happen as poor Rob got off-line in the village of Union Mills during Thursday afternoon practice session, clipping the kerb and ultimately crashing, sustaining grave injuries from which he died a couple of weeks later.

My youngest daughter, Katherine, had become friendly with the nephew of Chris East, another classic competitor and great pal of John Goodall. Chris advocated absolute originality, and his beautiful Matchless G50 was an example of this to all who gazed at it. He was very experienced around the TT course, and had several top ten finishes to his credit.

On Senior Classic race day in 1998, Chris was going well, but crashed on the second lap at the very tricky Douglas Road corner entering Kirkmichael Village, the reason for which has never been fully explained. The bike just seemed to lose rear wheel traction and, after falling off and sliding into straw bales, the bike clouted Chris. He was very seriously hurt as a result, and died a few weeks later.

Chris utilised a primary chain and, given its oiling system, it was possible that oil from this could have got onto the rear tyre. Most of us used toothed belt drives for primary transmission, so avoided the need for an oiling system.

Tim Johnson was another good friend of mine from my Velocette and Vintage racing exploits, and another rider who loved originality, spending years trying to achieve the fastest Velocette lap at the Classic Manx races. Eddie Dudman sponsored Tim with a quick Velocette and a very original Manx Norton.

In 1999, Tim decided that he could take the whole of the Barrowgarroo section flat out in top gear on his Velocette: like all of us, trying to shave seconds from each lap. This time, however, it was a step too far, and Tim and his bike crashed just after the crossroads at the top of the section, both of them sliding an awfully long way down the road, with neither meeting anything too solid, fortunately. I wondered what had caused the long green streak down the hill as I passed it at high speed later in that practice session, and ultimately learnt that it came from Tim's fairing. I guess Eddie's fibreglass repair kit was soon depleted!

Poor Tim died after falling from his Aermacchi at the Black Hut bend on the mountain section in 2005, in a fine third position in the MGP Junior Classic race. Travelling at high speed he attempted to take avoiding action when passing a rider he was lapping, who suddenly changed direction as he was slowing with a mechanical problem. This manoeuvre put Tim off the racing line and he had to lay down the Aermacchi to avoid hitting the other rider, suffering fatal injuries as he did so.

Speed differentials between the fastest and slowest riders often cause issues and sometimes accidents. I have certainly had my share of near-misses when inexperienced riders I was overtaking or lapping suddenly decided to alter their racing line, or brake suddenly.

The Isle of Man TT Circuit can be an unforgiving place …

CHAPTER 11

THE PETTY NORTON

DON WILLIAMSON WAS A FRIEND OF STUART JUKES; BOTH VINTAGE Motorcycle Club pals from the St Albans area and Excelsior Manxman enthusiasts. Don had approached Stuart whilst watching the Manx Grand Prix races in 1997 to say that he would like to get involved with a rider, contributing sponsorship in a small way. The pair discussed several options and, luckily for me, I was selected, I'm told, for my consistent lap times and good bike preparation.

Don owned Braye Precision Ltd, based in North London, which manufactured high precision components, typically for Formula One teams. Don spoke to me after the Senior Classic MGP race, and I readily accepted his kind offer of sponsorship. Don told me he wasn't interested in becoming involved with a reckless or brave rider, and wanted me to carry on, but hopefully with his assistance improving my results. He was especially interested in the Manx GP as he had friends on the island and visited every year. Don thought I had the potential to do well, given a little help.

True to his word, Don's company paid for tyres and other running costs for a couple of seasons, and then, just after the finish of the 2000 Senior MGP race, whilst I was enjoying a pint of Okells in the paddock beer tent, he wandered in and announced that he'd bought me a better bike for the following season. Unbeknown to me, he had been talking to Brian Richards, a well known and respected sponsor, and they had done a deal. Brian had been running a replica Petty Norton since 1997, and had enjoyed considerable success with both Bill Swallow and Bob Jackson racing the bike for him in Manx GP races. The bike had a great history, having won the Senior MGP in 1999 ridden by Bill, and finished second in three other MGP Senior Classic races. It had finished second in the 2000 Singles TT, again ridden by Bill, but utilising a 570cc conversion that involved a special crankshaft.

I was flabbergasted but so excited. I did a bit of networking and spoke to both Bill and Brian. Bill told me that he was a little fed up with the bike consistently leaking oil, and Brian told me that he had originally built the bike using an Andy Molnar motor, but had switched for 1999 to a Summerfield unit; one of very few that utilised very large experimental valve pushers, and was quick! Brian kindly offered any help he could with running the bike.

Don and I travelled to the Summerfields factory in Derbyshire to collect the bike, which was in 570 form, having had its motor rebuilt by Jerry Summerfield as we planned to enter it in the Singles race at the 2001 TT. We met Brian there and took possession of a wonderful bit of kit. Don was happy for me to store and prepare the bike at my house, and I spent many happy shed hours examining and slightly improving the machine in my own way. There were just a couple of small details that I wanted to alter, which I cleared with Don.

I raced my own bikes during the first part of the 2001 season, but then disaster: the TT and the Manx GP were called off due to foot-and-mouth disease. I was mortified. Don and I had a long discussion about the way to progress, and decided that we would enter the bike for the Classic race at the Dundrod 100 races over the Ulster Grand Prix course in Northern Ireland. I knew the course well and anticipated a good result. The motor, of course, had to be converted to its 500 specification so more trips up-north were undertaken.

Prior to the Irish event I raced the Norton at Donington and Chimay with some success. The bike had a large 40mm Gardner flat slide carburettor that proved difficult to set up as weather conditions varied. At Donington it was hot and humid, and the bike ran rich, which caused the motor to vibrate and bothered me. In Chimay things were better in moderate weather conditions, and the quick nature of the course suited me. Better results followed.

I had some trouble with my Seeley front drum brake, which we had fitted to meet IHRO regulations. Heavy use got it a little hot and bothered, and the sliding fulcrums began to stick, preventing the brake shoes releasing. A bit of careful spannering and lubrication cured the problem, though.

Practice at Dundrod went well with the bike running beautifully, and Don and his ladyfriend flew over on a scheduled flight to join us for race day. This surprised me a little as he owned and regularly flew a lovely French Aerospatiale four-seater light aircraft.

Race day weather started off fine but gradually turned wet, and riders soon found to their cost that the white lines painted around the road course were not anti-skid. In fact, they were lethal if the surface was at all damp. My Bavarian pal Reinhard Neumair competed in the first 350cc Classic race of the day, returning to the pits saying it was too slippery on the white lines to race properly, and that we would have to be very careful in the 500cc race later. Soon after a 125cc rider crashed near to the finish line, and his bike hit a spectator. There was a long period of discussion amongst officials and the meeting was called off.

Blimey, what a financial disaster for riders and their teams. We had driven to Stranraer from Hertfordshire to catch the ferry, and Don had forked out for flight tickets and car hire — ouch! Poor Reinhard had come much further than that. It was a great pity as I loved the circuit and fancied my chances for a good result in front of my sponsor.

Over the next few years I enjoyed several flights with Don in his plane. I was sometimes instructed in the use of the controls once we were airborne, and learned a little about flying. Don's plane had a six-cylinder engine, which made it quite powerful for its size. One year he offered us a flight to the Isle of Man to see a couple of days of TT racing. We drove to Elstree aerodrome where Don kept the plane, and had a coffee whilst he did all of the necessary pre-flight checks. Shelagh is a nervous flyer, and was distinctly concerned about her first light aircraft flight.

Before we boarded Don took me aside and told me that a micro switch on the landing gear was faulty, but that the mechanic had advised him all would be fine as long as he left the landing gear locked down for the entire trip. This would reduce our air speed a little, but the switch could be replaced at a later date. He told me that there would be a red warning light glowing on the instrument panel, indicating that there was a fault, but I should ignore it and not mention it to Shelagh. I did as I was told. Shelagh soon spotted the glowing light, however, and questioned its relevance. Don fudged the truth a little and she calmed down, although we had to own up eventually, and the trip home was a little tense!

At Snetterton the bike performed well and I finished well up in the four races I entered. As I cleaned the bike after the last race I spotted an oil leak from the magnesium crankcase, around the oil pump; a not uncommon occurrence with Manx Nortons — and ours had certainly earned its keep over the last couple of seasons, especially in the hands of Bill Swallow. I contacted the Summerfields and they agreed to strip and rebuild the motor with new cases. The bill was high but Don and I agreed to sell them the 570 crank as the powers that be (the ACU) had decided to end the Singles TT, so I would never get to use the large format motor, anyway. Selling the crank for £750 reduced the £1150 bill to £400, which Don's sponsorship funded — phew! I was very upset at the demise of the Singles TT as I dearly wanted to compete at the TT races; I wasn't sure I would get another chance.

I returned to Snetterton to test the rebuilt motor, and enjoyed a nice sunny outing at a Track Day organised by No Limits Track Days; the owner, Mark Neate, generously allowed us to steal some track time when his sessions were not full up. Over the years we were to frequently take advantage of his kindness, and he refused all offers of payment. Thanks, Mark. The only condition we had to comply with was not to use the same garage as he did for his temporary office as our classic bikes were slightly — okay, much — louder than the modern kit he normally catered for.

I enjoyed parts of the Snetterton track, particularly Corum Curve which Charlie Sanby had coached me around some years earlier in our Seeley days. Charlie was superb around Snetterton, and I enjoyed watching him pull away from me as he used every inch of the track around this notoriously fast bend. Our Seeleys were roughly equal in performance but, boy, was he brave and skilful there. Following him I quickly realised the difference between amateur racers like me and professionals, even though Charlie was around 50 years of age at that time.

After a particularly good session at a No Limits day, two riders turned up in our garage, wanting to look at the Petty Norton as they couldn't recognise the make of bike they had been dicing with. Both commented that their R1 Yamahas could eat our bike along the straights but couldn't get near me around Corum Curve. They were amazed at how narrow our 'classic' tyres were compared to the very wide items their modern sports bikes used. I puffed out my chest at the idea that I could still teach these youngsters a thing or two about racing motorcycles!

Practice at the 2002 MGP was traumatic, as the Norton continued to leak oil from the timing case cover. Brian had told me to drain the cover after each race, but other riders said that this part of the motor should be dry. After the second practice session I grasped the nettle and ordered a new lower timing pinion and a new brass bush. These arrived quickly by post from the Summerfields, and Nick Magnay, a pal of Stuart's, made us an ignition timing device and split the bush in half so that we could introduce an O-ring seal between the two parts of the bush. After a lot of effort this modification worked perfectly, and our main oil leak issue was resolved.

We continued with practice and my lap times were quite good. We checked fuel consumption carefully, and kept examining the bike for oil leaks, but found none. As a Petty back-up, I had taken the Seeley G50 to the island, and on the Thursday, gave it a run after completing a couple of good laps on the Petty, with a best lap time of 94mph. Both bikes seemed fine and, with the 350 Seeley 7R also performing well, we were in a good place. Okells was again taken.

A cautious lap on the Friday evening allowed us to run-in a new primary drive belt and tyres; then it was an early night ready for race day combat.

The race was a delight, with the Petty running perfectly and a best lap time of 97.19mph. I had been second fastest to Bill Swallow through the start and finish speed trap at over 122mph. At one time I had been on the top six leader board but ultimately finished seventh. Don and the whole team were delighted. I was elated!

Don and I had a deep and meaningful discussion regarding engine builders, and a decision was made to use Gerry Kershaw for future motor work. He was a Norton man through and through, and came highly recommended by my racing pal Wattie Brown. Gerry built motors for Andy Molnar, and he and I had chatted frequently over the years, with Gerry providing generous advice. I didn't know it at the time but Gerry was to build my Norton motors for the next ten years. We remain the best of friends: he sure knows his Manx Nortons.

The 2003 MGP was not one of my best. The Petty seized its piston twice in practice, and after the second major engine strip we put the bike to one side and I raced the Seeley G50 instead.

I delivered the Petty motor to Gerry that autumn and he advised us to switch to an Amal GP carburettor, as this would simplify fuelling adjustments, making them less critical when weather conditions varied. I collected the rebuilt motor in early July 2004, and a test session at Mallory Park showed that all was well. Later that month Dave Carter and I travelled to Mettet in Belgium where I enjoyed a couple of good races on the Petty; setting us up for the forthcoming MGP.

Practice on the island went well, with the usual test session at Jurby Airfield to refine fuelling. Dave Carter was suffering from a heavy cold, so we dosed him with Okells to try and cheer him up. My morale was boosted on the Wednesday evening when Wattie came up to me after the session to comment that I was "going well" over the mountain. Wattie has a superb record over the TT circuit, so that was praise indeed. After the extended Thursday afternoon practice session I met Frank Rutter, who was well battered and bruised after falling from his Seeley in Kirkmichael village: not a place I'd choose to have an accident. I also found out that Wattie had fallen off at Creg-ny-baa and had a deep wound in his back caused by a footrest digging into it as he slid down the road. Neither man would race that year.

The race went okay though I wasn't at my best, and could manage only 16th place, with slightly slower lap speeds than the previous year. At one point in the race I was following Ted Edwards on his Weslake, and we were negotiating the fearsome drop down Bray Hill when the lower side panels of his lightweight fairing blew off at over 120mph. I was close behind him and thankful to miss the debris as I had no time to take avoiding action. I then had a great dice with Reinhard Neumair until his Manx Norton motor expired with a broken piston: his second piston failure of the week!

In 2005, ever-keen to improve the Petty, I decided that the bike needed electronic ignition and a more modern carburettor to improve mid-range power. The opposition used these components, and with some sponsorship backing I bought a PVL ignition system from Dick Linton, and Gerry Kershaw lent us a 40mm Amal Smoothbore carburettor. Gerry advised me regarding the fitting of both items.

Dave Carter and I took the Seeley G50 to Mettet in mid-April, and paid the price of such an early date in the year as the Belgian circuit near the Ardennes was shrouded in mist, with constant rain. The meeting was called off without a race having been run. We both slept in my gazebo but the roof started to leak, so we left the circuit early on the Sunday morning feeling very miserable and thoroughly damp.

Gerry had serviced the Petty's motor over the winter and I collected it in mid-May. We saved the fresh motor for the MGP and, apart from a Mallory Park test day, it was in new condition when we arrived on the island.

2005 has sad memories for me regarding the Manx races. Geoff Sawyer, a racing friend, had bought my Seeley 7R the previous autumn, and, during an evening practice and whilst negotiating the tricky right-hand bend into Union Mills, sadly, he crashed and died. When I heard the news I was upset at the thought that he had died whilst riding my old bike, but it transpired he was on his own Seeley G50. There was never a satisfactory explanation for why the accident happened; certainly no mechanical fault was found. Very experienced around the mountain course, Geoff was apparently on the correct line, but spectators said something evidently caused him to lose control as he entered the corner.

Later in the week John Loder, another very experienced classic rider, crashed and died whilst negotiating the 33rd Milestone bends coming down the mountain. Damp conditions probably contributed, but knowing this did nothing to make his death any easier to accept. I think we all started the races slightly cautiously that year, though nothing seemed to make us doubt our own ability to conquer the track: we simply carried on and put the tragedies to the back of our minds. Our families thought we were hard, but nothing would stop us, and many marriages suffered. How Shelagh dealt with it I'll never know, but I am eternally grateful to her for doing so.

Practice wasn't too bad. Small issues arose but we managed to overcome most, except for a tendency for the motor to hold back after a long spell on full throttle. We decided that the float chamber wasn't able to pass enough fuel, and Bob Johnson, whose Honda I was now riding in the Junior Classic races, spent many happy hours filing and grinding the inside of the float chamber to increase flow through the carburettor. We even removed the small mesh filter. This work did improve matters, and I was hopeful that all would be well for the race.

I finished 13th at an average speed of 96.241mph, amongst good competition, and the fuelling issue only raised its head on the last lap.

The team seemed well pleased but my happiness took a dive when two other racing pals died during the Junior race a couple of days later. I had just started chatting to Eddie Byers and his lady sponsor when Eddie crashed at the difficult 27th Milestone section on the mountain, and Tim Johnson fell off at The Black Hut bend, also on the mountain. I still see the rider who caused poor Tim's crash at Classic Motorcycle Racing Club race meetings, but can't find it in my heart to even talk to him, let alone forgive him.

The following winter's rebuild of the motor soon bought bad news from Gerry: the crankshaft was cracked and needed replacing. Large amounts of money changed hands and the Summerfields provided a new crank, which Gerry fitted.

As soon as practice began on the island in 2006 I discovered that the bike seemed to have developed a vibration, and no matter how we adjusted the carburation, it remained in the background, and my hands soon had small blisters. There was some paddock discussion regarding oversized fuel tanks, and we spent some time getting ours accurately measured, discovering that it would hold 23.41 litres; the limit being 24 litres. In previous years I had finished with very little fuel in the tank, and was anxious to have the maximum possible load on board, as we thought that the new vibration might be making the carb flood a little at top speed. This, of course, would lead to increased consumption.

The bike seemed to hold back again during the Wednesday evening session, so Bob and I stripped the top off the motor and cleaned the piston to allow a little more clearance. In hindsight, though, I think it was fuel starvation, as we had suffered the previous year. I considered swapping back to the Amal GP carb but a couple of the practice sessions were rained off, and we ran out of time to test a different setup.

I started the race slightly nervous about the vibes but the bike actually ran quite well, despite this. I finished in 13th position at an average speed of 96.22mph, and was promoted to 12th place when another rider, Paul Coward, was disqualified for having an oversized fuel tank, 0.2 of a litre too large. In the parc fermé after the race, we noticed that two of the smaller fins had broken off the cylinder head, next to the exhaust valve, and disappeared into the depths of the fairing, from where we recovered them. I wasn't imagining that vibration! We sent the crank to a specialist company for balancing that autumn, and were told that a huge amount of weight had to be added to one part of it to get it in balance.

My finest laps in those last two MGP Senior Classic races had been at just over 97mph, which seemed about the best I could do unless the weather was good, with dry roads and everything running perfectly ... which was asking a lot on the island. I don't think I was ever going to be capable of lapping at over 100mph on a single: 98mph was a possibility, but by this time I had seen too many accidents, and certain sections of the track I held back on slightly. I really enjoyed riding the course, but didn't have a death wish ...

The postscript to the Petty is interesting. After the 2004 MGP I found cracks in the tubes below the headstock of the frame. I spoke to my fabricator pal, Paul Duncombe, and he said he could repair it, but that other cracks were likely to occur as the T45 steel tubing was reaching the end of its raceworthy life. I again went cap in hand to Don Williamson, and we agreed to approach Roger Titchmarsh in Yorkshire, who had made my Seeley frames, to see if he would make us a replacement. Roger said he could, and it would be completed in time to test the bike prior to the MGP. Fortunately, Don's sponsorship contacts would bear most of the cost. I was also having problems with the exhaust system sitting directly under my right leg, so got my friend, Brian Barrow, to make us a new oil tank that would let the exhaust pipe pass through the frame tubes, thus allowing my leg to sit further in.

Brian is an absolute expert at forming exhaust systems, and had made several for me over the years, all to a very high standard. He produced a serviceable oil tank and a nice new exhaust system to go with it. I used this oil tank for a short circuit meeting or two in 2006, but was worried that we had seriously reduced the capacity where the exhaust ran through it. A full five pints would be needed for the MGP race.

Paul Duncombe did repair the original frame most proficiently and we waited patiently for the new one to be ready. Roger kept us waiting until the last minute for the frame and, in the end, I went to his workshop in the wilds of Yorkshire, with my son-in-law, Simon, and we waited whilst he finished the job. We had just two weeks until MGP practise began. I spent some time frantically putting together the bike, and we managed a brief testing session at Mallory Park before leaving for the island. Roger makes a wonderful frame, but his timescale can stretch, and we never did get a new swinging arm so had to use the original one. The Manx Grand Prix waits for no one!

Soon after, I contacted a very skilful fabricator called Angelo from York, who made aluminium tanks for Fred Walmsley, and asked if he could make us an oil tank of similar design but increasing its width, and also make us a new fuel tank with a capacity very close to 24 litres. Our original fuel tank had already suffered some leaks and the repairs were not great. The fabricator agreed to make the tanks but opined that they would not be cheap due to their complexity. I gulped and said "Go ahead."

I had been generously sponsored for several years by the company of my Velo Club pal, Roger Yates, and his sponsorship helped to pay for the tanks. (Roger continued to sponsor me, through his company until I stopped racing.) After a couple of trips to York for measuring and fitting sessions I eventually collected both tanks, which looked wonderful and fitted well. I was slightly bothered by the fact that the large fuel tank relied on rather small spigots in the base of the tank for positive fore and aft location, and two hoover belts to hold it down, but it was too late by this time to change any design features.

The story of the 2007 Senior Classic Race is a painful one for me. The new oil tank cracked around its front face in the second practice session and, after welding a repair, cracked again in the next practice session, so we were forced to use Brian's prototype oil tank.

In the race, which took place on a lovely sunny day, I got off to a flying start and the bike was running beautifully. I leapt Ballaugh Bridge, taking off in fine style and landing firmly. A mile or so further on I smelled race fuel and, looking down, saw fuel leaking from the bottom of the tank, wetting my leathers. I kept going as far as Parliament Square in Ramsey, but, on stopping, immediately realised that my race was run without completing even one lap. There was fuel everywhere and the tank had a pair of holes punched in the base. I poured what remained of our very expensive race fuel down the drain outside the chip shop, and prayed that no one would throw a cigarette end after it. I was mortified and very pissed off! I didn't even have any cash with me to buy chips.

I hadn't practised with a full tank of fuel, and even if I had I doubt whether I would have jumped the bridge so aggressively in practice. In the race the extra weight of the fuel in the tank caused it to slightly lift up from the frame as I jumped the bridge, stretching the hoover belts. As the bike returned to earth the tank also dropped, but the two ¾in long spigots just missed their sockets in the base of the tank, and punched neat holes right through it. If only we had used a strong, full-length strap attachment instead of the hoover belts, or possibly longer spigots — hindsight, eh? That bike had never achieved its full potential for us, no matter how much money we threw at it.

2008 was bound to be better — wasn't it …?

CHAPTER 12

MEETING 'BOBBY LAD,' PLUS THE TT!

IT'S NOT OFTEN THAT YOU MEET SOMEONE AND REMAIN FRIENDS for life. Early in 2003 I wandered into Lloyd Coopers in Hemel Hempstead. I used an Arai crash helmet, and had taken a fancy to a smart Arai tee shirt I'd seen whilst browsing the web. I found out that I could only buy one through an Arai dealership, and Lloyd Coopers happened to be my local dealer.

The person who served me that day was the workshop manager, Bob Johnson, a Geordie about ten years younger than me. We got chatting about racing in general, and I learned that he owned a lightly-tuned Honda VFR 400 bike in race trim that he used for track days, as he was an instructor with No Limits Track Days. Bob had been an army staff sergeant with REME for a number of years, and also chief mechanic for a successful British Super Sport team — a racing nut, just like me! During our conversation I told Bob that, for some years, I had wanted to have a ride at the TT on a modern bike, and he suggested that with a little extra preparation, I could enter his VFR in the Lightweight TT.

To my delight Bob also told me he was considering building a Honda K4 350cc classic racing bike, and perhaps I would ride that for him at the MGP in the future? The initial plan was that he would race the bike at short circuits, with me road racing it.

My Seeley 7R was a delight to ride, especially around the TT course, but with only 34bhp, it was severely handicapped against the now-prolific K4 Hondas that, although slightly heavier, produced around 45bhp.

I offered to put some money into the project, and our partnership took off. By racing a classic Honda I felt I would be joining the enemy, but the world was moving on, and the next generation of classic racers wanted something more reliable and cheaper to run than our clunky singles. There were plenty of road-going K4s for sale, and race parts to increase performance were also available. This was the future, and I didn't want to be left behind.

I put in an entry for the 2003 Lightweight 400 TT supported by my MGP record, and this was ultimately accepted. I tested the VFR at Brands

Hatch and found it a pleasure to ride although, in truth, I was slightly too large to easily fit on it: it was designed for small Japanese riders. On modern racing tyres, with twin disc brakes and very linear power it was lovely to ride at high speed, and felt on a par, power-wise, with the Petty Norton, having about 60bhp.

The thought of racing at the 2003 TT was so exciting for us, and it seemed so simple: we had just the one bike to fettle, and Bob would do most of that. My job was to concentrate on qualifying and honing my skills around that lovely course. I would have to adjust my braking points as the VFR stoppers were so powerful, and get used to fatter, stickier tyres. The bike's motor and gearbox seemed silky in use, and handling was perfect. The bike had a racing exhaust system and race bodywork, and was not much quicker than a standard model, so we suffered a speed handicap against the fully race-tuned 400s at the front of the field. I hoped that my course knowledge would enable me to keep the little bike's throttle wide open, and finish somewhere in the middle of the result sheet, although Bob's bike had a good deal less power than the 80bhp of the frontrunners.

Bob had stripped and serviced the motor prior to the event and was confident that it would go the distance. He sourced a spare motor for us, and we even borrowed a full spare road specification 400cc VFR from my engineer friend, Phil Harding, to cover all eventualities.

2003 was the year that, sadly, David Jefferies died during the Thursday afternoon TT practice session. I was sitting on the Honda waiting for our session to begin, when the news filtered through that there had been a serious accident at Crosby, and the practice session had been stopped by the red flag. Practices were cancelled for the rest of that day, and we gradually learned the full story. It was a tragedy for the entire racing fraternity. Jefferies was a fearless hero, and his loss affected us all in some way, but, as is the way of the island racing folk, racing carried on.

My problems started as soon as I signed on. The officials rejected my national licence even though I had been assured prior to leaving the mainland that it was sufficient for the TT. I argued for ages, but they were intransigent, and ultimately I had to have a full medical at Nobles Hospital in Douglas that cost me £50, which the doctor requesting the medical promptly put into the nurses' charity fund!

We set up our workshop in Pat Kerruish's garage in Tromode, just outside Douglas. Pat's husband, my Manx pal Bush (David) Kerruish, had died from a sudden heart attack the previous year, but Pat had insisted that we could use the garage attached to her house as we had in previous years. I did miss Bush; his wicked sense of humour and enthusiastic encouragement was uplifting. Don Williamson's pals, Julian and Maree

Harper, offered us digs in their lovely Georgian townhouse in Douglas, which it would've been rude to refuse, eh?

After 'work,' my team often needed a drink because of all the trials and tribulations we were facing and Julian's wine cellar took a battering. He smiled through it all, however, and simply opened another bottle. A very generous and kind man.

I had a good week of practice though the bike was plagued by fuel starvation on the long flat out sections of the course. Rolling off the throttle brought the motor back on-song, but momentum had been lost and, with that, slower lap times resulted. Bob couldn't travel over for the practices but manned our phone 'help line.' We tried everything including buying some new, very expensive sparkplugs. I had to buy a box of 6 at a cost of £75 as Dennis Trollope, the paddock spares supplier, had to have them sent to the island by special delivery. We stole ignition components from the spare bike, and did everything we could think of, including stripping and cleaning the four complex carburettors, and also changing their settings, in an effort to resolve the issue. The bike still held back on the long straights now and again, however: very frustrating. By Tuesday evening I had qualified the bike on speed with a best lap of 97.99mph, but felt I could have gone a few mph quicker if only it had run properly.

Bob arrived at the end of practice week, and spent hours checking everything he could think of that might have caused the problem. Race day dawned sunny but windy, and I thoroughly enjoyed the pageant that was the starting ceremony of a TT race. It was one of the greatest days of my life.

Bob had suggested that I leave the bike in fifth gear instead of sixth all the way up the mountain, and just rev the nuts off it (if you say so, Bob): that means 15,000rpm. Good job it had a rev limiter in the ignition system. I had a good race, including a couple of dices with other riders, but the fuelling problem kept recurring, and my final result was slightly disappointing, but at least I had finished a TT race. I was well off replica time and finished 25th out of 46 entries, at an average speed of 94.53mph. No one had gone faster than their practice times due to the windy conditions, and even if the bike had run properly I think I could only have managed 21st — still outside replica time — never mind, eh?

At the prize-giving ceremony at the Villa Marina, where I received a coveted TT finishers medal, Bob and I spoke to another VFR rider, who told us that the standard fuel tap would never pass enough fuel for sustained, flat-out running, and that all the regular VFR racers fitted an aftermarket, high-flow fuel tap. Interesting information; just a bit late for us!

Bob and I spent the rest of 2003 and the spring of 2004 sourcing and buying various components for the K4 race bike. The K4 dates from 1972, and I didn't fancy using such an old frame for a rigorous course like the Isle of Man. Frames can rust from the inside out, and we wouldn't know the history of any genuine frame that we could source. We did consider using a Drixton replica frame, made by Asa Moyce, but there were slight doubts regarding its eligibility for the Classic MGP, so we decided against it.

Bob suggested buying a TAB replica frame kit from Terry Baker, who had raced and now marketed copies of a frame he had fabricated and used himself during the early '70s. We visited Terry's farmyard workshop in rural Wales and invested a large amount of money in a frame, fuel tank and fibreglass bodywork. Terry was a lovely bloke. He manufactured frame kits and various designs of aluminium tanks and other race kit items. He promised early delivery and we left Wales feeling we were at the start of a good project.

Bob located a donor bike and delivered the motor to classic Honda tuner Ken Garfield, who would build us a full specification race motor. Bob also sourced a genuine pair of Ceriani forks and Mikuni carburettors, and set about lightening a pair of K4 wheels. We duly collected the frame kit and Bob set to making a lot of the smaller fittings, including fairing and tacho brackets, plus the footrest hangers. We spent some time making sure the riding position was similar to that of a Seeley and got close to it. It soon began to take shape.

Bob's boss, Gordon Heal, had come over for the 2003 TT with Bob, and after the race hinted that he might be able to supply me with a bike for the 2004, 600cc Production TT. I knew I had the Isle of Man experience to finish well on a 600 proddy bike, and racing a brand new machine promised reliability and a quick ride, as good as the opposition. Getting in some TT course mileage and then following that with the Manx GP in the same year had to improve my results in the MGP races, which were still very important to me.

To my delight, Lloyd Coopers agreed to enter me on a Honda CBR 600RR, and when one became available in early spring, let me run it in and get used to it. It was a brilliant bike to ride.

Bob had a pal, Chris Allen, who owned a very 'trick' 400cc Kawasaki, and Bob somehow coerced him into allowing me to race it at the TT. The Kawasaki was quick enough to finish near the top of a British Championship, and came complete with works-type carbs and airbox, plus a very special ignition system. It had been breathed on by a well known tuner, and really was the business. All I had to do was buy and fit a new pair of tyres and it was ready to go.

I tested it out on a couple of short circuit practice days and loved every minute of it. Very strong, linear power, and around 80bhp. I did some serious fitness training, and put in a double entry for the 2004 TT races, attracting local press coverage: "Local copper to race for Hemel Hempstead motorcycle dealer at TT," I tried to contain my excitement.

Bob was as good as his word and put in some hard work, after shop hours, fettling the Kwak. Then I was dealt a hammer blow when the ACU turned down my production race entry, and agreed to the Lightweight entry only. No reason was given and there was no appeal process. When I looked at the accepted entry list it seemed to me that the ACU preferred Manx or foreign riders, with previous experience not counting for much. By this point I had competed in over 30 MGP, TT and Ulster GP races, and finished in the top ten several times on both courses. Boy, was I miffed!

I apologised profusely to Lloyd Coopers, who were very good about it. Bob had even bought a Yamaha R6 600cc trackday bike for his use and to give me some track time on this faster bike. We did enjoy an outing on the Brands Hatch GP circuit prior to my TT entry refusal, and agreed that a 600 race bike was awesome at high speed.

Anyway, I still had this superb bit of kit for the 400 race, and our scheduled trip to the island soon arrived. Bob couldn't travel with us due to work commitments, so Dave Carter and I settled into our digs and sorted out the garage at Pat Kerruish's. My daughter, Katherine and her partner (husband-to-be), Simon, joined us, with Shelagh scheduled to arrive at the end of practice week.

Saturday evening practice went well for the first lap, which I ran at a steady pace. For the second lap I gave it 'the berries,' and all went brilliantly until I felt a loss of power at the end of the Crosby straight. I cruised to a halt and found that the rear of the bike was smothered in oil. I phoned Bob and he advised us to start stripping the motor, and we soon discovered that one of the sparkplugs had aluminium particles all over it. Further investigation discovered a very damaged piston with a peppered top, and missing part of its skirt, which, fortunately, seemed to have found its way out of the exhaust port to freedom.

Paul Marks, my old MGP racing pal, had made contact and, as he was well into modern bikes, we recruited him to help with the repairs, as he'd foolishly volunteered. The bad news was that Monday was a bank holiday and we didn't have a spare piston. Bob promised to get on the case first thing Tuesday, and we set to cleaning all the motor parts. Very fortunately, I had sold my lovely Seeley 7R to Geoff Sawyer after the previous year's MGP, and we met up on the ferry. He let slip that he was also competing in the 400 TT on a VFR, but had brought with him a spare 400cc Yamaha. I even had his mobile phone number — phew!

Geoff agreed to let me borrow the Yamaha for a couple of practice sessions providing I fitted it with a pair of new tyres. I'd just forked out for new rubber on the Kawasaki, so the £200 I spent with Ernie Coates at his paddock-based emporium hurt a little. Beggars can't be choosers, however; good job I'd sold Geoff a nice bike ...

On Monday morning a few tasks were carried out to get the Yamaha ready to ride, and Stuart Jukes and his ex-grasstrack sidecar racing passenger 'Digger' (Dick Howling) offered to help out. Yes, Digger is an Aussie. Geoff had asked me to keep the revs down from 15,000 to 12,000 on the Yamaha, and that made for a boring session, but all the laps counted towards qualifying for the race. Tuesday brought the news that the only piston available was in Holland and Bob would bring it over on Wednesday to fit it in time for Thursday's afternoon session. The only ferry he could get was due to arrive at 8.00pm, and Simon and Paul offered to help as it was likely to be an all-night session. What a great set of lads!

Early Thursday morning found the bike complete. After several attempts to get the valve timing correct she fired and sounded lovely. We had also fitted a new induction rubber on the faulty cylinder and added larger jets to richen the fuelling, as we believed it must have been running weak. An ignition fault was ruled out because the coils were paired up, and the problem was with one piston only. We then received the bad news that Thursday's practice was cancelled, and the option of a session on Friday morning was not taken up. Bother and bother again! (not the actual words we used). I still hadn't done enough qualifying laps.

On Friday afternoon we managed to get onto Jurby Airfield and run in the new piston. We then rushed off to the pits, leaving Stuart to relieve himself without the cover of the van: spectators had a laugh at his 'small' embarrassment! At the pits for scrutineering, Paul Marks told us that Richard Britten (a fast and very popular Irish rider) had fallen off at Creg-Ny- Baa, but appeared to be okay. Whilst wandering around the warm-up area I bumped into Richard, and said I'd heard about his little excursion. "Yes," he smiled, "I was on my arse." Obviously okay then. (Sadly, Richard died at a Southern Irish race meeting the following year.)

Friday afternoon and I was at the front of the queue. The bike wouldn't start and the boys had left the quick-start aerosol a hundred yards away. I lost the plot and shouted and swore at them from inside my full-face helmet. I did get away eventually, but at the end of the Crosby straight lost power: I knew it was all over for the Kawasaki. I cruised into the car park of the Hawthorn pub, and some nice folk bought me a pint of lager. I followed this with a couple of pints of Okells, and the world didn't seem quite as bad as it had. The boys soon recovered me and the bike and we went for a meal. I apologised for losing my temper; all was forgiven. Whilst it was running the bike was wonderful, and we were all mortified about what had happened.

On Saturday morning I went along to Geoff's digs, and managed to do a deal to hire the Yamaha for the race. It wasn't cheap, but what else could I have done? His only proviso was that if his bike failed in the last practice session he wanted the Yamaha. I also had to promise not to beat him, which was highly unlikely as the Yamaha was untuned and a real pudding! We spent a lot of time trying to improve the Yamaha in any way possible to be sure it would finish, and I just managed to qualify in the last practice session.

I spoke to a classic racing pal prior to the race. Colin Breeze raced Petty Nortons for the Summerfields, and was a consistent winner on short circuits, and very experienced around the island, having won the Senior Manx GP in 1999. Ever-smiling and a lovely bloke, Colin was relaxing in the warm-up area before racing his 1000cc Suzuki in the Formula 1 race. I wished him luck and, after a brief chat, went on my way. In this race Colin crashed at the difficult Quarry Bends section and sustained fatal injuries. Everyone involved in classic road racing would miss his cheerful, competitive presence. The TT circuit is so unforgiving, and punishes even a slight mistake.

The race went okay — I suppose — at least the weather was kind. Riding a non-competitive bike is never much fun, but I did all I could, finishing 37th at an average speed of 96.09mph: faster than the previous year, but near the back of the field. Geoff failed to finish, so I took a bit of stick from him when we returned his Yamaha. In its wisdom the ACU decided to drop the 600cc Production and 400cc Lightweight races from future TT programmes, so that was the end of my short TT career. Not exactly glorious, eh?

Once we got home Bob and Chris Allen stripped the Kawasaki motor, discovering that, at some stage in its life, when the motor had been ported, the tool had broken through from the inlet tract into the socket for a stud holding one of the carburettors. This enabled a tiny amount of air to leak down the stud when the motor was running hard, which, in turn, caused that particular cylinder to run weak. Only the miles of flat out running around the TT circuit had revealed the fault; it hadn't shown up on short circuits. The pin-hole was all but invisible without a magnifying glass, so we would never have found it when we stripped the motor in Pat's garage. Shit happens, I guess!

Perhaps I'd be better off sticking to classic hardware, rather than modern stuff ...?

CHAPTER 13

THE PATON PART 1: 100MPH!

IN 2007 DON WILLIAMSON FLEW SHELAGH AND ME OVER TO THE island to spectate at the Centenary TT races. On Senior race day there was a display of Italian Paton racing bikes in the paddock area, and a pal of mine, Steve Linsdell, was racing Paton's unique GP 2-stroke bike in the race. Paton had been formed by Lino Tonti and Giuseppe Pattoni in 1958, and became famous for manufacturing and racing twin cylinder machines in the Grand Prix during the classic period. Giuseppe's son, Roberto, had kept the business going after his father's death in 1999, and in 2006/7 had returned to limited production a 500cc version of the company's classic race bike (on which TT ace Ryan Farquhar won the 2007 Senior Classic MGP race on a bike entered by Roger Winfield).

We were wandering around the busy paddock when Don approached us, calmly stating he'd bought us a Paton to race in the following year's Manx GP! I knew roughly the huge amount of money that the bike would've cost and was gobsmacked to say the least. Don reminded me recently that I'd actually said to him "You must be effing mad!" Shelagh was speechless — and mortified. Although little discussed, she wanted and expected me to stop racing on the island after my 60th birthday in 2008. There had been an age limit to racing until a few years previously, but Adam Easton, one of the older riders and a racing friend of mine, had taken this issue to the European Court of Human Rights and won his case, so now there was no limit. Ironically, and very sadly, Adam died, aged 71, after crashing his Manx Norton on the bends approaching the Cronk Y Voddy straight in the 2011 MGP. There was no real explanation for his accident: all that's known is that he collided with a grass bank and fell from his bike.

I had kept quiet but knew that I was 'under the cosh' to stop whilst I was still healthy, and now poor Shelagh's plans had been foiled, as this purchase by Don changed everything. Shelagh went very quiet whilst I became both extremely worried and excited, unsure whether I could do credit to such a sophisticated and quick machine. Don assured me he had faith in my ability to do so, however, and said that it would give me a chance to achieve my ambition of a 100mph lap.

Don had a quiet word with Shelagh and, begrudgingly, I was allowed to continue my Manx GP career. Don did say that if Shelagh wouldn't support our efforts he wouldn't let me race the bike. Don is a sensitive man with a very human side to him. He has been a great friend and supporter for many years now, and I owe him a good deal.

In early 2008, Don and I flew to Italy by scheduled airline, and spent some time overseeing the gradual construction of our Paton BIC 500 in the company's small, but immaculate workshops (BIC = twin cylinder). It was the 13th 500cc Paton to be built, which I was very happy about as I considered 13 to be a lucky number for me (I think they numbered it 14, though). In recent years Paton had built three or four replicas suitable for parading, and our bike was about the third built to full racing specification. Don spent some time discussing the technical specification and design of the motor with Paulo, the English-speaking PR and salesman. Don planned to maintain the bike himself, and was keen to understand its foibles before he got his hands dirty.

Don took delivery of the Paton in early April of 2008, and in his nice new workshop/garage we added our own detail modifications. I had been generously sponsored for some years by Falcon Shock Absorbers, and was keen to use its rear shocks, to which Don agreed, and we also began a programme of lockwiring, seat and control position adjustment, and so on, to take the bike to our own safety and comfort standards. Don was brilliant, he just accepted my need for attention to detail and allowed me to alter anything I deemed necessary. I soon began to feel very happy about the whole project, and we eagerly awaited the first scheduled outing at Mettet in Belgium in May.

A trip to my local dyno in Aylesbury showed that the bike was delivering 74bhp at the rear wheel, which I was very impressed with, albeit slightly concerned also as Manx GP regulations stipulated we use the same narrow rear tyre that the Seeleys and Petty Norton had used. I would have to be cautious with that amount of horsepower available on demand. Bob Johnson had been very involved in the Paton's preparation, and was as keen as I that the project should be successful. Don, Bob and I had several pub discussions to plan the way forward.

After a successful test day at Mallory Park in late April, a couple of weeks later we travelled to Mettet in Belgium for what turned out to be a very sunny race meeting with the Paton. I was a bit worried about this first outing with the bike, but regular visits to the gym over the winter meant I was fit, as I'd anticipated the bike would test my skills and physical fitness.

I travelled to Belgium with Bob in his Fiat motorhome, Don following in his car with his partner, Steve (Stephanie). Don had organised tickets for some of his Dutch business pals and their wives, and they would arrive on Sunday. We had spent over £600 on race fuel, Eurotunnel tickets and entry fees: no one said this classic racing would be cheap (have I mentioned that before ...?).

I had entered both IHRO and Belgian Classic races, so would have plenty of track time. The Belgian races were clutch starts but the IHRO events were push-starts. After practice we discovered that the Paton was a thirsty beast, and also had a slight oil leak from a cam box cover. The latter was easily fixed with a little silicon sealant, and a note was made to keep a close eye on fuel consumption.

The first Belgian race on the Saturday went wonderfully. I got a reasonable start and soon began to realise how quick the bike was, adjusting my braking points accordingly. I overtook a few bikes to finish third: a podium on our first outing — brilliant! In the IHRO race the bike took a fair bit of pushing before it fired, and we eventually finished fifth behind a couple of other Patons ridden by experienced pilots. Everyone was happy, and Don treated us to a nice meal to round off the day.

Sunday morning's Belgian Championship race went so well. I got a good start and gradually worked my way up to third place, where I had quite a battle with ex-GP rider Tony Smith on a Matchless G50, and my friend and ex-Manx Grand Prix winner Dave Hughes on a lightweight Manx Norton. Tony even resorted to weaving along the main straight in an effort to prevent me passing, but I simply waited until he weaved left and then, using the Paton's superb power, squirted it up the right-hand side — that'd teach him, I thought. I won the race after just managing to pass Dave Hughes approaching the final chicane. Although I'd had a few good results, this was my first road race win since 1977.

Don was almost crying with delight; Bob was grinning from ear-to-ear, and Don's business pals were impressed. I had ridden well: a good bike brings out the best in me, and my confidence had been boosted. What a moment: we lived on that for weeks afterwards.

The following IHRO race was a bit of an anti-climax as I again took ages to push-start the Paton, and could manage only another fifth place. I had started dead last. Everyone was pleased with the overall results though, and we returned home a happy team, anxious to have another go at Chimay. In July we travelled to Chimay for the annual meeting that included a Paton celebration. 2008 was a special anniversary year for the Chimay circuit, and the original was to be used for the first time in many years. This was right up my street as the circuit was very fast, double the length of the later one, and flowed beautifully.

I spent a lot of money on entry fees for the Paton, Bob's Honda, and my own Manx Norton that I had recently built, having sold my Seeleys. I really liked the challenging nature of the Belgian road course, and the long, flowing downhill section towards the final bend really tests a rider's nerves, skills and speed of his bike. Gearing for this section is equal to the Isle of Man, it's that fast. The final 'S' bend on this section demands a very late apex, which numerous riders fail to get right, paying painful and sometimes fatal consequences. The longer original circuit also included a slow right-hand bend in a small hamlet, followed by a fast section with a slight left-hand bend past a chapel. I spent the entire practice session trying to do this fast section flat out on the Paton in top gear, and managed it eventually. Really thrilling; everyone agreed that it was a great track.

There were Paton parades, and I had a camera fitted to our bike to record one of the races, that I watch now and again to relive the buzz (including my terrible push-start). In one of the Paton parades Phil Read turned out in an anorak rather than leathers. His Paton was also the only one not in Paton green, but red. Shelagh was disgusted at his lack of respect.

I spent some time talking to Fred Stevens, who rode Patons during the classic period. He told me that they had two and four valve versions of the 500cc motor, and ran either depending on the nature of each track. He said they never told anyone which motor they were running. The legality of the replica four valve Patons has been discussed many times, but Fred assured me that they were used in the period, and said he had sworn an affidavit to that effect.

I had a good meeting in dry conditions, and the Paton ran well to everyone's relief, as the next outing would be at the Manx GP. After a spot of jet changing and gearing alterations I achieved fifth and seventh places in good company. Push-starts were still an issue, though. The Paton had very light flywheels as it peaked at nearly 11,000 revs, and if I got it wrong and opened the throttle slightly too much, it stopped dead and I had to begin pushing all over again. My notes say that I overtook Phil Read in one race — how did that happen? (Perhaps he had a problem?)

Our next outing to the Manx Grand Prix was recorded by Shelagh, in diary form, for a magazine article, and makes a valuable addition to this book —

I have had a love-hate relationship with the Manx Grand Prix for the last 25 years. The Isle of Man is a most beautiful island; the kind of place I like to be. Two or three times a year the roads are closed for the road races, and the island becomes exciting and exhilarating — and, if the truth be known, a bit scary for those who race — and me. The Manx is the event of the year in our racing calendar, and on August 14th, we pack half the house into a very small, two-berth caravan and set off to Heysham to catch the ferry.

After a fairly rough crossing, with Andy and Bob sleeping through it, and snoring all the way, we arrive in Douglas at 6am. We then get to the pits as soon as possible, and find the space allocated for us to camp for the next 16 days. Fortunately, it isn't raining and we manage to get our campsite set up by 9am. Time for a nice big breakfast at the local greasy spoon, then it's shopping to fill the cupboards with provisions. As it's raining Andy and Bob come with me, desperate for something to do. It rains all night.

Today is Friday, and signing-on day, meaning a lot of hanging around and chatting to people you haven't seen for a year, or since the last race meeting (I don't know what they find to talk about, but it starts on Friday and doesn't stop until ...). It rains all night again.

Saturday, and everyone wakes in anticipation of practice this evening. Andy and Bob are off to Jurby Airfield to run-in the Honda, as its motor is all-new. They get lucky as it doesn't rain until later in the day, and doesn't look like stopping. Eventually, practice is cancelled. Go to the pub.

Sunday is 'being bored day,' with riders who are champing at the bit to get out on their bikes: by this time, you can feel the tension in the pits. Everyone speculates about what is going to happen tomorrow if it's wet. Good friends who live in Ramsey invite us for Sunday dinner, which is lovely. The sun comes out, and we go for a walk afterwards; hopes running high for practice tomorrow. What a difference the sun makes!

Monday. The boys have to take the Paton to Jurby to bed-in the brakes. They get lucky again as it stays dry long enough for them to do what they need to. A bit of air in the system gives Andy a scare at over 100mph as the brake lever pulls back to the handlebars, but the boys soon sort it out. Andy decides that he will not practise on the Paton even if practice goes ahead as he doesn't really want to ride it in the rain the first time round the TT course, and get it full of water. It is still very wet, and eventually practice is cancelled again for the classics, though the newcomers get one lap, taken round by a travelling marshal. The atmosphere in the pits is very subdued. It's very muddy and I hear someone say they think they have trench foot!

Tuesday, and at last the roads look as though they will be dry enough to practise. Andy manages to do 3 laps: one on the Paton and two on the Honda. Heart in mouth I watch from the grandstand with Steve, Don Williamson's partner. The Paton is much faster than anything Andy has ridden before, and it worries me that he has to learn to ride it. He knows the TT course very well, of course, but this bike is capable of much more, and arriving everywhere much faster than anything he's ridden previously (it's also worth more than £50,000). It's getting dark by the time Andy returns to the pits, and he tells me the street lights were on in Kirkmichael! He has managed to get both bikes round in qualifying time so that reduces the pressure a bit. The atmosphere in the pits has now lightened and the tension has gone, thank goodness. It looks as though we might have a few days of better weather, and everyone is very relieved to be getting in some laps. Unfortunately, Doug Snow came off at Alpine Corner, a very fast part of the course. Andy says he went past him and thought it looked very serious if not fatal; we are all very worried. I saw Doug's mum in the pits the next day and she said he was okay, with a broken bone in his heel and a bit battered and bruised generally — how amazing is that?

Practice progresses without too many worries apart from Chris Swallow having a Menani rear hub break up (the Paton has Menani hubs!). Send for a wheel builder. Don finds an expert who has a good look at the wheel and makes some adjustments, then gives it the okay. Everyone is satisfied that it's safe.

Don has bought Steve a stopwatch, and we have been timing Andy's laps from the grandstand: he's getting progressively faster as he gets to know the bike. Thursday evening he does two laps on the Paton, going through the speed trap along the Sulby straight at 135mph, with a first lap average of almost 99mph, and a second lap of 100.064mph. Steve turns to me and says "That lap was 100mph" as if Andy does it every day! Don is absolutely ecstatic as this is the one thing he hoped Andy could achieve on the Paton. He had done it, and our pit crew are absolutely buzzing. Needless to say it's straight to the beer tent to await official results. Andy's friend, Derek, has arrived from Portugal. Andy's mechanic for many years before he went to live abroad, Derek was so pleased to be there. Andy definitely did do it, and has it in black-and-white on the timing sheet: we've great expectations for the race.

Causing us some concern is whether or not to have a pit stop for fuel, and this is debated uphill and down dale. Fuel is measured in and out of the bike, and eventually it is decided that a pit stop will be needed, which is something we aren't used to doing, so is causing a bit of tension in the pit crew of Bob, Don and Stuart. Everything is done to try and avoid a pit stop, even blowing the larger spare tank with compressed air to give it more capacity, but a pit stop is inevitable if the race is going to be 4 laps.

On Friday our daughter, Katherine, her husband, Simon, and 6-week-old baby, Emily, arrive. Andy didn't know they were coming so is really surprised to see them. Practice goes well with two more laps of *around 99mph in the bag, again in the damp and with a full fuel tank. Both bikes need only final preparation for the big day as the forecast for bad weather turns out to be correct, and the session scheduled for Saturday evening is cancelled.*

The weekend always drags by with everyone waiting for Monday to arrive, keeping everything crossed that the weather will be kind. Andy and I have a bit of time to go out on our own while the boys do the final tinkering for the races. Then, early on Sunday morning, Andy wakes up and says he wants the exhausts on the Paton changed, and phones Don at 7.30am to tell him. Don comes up to discuss the pros and cons, and it's decided that they should be changed for a silenced system that will give more mid-range power. That puts paid to a nice restful day, so I go to church and leave them to it.

My heart sinks when I look out of the window on Bank Holiday Monday to see a by-now familiar grey sky and wet roads. It isn't actually raining but is very damp and misty. Due to start at 10.15am, the race is postponed until 12 noon, then postponed again and again until 6pm. By the time the bikes are warming up on the Glenclutchery Road I can hardly breathe, Andy seems remarkably calm, and has almost given up any hope of racing today, I think. One good thing is that the race has been reduced to 3 laps, so a pit stop is not necessary — hurray!

At last they're off, Steve and I are in the grandstand with my daughter and son-in-law and other friends. Andy selects a false neutral on the startline but quickly gets going. There are damp patches on the road, and some places remain very wet, still. We wait anxiously for the hands on the rider clocks to tick round ... he's through Glen Helen, the first commentary point, and we hear his name mentioned, then he's on to the next point and again we hear his name mentioned. I notice that the clocks of John Goodall and Bill Swallow have not rotated but haven't heard that they have stopped. Andy's first lap is done at 94mph, which we think is a little disappointing though he has gone up a few places. The poor conditions are affecting everyone's speed, it seems: Ryan Farquhar on another Paton was doing 109mph in practice but achieves only 103mph in the race. Andy's next lap is better and he moves up a few more places. The last lap is very exciting, and I don't know whether to laugh or cry, egg him on or wish he would stop. It's announced he's seventh, and then we can't believe it when we hear he is chasing fifth place. He is on the lap leader board twice.

At last the race is over and the phone rings before I get down the grandstand stairs: it's our friends on the mainland ringing to say congratulations on fifth. Andy says that when he came in to parc-fermé he wondered where all the other bikes were: he didn't realise he was fifth (out of 73 entries and at an average speed of 97.152mph). There are tears of joy and relief. One of Andy's friends, Swiss classic racer Franz Glauzer, was watching at Hillberry where Andy told us he had had a big slide on the last lap, and thought it was curtains but managed to hang on. Franz says: "There must have been many angels watching over him!" The big slide at over 100mph was also seen by Dennis Trollope's rider, Neil Kent, who was marshalling there. All of the marshals thought he was going to crash and jumped up to get out the flags. The fuel debate was settled in that Andy would not have had enough fuel to do another lap so next year, if there is a four-lap race, there will have to be a pit stop. Big celebrations in the beer tent!

Unfortunately, it was bad news for John Goodall, who we had known for many years. He had tuned Andy's own bikes for a long time, and was always very helpful and supportive to him. He will be sadly missed. I'm sure the news that John had died in an accident at Ballacraine, after crashing on spilt oil, affected the riders and the rest of the racing. All I wanted now was to go home and be safe.

Andy usually looks forward to his 350 race, and he really wants to get a good result on Bob's Honda, but it has been raining again and the race is delayed from 10.15am until 3pm. Although there has been ample time to get the roads ready for racing there are damp patches and oil spills all round the course. Andy doesn't like the wet, and oil rainbows were evident around several sections of the course, so he was really worried about sliding off. This race is also reduced to three laps, and Andy finishes 20th, though felt he could have done much better if conditions hadn't been so awful. One of the riders said he had been racing in the IOM for 30-odd years, and had never seen such bad conditions. I feel sorry for Bob as the result for his bike isn't as dynamic and successful as that of the Paton. Lap speeds were down and everyone was being careful. I was more than happy we were going home in one piece and with two bikes that were ready to ride again.

Andy always calls the Manx a 'holiday,' but I wouldn't call cooking on three gas rings in a small caravan, and shopping for up to six people for the first week a holiday! It did have its good parts, of course, and we have made some very good friends and acquaintances over the years, which helps make it special. The IOM has a lure that can't be put into words: love it or hate it; I do both.

Shelagh Reynolds (the wife!)

CHAPTER 14

THE PATON PART 2: JOB DONE!

THAT 2008 SENIOR CLASSIC RACE IS A FANTASTIC MEMORY, although the weather and track conditions were a great disappointment, and I felt I could have lapped a few mph quicker given a full week of practice and a dry track. Even so, in the damp conditions, at 135 mph, I had been fifth fastest through the Quarry Bends speed trap, which I was well pleased with. On my 100mph practice lap there had been a lot of cement dust in Kirkmichael, so I had to slow down there; I was also blocked a little by Mark Parrett at the Gooseneck, and lost some momentum as I began the climb up the mountain.

We were very worried about fuel consumption over four laps, and Steve Linsdell had used his compressor to blow out the Paton's fuel tank to try and increase its capacity slightly. It worked and we measured it at 23.7 litres, very close to the 24 litre limit, but by the end of practice we realised that I would have to stop for more fuel so it was all in vain. The bike was using between 6.1 and 6.2 litres per lap by our calculations.

We had brought a quantity of race fuel to the island for the Manx GP. Not wanting to be excluded at the end of the race I decided to have this analysed by the scrutineers during practice. They checked our sample twice and informed us that we were "pushing the window" as the results showed it to be 101.7 octane: the limit is 102! We diluted it slightly with 98 octane petrol to be on the safe side.

Taking Bray Hill flat out was thrilling to say the least, and I managed this by the Thursday practice session. My speed must have been approaching 130mph down that steep decline, and I had to really hang onto the bars to keep the bike on the racing line.

By the Thursday we had managed only a few laps of practice. The classic bikes were always the second session, which meant we had the least sunlight and sometimes an abbreviated session. I went to see the Clerk of the Course, Neil Hanson, to ask if the classics could be moved to the first session for the remaining practices, which is what happened. Neil was a solicitor; not popular with all of the riders, but I had frequently spoken to him over the years, and he had always listened to what I had to say. He had some very difficult decisions to make during practice and race weeks, and couldn't please everyone all of the time.

On the Friday evening I did two laps, one of which was at 98mph-plus from a standing start, so everything was looking good for the race. On the Saturday Bob and Derek were preparing the Paton, and noticed, fortunately, that the front tyre was de-laminating. Ryan Farquhar's sponsor, Roger Winfield, had a spare tyre for their Paton, so we bought and fitted that. Good spot, boys! Evening practice was cancelled so we adjourned to the pub for a couple rounds of Okells followed by a lovely Chinese meal at the flat that my daughter, Charlie and her partner, Simon, were renting They had arrived on the Friday, and everyone but me knew they were coming, so it was a big but pleasant surprise. The weather forecast for Saturday evening (and the next few days) was poor: sure enough the session was cancelled.

I was worried about the Paton's lack of performance, particularly in damp track conditions, and slept very fitfully that night. At 7.30am on the Sunday I'd decided on a course of action, and phoned Don to tell him I wanted the silenced exhaust fitted, as that would clean up carburetion at low revs. The very slight loss of power would make very little difference to my lap times. I wasn't too popular with Bob and Derek, who thought they had finished spannering the Paton, but they set to and swapped the exhausts. We then travelled across the island to Jurby Airfield, and ran the bike up and down the runway to finalise everything. It seemed fine.

As predicted Monday's race day dawned damp and misty, so a delayed start was inevitable. Initially, the 10.15am start time was moved to noon and eventually to 6.00pm. There were still some wet patches around the circuit, and the first lap had to be ridden with caution to establish where these were: my first lap time of 94mph reflected this (my second and third laps were both just over 98mph).

I had started a few places behind John Goodall, and was very surprised to come across him on the ground, in the middle of the track, just around Ballcraine corner. Marshals were waving yellow flags on the approach to the corner, so I slowed right down as I approached. I trickled past the marshals attending to John, assuming he would be alright as the bend is not known for serious accidents, and has a lot of straw bales to protect riders from the stone walls on the exit. It transpired that Bill Swallow's Aermacchi had suffered an oil leak and, although Wattie Brown, the rider following behind Bill, made it safely around the bend, poor John skidded on Bill's oil. John was laying just beyond the last straw bales, and I'm not sure if he hit the wall or his bike hit him, causing ultimately fatal chest injuries.

I had a couple of incidents myself, including jumping Ballaugh Bridge very firmly, my foot missing the footrest as I came down to earth. My sponsor, Roger Yates, was watching, and told me later that I'd worried him a little (didn't want his investment damaged?). On the last lap I was behind Chris Swallow, Bill's son, approaching The Bungalow up on the mountain. Chris was really trying, and made a small mistake as he negotiated this tricky bend. I had a very clear view of him gracefully tumbling from his bike onto the grass — unhurt, luckily.

By now the sun was going down quite quickly, and although it was fine up on the mountain, as I descended it became a little gloomy. Shelagh has described my big slide at Hillberry very well but, in mitigation, the marshals told me that they had noticed damp tyre marks appearing on the road surface as dew fell, just before I arrived. Under the trees, the tarmac has a lot of green moss on the surface, and I think I found some of it. Fortunately, I had allowed about a foot of spare track around all the difficult sections, thinking that, if I got the bike out of shape, I would have a little 'recovery' room before I hit a kerb. I needed it at Hillberry that day!

I think it was while we were on the island that Steve Linsdell mentioned the Paton gathering at a race meeting at Franciacorte in Italy in September. Steve offered to transport our Paton in his van: all we had to do was book a hotel and flights. Sounded too good to be true and, after discussions with Don, we jumped aboard. I checked out the circuit on YouTube and it looked a little like Snetterton to me. After a pleasant flight, we hired a car and went to look at the circuit.

Ah! It wasn't at all like fast and open Snetterton ... contained within quite a small area, it consisted of medium-length straights and several series of tight and twisty sections. We went to see Steve Linsdell and Roger Winfield to ask their opinion, and Steve told us they were fitting a wider rear tyre, as their riders would be on the edge of it for so long. The tyres they were going to use were not allowed in classic racing in the UK, and we certainly hadn't got one. They had no spares, either, and there were none for sale at the circuit: I was lumbered!

Practice proved troublesome. Lea Gourlay and Oli Linsdell were determined to beat each other to the win, and I was destined to be an also ran. My confidence was very low, which wasn't helped when Lea clipped me on a bend at the back of the circuit as he chased Oli, who had just passed me. I ended up almost falling and went onto the grass. I soon realised that I was going to be lapped in the race as the circuit was very short, and the pair of them were lapping a good deal faster than I could. The track lacked grip and, after a lot of serious thought, I decided not to ride the next day.

I'd had a good year, our bike was in good nick, and I was convinced that if I did ride, I'd either fall off or get knocked off by the quick boys. In hindsight I'm quite ashamed I decided not to ride, but that was it. Shelagh and Oli's brother, David, supported my decision; Don was dismayed but didn't push the issue.

Race day dawned and the competition between Lea and Oli was obvious. In trying to get ahead, Oli crashed approaching the third corner, though I don't know whether he fell or was pushed ... Lea just cleared off and won easily, with two other Italian Paton riders finishing near the back of the field. I didn't enjoy watching, and the atmosphere between myself and Don was cool.

Roberto Pattoni was there to promote the Patons, and was very nice to me even though I didn't compete. He invited us all to a meal at a nearby restaurant, where around twenty of us sat down to local cuisine that included donkey meat, which I tried.

The journey home was a little strained. I focussed on the next season as I was sure I could improve my results once I'd acquired more experience on the Paton.

Our first outing in 2009 with the Paton was at Mettet, where we ran the bike with the silenced exhaust system. I qualified fifth in class for the IHRO races and the bike seemed fine. In the IHRO race I finished eighth in good company, and followed that with fifth in the Belgian Championship race.

In the second IHRO race I was going well but felt that the motor was vibrating slightly, so decided to stop in case damage was caused. When we got home Don stripped the motor and, on examining the gearbox, found that two of the gears had a lot of premature wear. He spoke to Paton in Italy, whose advice was to send the crankshaft there to be rebuilt, and fit new pistons as the bike had done its quota of miles after the MGP. Paton only had gears from the same batch as potential replacements for our worn ones, so Don arranged to have a batch made by our sponsor Terry Grubb's firm, which specialised in gear production, After an inspection it concluded that our original gears were slightly faulty.

Don stripped the motor and fitted the replacement parts when they arrived. He generously supplied replacement gears for their Patons to both Roger Winfield and Steve Linsdell, as they were likely to have the same issue at some point. The bill for our motor's parts was horrendous, the two pistons alone costing over £1000!

In July we travelled to Chimay again, disappointed not to be on the longer track, which was not being used as there were problems concerning access for the emergency services. I doubt the long circuit will ever be used again; we were very lucky to experience it the previous year.

We had some small problems with the Paton in practice, including the clutch coming loose, so I didn't qualify very well. Roger Winfield kindly lent us a larger rear sprocket as I couldn't reach maximum revs in top gear, and I fitted the open exhaust system, hoping this would improve the revs. It certainly 'improved' the noise, and I was asked to stay at the back of the warm-up area as the moustachioed controller — who swore at me in Belgian — couldn't hear his radio whilst I was blipping the beast. A couple of times I spotted spectators covering their ears as I passed them through the flat out downhill section on max revs. Good job I had moulded earplugs, though my ears buzzed for the next 24 hours, even so.

Results were okay, but starting from the back of the grid didn't help. The Paton suffered from front brake fade, and I noticed that a couple of the other quick Patons — those owned by Roger Winfield and Steve Linsdell — now had larger diameter drum brakes than those supplied as standard. I wasn't too bothered as we could fit the disc brake setup for the MGP, which was always our main target.

The 2009 Manx GP threw up numerous points for discussion regarding the future of the races, and tested entrants' strength of character. Most days it rained, and on some it poured all day. The local council provided plywood boards to enable competitors to walk to their tents and caravans without disappearing in a quagmire, and also provided a tractor service to extricate our vehicles if they became bogged down. Not much fun, especially considering the cost of competing!

Saturday practice was dry but untimed, so we ran the 350 Honda and I did two steady laps to bed in the rings and other new parts. This year Bob Johnson, the bike's owner, had fitted a heavier crankshaft that made the bike feel very smooth and torquey.

Sunday was very wet again and, after some discussion in the pub, I elected to run the Paton in the dry conditions forecast for Monday evening. Practice went well, though the rev limiter was coming in too early at 10,500 revs, and, in dry but windy conditions my best lap time was 98.684mph. The following morning Don altered the ignition settings to return the rev limiter to 11,000.

Tuesday's session was again dry. I did two more laps on the Paton but, although I thought I had ridden well, I failed to go any faster: my best lap was 98.328mph and I went through the Sulby speed trap third fastest, at 137mph. My pal, TT star Oli Linsdell, was quickest at 145mph on his Paton, so I wasn't doing too badly through that section. At The Verandah up on the mountain Brian Spooner flew off the road, fortunately, without serious injury. In hindsight, witnessing the aftermath of the crash might have slowed me a little.

I decided the Paton was under-geared, and asked the boys to fit a rear sprocket with one tooth fewer.

Wednesday dawned wet and stayed that way. It was decided that practice would be untimed, but I elected not to fill a motor with water. Returning riders told me conditions were terrible so it was a good decision; experience does pay off, occasionally!

Thursday practice (all practise now took place during the evenings) was cancelled due to rain, and I still hadn't qualified the Honda on time. I was a little short of track time and getting worried as the forecast was not good for the next few days either!

Friday dawned damp, and wet patches were evident all around the course as I managed two laps on the Honda within qualifying time. Bob checked the sparkplugs and found the fuel settings to be good. We agreed to alter the gearing by adding one tooth on the rear sprocket as I had been unable to reach maximum revs on the long straight sections. I told Bob I'd stick my knees out on the downhill bit if I thought it was going to over-rev!

Do I sound as if I'm repeating myself when I say it was damp again on Saturday evening for practice? We had new rear tyres on both bikes: soft compound for the Honda and a hard compound version for the Paton. I did a single lap on the Paton to bed in the tyre but didn't enjoy it as the roads were so difficult to predict, grip-wise. Junior race favourite Ryan Farquhar fell off his Honda just above Guthrie's Memorial on the mountain, injuring a hand and bruising his leg.

Well, that was practice, and a fat lot of good it had done me. I was no faster, although both bikes seemed fine.

On Sunday Bob spent several hours race-preparing the Honda, and Don changed the oil and carefully checked everything on the Paton. Monday was forecast as wet and, true to form, racing was cancelled. Bored, and frustrated by the rain, we all ate too many sweets!

On Tuesday the new Post Classic race took place in the morning, and we were on the grid, all warmed up at lunchtime, ready to go. Unfortunately, our race was delayed as a heavy spell of rain was forecast, but expected to clear in the evening, so we were for scheduled for a six o'clock start. Just before then, a motorcyclist decided to ram a minibus at high speed at Bishops Court near Kirkmichael (on the course), and our Classic Junior race was cancelled ... we had run out of time.

An hour later we were told that the next day's Senior Classic race would be a combined event, and riders with two machines like me would have to nominate which they would ride! How do you tell a good friend and sponsor that you have decided not to ride his bike? Bob took it very well, knowing that he would also have chosen to ride the Paton. (Bob was very fed up with the entire situation. The rain had really depressed us all, and we had spent hours doing nothing but getting damp!)

I went to race control and put Paton on the form. Other riders were choosing to ride their 350cc machines as they knew they would not win replica trophies in the 500cc class, as Ryan Farquhar and Oli Linsdell, on their Patons, were likely to beat previous lap and race speeds based on their practice times. Ultimately, there were 30 entries for the four-lap Senior Classic race. A number of my racing pals said they'd had enough of all the problems, and they would not be entering if things didn't change.

I went to see Roger Winfield, owner of Ryan Farquhar's Paton, and he suggested fitting a 'soft' rear tyre as it could end up a damp race, and the temperature was cool anyway. Bother! Off I went to beg our tyre supplier, Dennis Trollope, to remove the new hard rear tyre and fit a soft version. Another £140 spent. Dennis grinned, pocketed my money, and said "Of course, good idea," working into the evening to fit the tyre.

Wednesday dawned fine, with the race scheduled for a 1.15pm start. At twelve o'clock it was announced that the race would start 15 minutes early as rain was expected later. (There's a surprise!)

I made a good start and conditions were okay. I had no real 'moments,' and rode as firmly and fast as I could. I had a little battle with Paul Coward on a Honda, and passed a couple of bikes stopped by the roadside. Nearly everyone had decided to pit for fuel at the end of lap three in case it was decided to reduce the length of the race due to incoming rain. The single cylinder bikes didn't need to pit as they use less fuel.

This year a pit lane speed limit had been introduced, and was going to be policed! None of us classic riders had electronic speed control, so going slowly was the only option other than risk a time penalty. Our pit stop went very smoothly but seemed to take an age. Bob made sure I had enough fuel, and I got the motor started and was away cleanly, Don and Stuart Jukes (my Isle of Man-based pal) efficiently operating the starter motor and cleaning my visor. Stuart drove over the mountain to the paddock from Ramsey for every practise session, his input and enthusiasm very welcome.

This stop took its toll on my lap and race time, and my only flying lap was the second, when I had almost a full tank of fuel, so no 100mph laps for me this year. Going up the mountain on the final lap, someone held out a board with '4th place' on it. I had asked Oli Linsdell's brother, David, who was operating a board for Oli, to remind me to pit on the third lap but had not seen the sign. I thought nothing of this board, assuming it was meant for someone else. Just then it began to rain, and my last trip across the mountain was ridden with great care at slightly reduced speed. I later learnt that Ryan had a dry trip as he was so far ahead of us all.

I took the chequered flag, and breathed a sigh of relief, knowing the team would be pleased to see at least one finish. I pottered up the pit lane and was aghast when they directed me to the winner's enclosure: I had finished third! Never have I been so shocked; I had no idea I had been running fifth, but two riders had broken down on the final lap. You do need a bit of luck, sometimes!

I was interviewed for Manx radio and had loads of photos taken alongside runaway victor Ryan, and Wattie Brown, who had finished a brilliant second. Shelagh was the last to know and had taken herself off to the finisher's enclosure at the far end of the grandstand. She eventually arrived breathless and tearful, glad I was safe, to join us for another photo. It was then off to the pit lane podium for more photos and champagne — brilliant! I eventually made it to the beer tent, leaving the boys to strip the Paton engine to have its dimensions checked. Race rules stipulated they had to begin stripping it within 20 minutes of the end of the race, and they only just made it. Anyway, all went well, and we were legal, as were Ryan's Paton and Wattie's Norton. Stuart said it was obvious that Ryan's motor had higher compression pistons than ours, and therefore, a power advantage.

Third place in the Manx Grand Prix ... who would have believed it was possible? The brilliant Paton was a great help, but the team, plus all the fastidious preparation and my course knowledge also contributed to this wonderful result. The team was ecstatic, and bike owner Don was emotional and very happy. I was thrilled, but also sorry for Bob Johnson, whose pristine Honda stood ready to be ridden but unused, sadly. That evening, after everyone had left the pits, I went for a quiet walk on my own, determined to remember every detail of this day for the rest of my life.

Over the next few weeks Don, Shelagh and I had meaningful and sometimes difficult discussions. Shelagh felt that, at 61, I had achieved all I was likely to around the TT course, and I couldn't really find a good argument against this, although I tried hard. I did feel that, with a good practice week and a dry race, I could go a couple of mph over 'the ton,' but I was unlikely to win a Manx GP when up against the professionals now competing. Without Shelagh's support Don felt that our job was done, and he decided to sell the Paton to try and recoup some of his investment, which he ultimately did.

Early in 2008, I had been diagnosed with a chronic blood condition (Polycythemia Vera) that would handicap my fitness to some degree, and this seemed to confirm the decision to retire from the rigours of island racing. Short circuit races, continental adventures, and much excitement and mechanical mayhem would continue for a few years to come, though. I wasn't done yet!

CHAPTER 15

THE TAB HONDA

IF YOU HAVE A MECHANICAL BACKGROUND, YOU MAY NEED something to help you get through this chapter, which will be painful at times and exhilarating at others. In July 2004, the TAB Honda became a reality. The Ken Garfield motor complemented the Terry Baker frame kit and, with advice provided and some parts provided by Len Cooper, the bike looked a picture. Bob Johnson had managed to source a Ceriani disc brake fork slider from ex-racer and tuner Richard Peckett, and I managed to persuade Robin Packham to sponsor us with a pair of his brilliant alloy rear shocks.

With the best race frame available, original Ceriani forks, and the Falcons, we had a bike that ought to handle perfectly, but the first test at Snetterton revealed that, although the bike did indeed handle well, it was virtually unrideable because of excessive vibration!

We returned to Bob's garage, where he modified the head-steady, considerably reducing the vibrations. At the second test, I found that fuelling at low revs was very poor but a change of pilot jets improved matters; we were happy bunnies! The Manx Grand Prix would be the next outing for the bike and we were looking forward to the challenge.

After a rough crossing, we settled into MGP mode. It was nice to be handed a very loud but perfectly prepared Honda instead of having to sort out the bike myself. I completed one careful qualifying lap on the Honda, and although it was under-geared, all seemed well. The next day, Sunday, Bob played with the Honda whilst Dave Carter and I sorted out the Petty Norton. Bob modified the mountings for the ignition coils, changed the gearing, added a deflector screen to the fairing to prevent the bugs hitting my helmet visor, and made a slightly larger 'shark fin' chain guard, as the scrutineer had been a bit sniffy about the small one we had. We needn't have worked so hard, because Monday dawned and stayed wet, and practice was cancelled. Drink was taken!

Tuesday was a positive day. I completed two good laps on the Honda, the bike running perfectly and feeling quick. One of the rear exhaust mounting brackets had broken, but this was easily remedied with an extra rubber bobbin. Bob and I were delighted with the project and slept well that night.

By the end of Friday's practice I had lapped at over 93mph — faster than I had ever managed on the Seeley 7R — and the bike seemed fine. It always attracted a lot of interest, and Bob and his lovely wife, Anne, kept it immaculate.

Ken Garfield and Terry Baker came to see us. They were very attentive, and encouraged our efforts. The slight vibrations were manageable, and the motor remained oil-tight.

We didn't bother going out on the Saturday as conditions were poor, and instead concentrated on our race prep. Derek Cheesman had arrived from Portugal and took up residence in Bob's campervan as Bob and Anne were using my caravan. This was Derek's first trip to the island since moving to Portugal several years previously; he and Bob got on famously as they had similar backgrounds.

On race day we had a bit of trouble starting the bike: Anne's face a picture of stress but then delight when it fired. The race was pretty uneventful though the wind changed direction and was against us as we climbed the mountain, making our gearing too high. The carburetion also turned slightly rich due to the weather, and that made fuelling feel slightly woolly. I managed to hit the kill switch twice whilst attempting to adjust the clutch lever, though was able to bump-start the bike each time, fortunately. I resolved to move the kill switch for the following year.

On the last lap one of the three rubber mounting links that supported the tacho broke, making me jump as I was flat out in top gear at the time, and the instrument suddenly dropped. Fortunately, the remaining two rubber links remained secure. I finished 14th, won a silver replica award, and everyone was happy. A few pints of Okells were sunk in the beer tent and friendships cemented with new and old riders.

In 2005 I raced the Honda at a couple of CRMC short circuit meetings at Snetterton and Brands Hatch with reasonable results, with Snetterton proving a real experience!

On the Saturday we were not allowed to start our motors until 8.30am. We were due out in an early practice session, and I began to sweat when we started the bike and it stalled as soon as I tried to pull away. Bob checked everything, ignition, wiring, carbs, but to no avail. A fellow competitor, Rob Munro, came across and said the bike sounded over-geared, and the penny dropped: Bob had fitted the gear linkage upside down, and we were trying to pull away in top gear — numpties!

I just made the practice session, but it was a waste of time as the bike vibrated so much that I could hardly hold onto the handlebars. Bob got out the spanners again and found that the head-steady mounting was touching the frame. A quick spot of spannering (dropping the motor out of the frame) and a certain amount of filing resolved this, and we were back to normal.

By now I was beginning to panic as race-time drew near: good job we had parked near the toilet. Fortunately, my good friend Pete Sharples turned up on his Ducati Monster, and helped calm me down. He's a very placid chap, and a good companion in a crisis.

A couple of dry races followed with the bike running beautifully. I had a good dice with a two-stroke rider in the second race, and just beat him to the line. For the third race I decided I'd better get my head down and get away from him immediately. It began to spit with rain as our race started, but I got away well. After three laps of six I was going well and running in sixth place, but then it really rained! The guy in front of me fell off, and I had to go onto the grass to avoid his bike and him. As I slithered back onto the track, a riderless Honda overtook me and parked itself in the Armco barrier. Ouch! I regrouped and rode steadily from then on to finish fourth, returning to a very happy Bob in the paddock. That was it for us: it continued to rain, so we agreed to miss the last race and go home to de-stress!

In the following weeks we altered a few minor things on the bike and looked forward to the MGP. As is the way, as soon as I began practice around the TT course I decided that the footrest position was wrong and needed altering. With the help of Nick Magnay, Stuart Jukes' engineer pal, adjustments were made and all seemed fine. Practice went according to plan, but on the Tuesday I complained that the motor felt sluggish. Bob took it to the dyno that was set up in the paddock, and found that the ignition timing was retarded and required adjusting. The following day I completed two trouble-free laps, followed by a single lap on the Saturday evening. Prior to my going out, Bob had fitted a new visor to my helmet but, just as I was about to leave the warm-up area, it flopped off on one side. Some mechanic, eh? I slapped his balding head and swore gently at him — best not to upset your sponsor/mechanic too much, though!

The Junior race was a disaster. The start was delayed by mist, so, when I did get going, I gave it 'the berries' as I left the start line: 11,000 revs and determined to get in a quick first lap. The gearing seemed fine and I passed a few slower riders as I wended my way around the course. I overtook my pal, Pete Swallow, as I exited the Quarry Bends section, who mentioned later that our bike was quick but was smoking slightly as I passed him. Sure enough, a mile further on it called 'enough,' a loss of power and death rattle prompting me to pull off the course at Sulby Bridge, about halfway around the lap. Now a rattle and vibration at 120mph can be confusing so I started the bike again to check it out. No compression and a real rattle — race over. Bother, etc!

A kind marshal lent me his mobile phone, and I called all of the three numbers I carry with me in my leathers, but no reply from any of them! Eventually, my wife, Shelagh, answered and said "It's a bit noisy here at the grandstand." After another hour of watching my racing pals have a great time, Bob, Derek and Dave arrived to recover me and the bike. I had broken down about as far away from the pits as was possible, and with the roads closed for the racing they had endured a very tortuous journey to get to me. Poor Bob, a year's work and investment with little to show for it.

A post mortem on the motor revealed that a piston had broken up: one of a faulty batch, we later discovered. It had completed a year's racing without failing; what a shame it hadn't let go during the dyno sessions rather than in the big race. We even had a spare motor that we could have used — bother and bother again!

Bob took all this in his stride, and spent the winter and more of our hard-earned cash rebuilding the motor. Bob's pals, 'Big Dave' Pierson and Brian Loader, and his wife, Linda, threw some extra cash into our Honda pot, and continued to do so through the highs and lows of forthcoming seasons, earning our grateful thanks.

I raced the Honda quite successfully at Lydden, Brands Hatch, and Chimay prior to our next MGP adventure. At Brands Hatch I managed to topple off on the start line, much to commentator Allan Robinson's delight. Waiting to begin our warm-up lap we'd been instructed to kill our engines as there was an issue with the marshals' radios. Suddenly, we were told to start engines and complete our warm-up lap, as the radios had been fixed. Prior to this we had been starting the Honda on rollers, so I hadn't practised bump-starting it as almost all our races were now clutch starts.

Anyway, taking a few steps I gave the bike a good shove, dropped the clutch into first gear, and jumped onto the seat side-saddle as soon as it fired. Unfortunately, it immediately stalled and the rear wheel locked. I was leaning too far to the offside of the bike, lost my balance, and fell over at all but zero mph! I managed to throw my body underneath most of the bike to save it from damage but did scrape the fairing slightly. Back in the paddock and out of sight of the start line, Bob heard Allan laughingly describing my fall from grace over the tannoy. I got it in the ear from everyone after the race, and felt a little sheepish for dropping the bike. I suffered a certain amount of piss-taking for weeks after that incident. Bob is a cruel man!

At Chimay, several very high-speed accidents occurred, two of them involving friends. My Bavarian pal Reinhard Neumair very luckily escaped with a broken collarbone after clipping a tyre wall and falling off at about 130mph. Richard Adams fared far worse when he did a similar thing at about 100mph, breaking both collar bones, both shoulders, and front and rear ribs; puncturing a lung, and breaking three vertebrae in his neck, plus hand injuries. Phew! It wasn't the crash that did the worst damage, but being run over by a following rider.

After clipping the tyre wall and falling from his bike, Reinhard rolled down the middle of the track; if he'd hit the Armco barriers at that bend he almost certainly would have died. After hearing where the crash occurred I feared the worst, so was amazed to see him walking through the paddock, his arm in a sling, sipping a beer a few hours later. Lucky boy! After a spell in hospital in Belgium, Richard eventually recovered from his numerous injuries but lost a lot of strength in one arm. Apart from one last race meeting at the Goodwood Revival, that was it for him, and he concentrated on building and tuning his very special Velocettes and Manx Nortons, sponsoring quick rider Mike Russell to much success in numerous classic races. I remain very good friends with both of these plucky racers.

My Honda ride in the 2006 Manx Grand Prix culminated in one of the most bizarre retirements I've ever experienced. Things didn't start well as the first practice session was cancelled due to rain. The following Sunday afternoon, Dave Carter and I were testing the bikes at Jurby Airfield when I suddenly remembered that I was supposed to attend a technical briefing that afternoon. Attendance was obligatory, probably due to a new insurance requirement, but a team member could stand in for the rider and, fortunately, my future son-in-law, Simon, was in the paddock, and agreed to go in my place. Thank goodness for mobile phones. He reported back that he had learnt nothing that we did not already know!

I managed two good laps on the Honda on the Monday evening, but witnessed the debris that resulted from the big accident that Belgian rider Bart Crauwels had at Union Mills. He was on his Honda 350 and crashed outside the post office, subsequently severely injuring a foot, though recovering sufficiently to race again, I clipped a wall at Ginger Hall and made a mental promise to allow more room there in future. Tuesday's practice was halted at Ramsey due to mist on the mountain, and we were escorted back to the pits by travelling marshals.

I'd raced in worse conditions but, after the previous year's accidents, the organisers were putting safety first. On Thursday I managed another good lap on the Honda, but the rest of practice was plagued by rain. I had managed five-and-a-half laps in total. Good job I knew my way around the TT course; who'd be a newcomer?

Bob and Derek gave me the day off on Tuesday and Shelagh and I spent the day sightseeing. On returning to the garage they were still at it! The race engine had refused to allow adjustment of the tappets, and after much discussion they had decided to fit the spare motor as they simply didn't have enough time for extensive fault-finding. They eventually finished the job and, just as dusk was falling, we started the motor to check oil circulation which was delayed longer than we would have liked, but eventually the tell-tale dribble appeared from the cambox feed.

Race day dawned fine, and another good start lifted my spirits. I had to observe a 10,500 rev limit rather than the 11,000 that the best motor would tolerate. The gearing we had selected proved correct and my first lap was a good one at over 94mph. I overtook several riders and managed the bottom of Barrowgarroo flat out on the second lap, but 200 yards further on towards the 13th milestone the motor cut dead. The tacho dropped like a stone to zero and all was silent.

I coasted to a halt and parked the bike in the entrance to a driveway about half-a-mile short of Kirkmichael village, and frantically began stripping parts off the bike in an effort to correct the fault. I checked the ignition wiring, fuel and sparkplugs but couldn't see anything wrong, so gave up and walked to The Mitre pub in the village.

I called the team and could hear their tears and despair. It was too early for a beer but I was able to have a glass of water and a grandstand seat from which to watch everyone enjoying themselves. The team travelled across the island to recover me, and in the pits Bob began stripping the bike to try and find the cause of our demise. A short time later, having commented that he expected the cause to be ignition failure, he called me over: "It was ignition failure" he smirked. He then handed me the ignition rotor that contained the end of the broken crankshaft which had broken clean off, just outside the left-hand main bearing. The crankshafts everyone raced with had seen service in road bikes, and we rarely knew what mileage they had covered or the kind of treatment they had received at the hands of previous owners. Ours had decided to call a halt approaching Kirkmichael, and there was nothing we could have done to predict this. Racing lifts you up and drops you down. It was just our turn — again!

Bob had two motors prepared for the 2007 MGP and we arrived on the island ready for anything! Saturday's practice session was cancelled due to heavy rain, and on my first practice lap on the Monday evening the Honda dropped a valve as I approached Ramsey. It was our best motor and the damage was extensive. We were heartbroken. A year's wait, loads of money invested, and a wreck to show for it. Poor Bob spent Tuesday building one good motor from two. Our session was cancelled on Wednesday when sea mist rolled in. I heard that my friend, ex-Manx Grand Prix winner Dave Hughes, had crashed badly at Union Mills and, feeling very depressed, Bob and I shared a bottle of red. (Dave did recover, thankfully.)

We tested the Honda rebuild at Jurby on the Thursday but the evening practice session was again curtailed due to mist, so I got in only one lap on the Petty Norton. On the Friday I managed two laps on the Honda but had to stop between laps to repair the exhaust system, which had a separated downpipe joint. Thanks to help from a scrutineer and a mechanic from Martin Bullock's race team, a repair was swiftly effected, and the second lap completed. I later checked my Sulby speed trap speeds and found that the Honda had gone through at 117mph and the Petty at 130.6mph. Both good speeds.

That was it, seven laps in total. On the Sunday Bob checked the motor, discovering that it had a damaged camshaft and bearing plus a broken head stud. He chased down our engine builder, Ken Garfield, and managed to borrow the necessary parts from him to repair the motor. Pat Kerruish's lovely garage was a mess! I never knew that a Honda motor had so many parts; Bob was doing a great job at mix-and match. He and I were totally knackered, both bikes had tested us to the limit — goodness knows why we did this! Shelagh flew in to join us and calmed me down as I was a little on the frazzled side.

On Tuesday Bob and Derek did the final preparation on the Honda, Shelagh and I leaving them in peace to socialise in the paddock, where we chatted to Paton owner Roger Winfield and met his rider, Ryan Farquhar the TT ace. Ryan asked if I was quick ... everyone was very diplomatic!

Wednesday began fine, but windy, and I was up for a good ride after the Petty's frustrating demise during the Senior race on the Monday. I started well following the ritual firm good luck handshake from Stuart Jukes and "rev its nuts off" from Bob (he obviously hadn't considered the value of the motor parts we'd already destroyed during practice). I spent the race tucked in as much as possible and did wring its neck. After the first lap I hardly saw another rider, and tried to maintain concentration. Halfway through the third lap there was a slight misfire on the overrun, and I guessed that the exhaust pipe joint was trying to separate again, though I knew it couldn't come apart fully as Bob had fitted new mounting rubbers for the race.

The race seemed to take ages, and I longed for the frail little bike to carry me to the finish, which it did — and I just made the top ten. Competition had been strong but I had managed to add two-and-a-half mph to my best race average speed. tenth was my best Junior placing ever, and everyone was very happy. Bob was almost shaking with relief and exhaustion, but had the widest grin in the world. We hugged; the beer tent beckoned!

The 2008 MGP was a personal disaster for me when it came to the Junior race. Practice week had been dogged by very changeable weather, and I spent a lot of time getting used to the Paton and its high-speed capability. I completed two laps with the Honda on the Tuesday, encountering plenty of damp patches that required care to ride through. Rain put paid to any more play with the Honda, and I hoped that, with my previous experience on the bike, I could do it justice in the race. This was not to be, however. Conditions were horrible, the race was delayed from 10.15am until 3.00pm due to rain, and we were warned that there were damp or wet patches all around the course. Boy, was that right!

The biggest problem for me, however, was a trail of oil or fuel on the road that began at Ballacraine and continued through the very dangerous Glen Helen section. A rainbow of colours glistened on the wet road surface for a couple of miles, and were impossible to avoid in places, as they covered the racing line. I didn't fancy killing myself so backed off through that part of the course, losing any chance of a good lap time in the process.

My friend, Grant Sellars, had raced there for many years, and said they were the worst race conditions he had ever experienced on the island in thirty years. I finished the race 20th and outside replica time. Bob had prepared the bike beautifully, and my speed trap result in the race of 119mph demonstrated that the bike was in good nick. We'd hardly used it in practice, and then I'd failed to produce the goods in the race. I felt so sorry for Bob, who was obviously disappointed but took it well, trusting my assessment of the conditions. I'd seen too many accidents around that part of the course, and didn't want to become one of the statistics. There would always be another MGP race.

The following year — 2009 — we took the Honda to Mettet and Chimay prior to the MGP. The bike ran well at Mettet and I finished midfield at Chimay, where we experienced a small mechanical issue.

We took three bikes to this meeting: the Paton, my new Manx Norton (more of which later), and Bob's Honda, so were going to be busy. We used the spare motor in the Honda and I qualified 12th, though hindered by gearbox selection issues and a broken steering damper bracket. We found someone to braze on the bracket, and Bob played with the gearbox selector spring to try and rectify that problem.

The race on the Saturday went well and I finished in the top ten: the gearbox seemed fine. Sunday's first race was not so encouraging. I got a good start but, as I passed the pits after the first lap, Bob noticed smoke coming from one of the exhaust pipes. I slammed down the gears for the first corner after the pits and accelerated firmly towards the first chicane; negotiated that safely and accelerated towards the second chicane. As I did so I felt something peppering my right foot and the bike lost power. Whipping in the clutch I coasted to a halt wondering what had failed this time!

Initially, I thought that the front tyre had touched the mudguard and it was fragments of tyre rubber I had felt hitting my boot; wrong. I then spotted oil around the front of the motor, and gave up, waiting to be recovered. Back at the paddock Bob removed the fairing, exposing the motor, and cursing at what he saw. I wandered over to see what he'd found: the more we looked the worse it seemed. A very expensive con rod had broken and the piston had smashed into the cylinder head, bending the valves and damaging the head. The remaining lower part of the con rod had flailed about, smashing its way through the cylinder barrel and crankcase, bending one of the front frame down tubes. It was catastrophic to say the least and would cost a fortune to repair. Drink was taken, (by Bob, anyway, as I still had races to compete in). That poor bike tested our resolve to the limit. When it went it was a flyer, but when it blew it broke our hearts — and wallets.

Bob managed to repair the bike in time for the following month's MGP but, as you will have read previously, it was never raced, and would have to wait for the following season.

In 2010 we raced the Honda at Mettet in May and Chimay in July with excellent results, including a fourth at a cool Mettet and seventh at Chimay in blazing sunshine. Bob didn't give up on the bike, constantly trying to make it reliable and only ever fitting the best parts. We thoroughly enjoyed our continental jaunts, and felt that, with a little luck, a podium place was possible in this hotly-contested class.

I was keen to return to the Dundrod circuit and, because I'd retired from the Manx Grand Prix side of things by this point, we decided to give it a go. After a long and expensive ferry trip we set up camp in the paddock and got stuck into the practice sessions. The bike ran beautifully, and we correctly determined the gearing. I ended up fourth in my class, and looked forward to a good race as the weather was fine and the track one of my favourites.

There were a couple of small issues after practice as the head gasket seemed to be leaking oil very slightly, and a small crankcase through bolt had broken, requiring replacement. Bob tightened down the head and fixed the bolt prior to the race, and I went to the start line confident of a good finish. As I completed the warm-up lap, however, I felt the motor falter slightly. Bob was alongside my grid position and, as I came to a halt, I quickly explained the problem. Bob, bless him, said "Give it 'the berries'; I'm sure it will be okay, probably just an oiled sparkplug!" I did as instructed and got a flying start but, as I pushed it into third gear, the bike lost a lot of power and I realised my race was over.

That year at Dundrod only one classic race was run; the grid comprising three groups that were flagged off at timed intervals. The track is too narrow to let everyone loose in one go, so groups are made up according to practice times. I was in the second group, the front group comprising mainly larger capacity machines. When the bike failed I quickly realised that there was nowhere safe to pull over, and with another group of riders let loose behind me, decided I'd have to ride slowly to the first corner, Leathemstown, which was still a good half-a-mile away. I raised my left hand and rode cautiously, being passed at very high speed by the rest of the field. On arrival at Leathemstown I pulled off the track onto the grass verge and looked down. The lower part of my leathers were covered with oil and aluminium which had blown out of the carburettors: laying in the inlet tract of one cylinder was a valve head. Our race was run, another good engine knackered, more sad stories to tell — drink was taken yet again!

The following year, 2011, we again had motor trouble with the Honda at Chimay, plus the weather was wet. For the first time we entered the Belgian Classic TT at Gedinne. The weather in mid-August was hot and sunny and, with the motor rebuilt by Bob, we had some wonderful fun. The circuit was right up my street: fast and flowing, up hill and down dale, no run-off areas — challenging but brilliant. In the first race, I had trouble selecting second and third gears, but Bob adjusted the clutch and I had a great second race, finishing first in my class. Boy, were we happy! When that bike ran properly it was a rocket ship, and handled brilliantly.

Chimay was kinder to us in 2012, and after a damp practice session Bob adjusted the low throttle settings of the carburetion. In hot and sunny weather I finished fourth in my first race and third in the second.

There were now three chicanes around the Chimay road course, and refining the fuelling made it much easier to accelerate out of them. I was slightly handicapped as our motor had only five speeds, whilst some of the opposition had newly-available six-speed boxes, so their results were excellent.

A few weeks later we returned to Gedinne and, again in lovely weather, I finished first in our class in the first race. I'd had an enjoyable battle with a French guy called Alvaro Margulis, who commented to Bob after the race "I thought I'd follow Andy — but no!" A nice sideways compliment. In the second race I finished third after being badly baulked at the start, and poor Alvaro received a three place penalty for jumping the start: perhaps he had been keen to try and beat me?

2013 saw a change in the weather. I had to travel on my own to Chimay as Bob had to work, though planned to leave as early as possible on the Friday afternoon and travel overnight to join me. The head gasket decided to leak in practice and, to top that, the gearbox decided to stick in top gear. Fortunately, Ken Garfield, our engine tuner, was at this meeting, and helped me to sort these issues. Further investigation by Bob, when he arrived, revealed that the top engine mounting on the frame had fractured, but I managed to get sidecar racer James Walker to repair it for us with his welding kit. Poor old Bob — having had only little sleep, we then had to remove the motor to repair the frame.

I had a couple of good races the following day, finishing in the top ten both times, so not too bad at all. I always struggled to some degree through the chicanes that had been gradually added by the organisers to comply with insurance requirements introduced because of the then recent history of serious accidents at the circuit. I was quite a good road racer, but never as quick through fiddly sections or on short circuits: the story of my racing life, really.

We eagerly anticipated our trip to Gedinne, but the weather wasn't so good that year. I did have one really good, dry race, overtaking Reinhard Neumair on his Aermacchi and Alvaro on his Honda to finish fourth in my class: very satisfying. To be fair to Reinhard, his Aermacchi was no match for our very quick, later specification Honda, and I only just managed to squeeze past him on the run downhill to the chequered flag. In the second race I fell asleep to some degree and could manage only fourth again.

The following year Chimay experienced temperatures in excess of 30 degrees which the Honda did not appreciate. I qualified quite well in 14th place, but, in the first race, whilst going well, a piston

(continued on page 169)

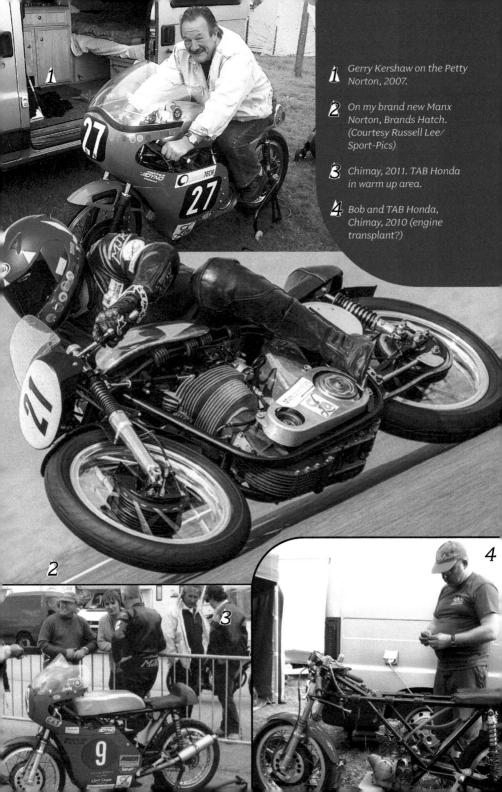

1 Gerry Kershaw on the Petty Norton, 2007.

2 On my brand new Manx Norton, Brands Hatch. (Courtesy Russell Lee/Sport-Pics)

3 Chimay, 2011. TAB Honda in warm up area.

4 Bob and TAB Honda, Chimay, 2010 (engine transplant?)

Petty Norton, final specification, 2006, showing 'those' tanks!

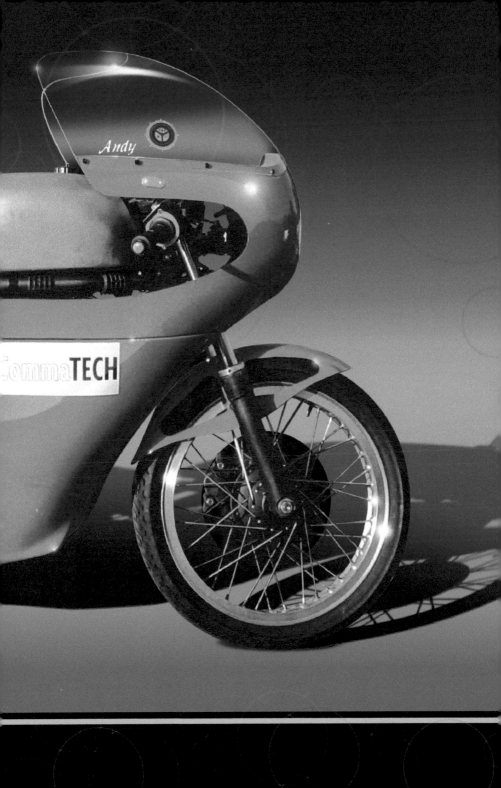

Above, left to right:

Looking smug on our new bike, with Roberto Pattoni at the Paton factory, Italy, 2008.

Paton gearbox discussion, with Bob, Don and Steve in Steve Lindsell's workshop.

The Paton at Chimay, mechanic, Bob Johnson 'possibly' hung over?

On the Paton, MGP practice, 2008, Bungalow. (Courtesy Russell Lee/Sport-Pics)

Enjoying Bob Johnson's TAB Honda at Greeba Bridge, MGP, 2009.
(Courtesy Russell Lee/Sport-Pics)

Insets anti-clockwise from top:

With Trevor Nation at Goodwood with my Manx Norton.

Don Williamson telling me I have just achieved a 100mph lap. MGP 2008. (Courtesy Don Williamson)

MGP 2009, scrutineering the Honda with Bob.

MGP 2009 podium with Ryan Farquhar and Wattie Brown.

Lansdowne race, Brands Hatch British Superbikes 2010 (me No21) — the first five riders are already out of picture! (Courtesy Anthony Beck Photography)

On Seb Perez's 1939 Velocette KTT,
Goodwood, 2010.

Lansdowne Donington, me 21, Redgate,
Pete Swallow up the inside again!
(Courtesy Russell Lee/Sport-Pics)

Racing my Manx Norton at Snetterton, eyes closing
(falling asleep?). (Courtesy Russell Lee/Sport-Pics)

Manx Norton at Silverstone being shadowed by Malcolm Clark. (Courtesy Russell Lee/Sport-Pics)

Goodwood revival, Phil and Derek Harding puzzling over Woden, Norton-JAP.

Stretching the throttle cable on the BMW RS54 at Goodwood revival, Pit straight. (Courtesy BMW AG/Gudrun Muschalla)

Me scrutineering at Portimao for GP originals and The Landsdowne Classic Series, 2018.

Aermacchi rebuilt, at MCN Day, Peterborough.

My TZ Yamaha, being expertly paraded by Ian Bain, Donington 2018.
(Courtesy Russell Lee/Sport-Pics)

Enjoying my Manx Norton at Snetterton.
(Courtesy Russell Lee/Sport-Pics)

The fan club. My daughters: Charlie, Julie and Amanda.

Andy Reynolds

broke up, with not too much damage, fortunately, though putting paid to any more racing that weekend. The Gedinne meeting a month later was marred by small mechanical problems, though race we did, producing a couple of fourth places. Socially, these Belgian meetings were wonderful, and we forged numerous friendships with riders and teams from many countries. Several of these were pals from my '90s IHRO period and MGP days, and we often shared food and drink whilst relating past racing tales (maybe sometimes exaggerating our achievements? It's what racers do!).

By now, most of our opposition had six-speed gearboxes so Bob kindly dug into his well-used wallet and, during the winter months, acquired a lovely six-speed cluster. Due to its late delivery we had no time to test it before our annual trip to Chimay, where — sure enough — it bit our backside and refused to cleanly select gears during the Friday afternoon practice session. Bob was not present as he had again to follow me to Chimay; not arriving late on the Friday night. Fortunately, Ken Garfield, our engine tuner, offered to have a look, along with our paddock neighbour, experienced racer John Cragg. After several hours of fiddling, filing and cursing, they declared the problem sorted.

On Saturday morning I had six gears available, and what a difference that made: a gear for every corner! My first race provided a fifth in class and a very enjoyable ride in good company. In the second race, I was stalking Bruno Leroy, a really good French rider and Classic MGP winner, but to no avail as the race was red-flagged before I could mount a serious challenge. Someone had lost the plot in a big way at the end of the back straight, which signalled the end of racing for us that weekend.

Gedinne, a few weeks later, enjoyed some welcome summer sun, Belgian style — very hot! This was to be my last event on this brilliant machine, although I didn't know it at the time. The Honda felt quick, and was quick. I qualified second and finished second in my class, delighting in handing the trophy to Bob (he never got his hands on my first place ones!).

As I write this, at the end of 2018, Bob has sold the Honda and another chapter has ended, but someone has bought a bike with a very interesting history!

CHAPTER 16

A NEW MANX NORTON

IN LATE 2005, I REALISED THAT MY REPLICA STANDARD specification Seeleys were no longer competitive; the lightweight, highly-tuned versions were dominating classic racing at all levels. The rules had been relaxed, and almost any modifications were now permitted. A series of races for standard specification, pre-1963 GP bikes was becoming popular, and I thought this would be a good direction to follow. This was the 'Lansdowne Series.'

I priced up a new George Beale replica traditional Matchless G50 rolling chassis with the intention of slotting my own G50 motor into it, but the price was extortionate and beyond my means. Thinking laterally, I placed an advertisement in *Classic Racer* magazine, cheekily asking for sponsorship on a suitable bike, receiving three replies, all of whom were offering original condition Manx Nortons.

Two were owned by elderly chaps who wanted their lovely bikes raced again after some years in storage. One of these had serious health issues, and the other seemed a little vague on the phone so I politely declined their kind offers. The third 'applicant' was a businessman from Northamptonshire, who said he had two Manx Nortons — a 350 and a 500 that he'd recently bought. He thought that the 350 could be made raceworthy, and would like to meet me to talk over the idea.

A week or two later I travelled to his palatial home, and there in the large garage was a very nice 350 Manx. Its owner explained that he was going to have it race-prepared by a well known restorer of Manx Nortons, and that if I was agreeable we would go and visit the restorer, who lived in the West Country, once he had started work on the bike. Some weeks later I met the sponsor at a services on the M40, and we travelled in his Porsche to the restorer's house. During the journey we chatted to pass the time, and I talked about my racing career and various Manx GP experiences. I probably dominated the conversation but my companion seemed happy to listen.

We arrived at our destination, and there was the bike partially stripped and looking good. I asked for a few items to be changed, and some additional lock wiring to be done, and was shocked when the restorer said that he didn't like using lock wire unnecessarily. My years of classic racing had demonstrated that if a part was able to become detached it would, and lock wire was a very efficient deterrent to this happening (often, it was used in conjunction with Loctite as back-up).

We travelled home in a reasonably good mood, and further discussions took place regarding race plans and general co-operation. I wasn't unhappy but did feel that I was, for a change, not totally in control of the bike preparation. I suppose I had made it clear to the other two that I was used to riding very carefully-prepared machines, and wanted this Manx to be of the same safe specification. Anything I was worried about could easily be sorted at a later date, I thought, and the sponsor and I parted on good terms to await delivery of the completed job in spring 2006.

A couple of months later, in March 2006, I received a phone call from the sponsor late one evening. Before I had a chance to speak he told me that our partnership would not take place as he was fed up with my "inane wittering" about the Isle of Man. He'd changed his mind about providing sponsorship, he said, and that was that. He put the phone down on me as I sat there, stunned. I did wonder if he had enjoyed a drink or two that evening, before he phoned me, as he sounded a little strange, but there was nothing I could do; he made that very clear.

My Manx Norton/Lansdowne Series plans for the 2006 race season were trashed and I needed to move on. I know that I can bore people to death about racing, but most 'racing folk' enjoy banter like this. I obviously got it wrong in this case ... As a footnote to this incident, over the following couple of years I chatted with two other classic racing pals, both of whom had ridden for this sponsor and been discarded as soon as a potentially faster rider became available. This may have been what had happened in my case, as the rider he ultimately recruited was younger and perhaps a little bit quicker.

I was racing Don Williamson's Petty Norton and Bob Johnson's Honda, so my two Seeleys were seeing little competition. One evening my youngest daughter, Charlie, rolled her eyes as I ranted on about this, and said "Why don't you sell the G50 and your road bike and just have the new bike?" I had promised Pete Clements that I would never sell the G50, but Charlie pointed out that Pete had always advocated moving with the times, and was sure he would have encouraged progress. I took a moment to ponder this, and concluded that she was right, so a plan was formulated. I advertised the Seeleys for sale along with my Honda CB1300 road bike. Bob, Don and Roger Yates encouraged me to go down this route, and it turned out to be one of the best decisions I ever made. Looks like not going ahead with the sponsor was a good move!

In the spring of 2006, I took the 500 to a race meeting at Oulton Park, and parked it in the paddock with a 'For Sale' sign attached to it. A few days later, I was contacted by someone who had seen the advert and he bought the bike from me for a little (well, a good bit) under the asking price. I advertised the 350 in *Classic Racing* magazines, but there wasn't a lot of interest; eventually, Geoff Sawyer, a Manx Grand Prix racing friend, offered to take it off my hands. He really drove a hard bargain, and I had to include an almost new Suzuki front drum brake that he'd spotted in my workshop. A few months later another pal revealed that he had bought the brake from Geoff for "good money" so I knew I'd been the loser in that particular transaction! I did have enough budget to build the Manx, though.

I took myself off to a Lansdowne meeting at Brands Hatch for some networking and window-shopping. I spoke to a number of racing pals there and asked for their recommendations regarding sourcing the necessary components to build a new replica 500cc Manx Norton. I soon had a list of the most critical parts and their recommended sources, and probably avoided making costly errors by doing so. At this time the Lansdowne Series competitors were all very experienced classic racers who loved and coveted their precious machines. There were almost no sponsored riders, and the camaraderie amongst the riders was genuine and wonderful to see. They actively encouraged me to join them, and I was anxious to fit in. The advice they provided was honest and I made copious notes. As I write this the Lansdowne Series is still very active, although a larger proportion of the competitors are sponsored, younger riders: my old pals are beginning to feel their age, and gradually retiring from competition, in some cases becoming sponsors themselves in order to keep their bikes on the track.

Returning from Brands Hatch I began ordering components based on the recommendations I'd received. Brian Penfold had raced immaculate Manx Nortons for years, and he suggested that I buy a frame from Richard Adams, a Velocette pal of mine, and an excellent engineer. Richard was in cahoots with Ken Sprayson, who had made the original Manx frames in the classic period, and they had the original jigs, so I felt confident that an excellent product would be forthcoming. Dick Hunt's brakes and hubs were recommended by most riders, and, as I knew Dick well, that was an easy decision. One bike at Brands had a TAB (Terry Baker) Norton Dominator-style fuel tank, the shape of which I really liked: as I had met Terry when Bob Johnson and I were sourcing parts for the 350 Honda, this was also an easy call.

TT Industries gearboxes from New Zealand were becoming popular as they looked classic, but had more modern design internals and were less prone to missing gears. Boy, were they expensive, though! I bit the bullet and ordered a new lightweight version with a magnesium casing, which proved another great decision. Robin Packham offered to sponsor me with a pair of his lightweight Falcon shocks and I readily accepted his kind offer. Over the years we have become great friends; he really has helped me out and, in turn, I've done my best to be a good ambassador for his excellent products.

I turned to Gerry Kershaw, who prepared Don Williamson's Petty Norton motor, for advice regarding the motor, and he suggested there was little to choose between a Molnar motor and a Summerfield version, but that, as he was currently working for Andy Molnar, this might be the easiest route. I happily agreed, and Gerry took delivery of a new motor in its component parts ready for him to build. My MGP pal Pete Swallow offered to make up a set of forks and a primary belt cover and, as his workmanship is second-to-none, I asked him to press on. I already had a spare NEB belt-drive clutch and a spare Krober tacho, which pretty much completed the 'kit'!

Patience has never been one of my virtues but, as nearly everything I had ordered was bespoke, I had to await delivery news. An initial issue was when Ken Sprayson was taken ill and Richard Adams had to complete the frame and swinging arm. Richard had quite seriously damaged an arm in that Chimay crash, and I felt bad about pressurising him. He ultimately did me proud, however, and I duly collected my order towards the end of the summer. Other parts began to arrive, and the excitement of the 'build' started. Gerry Kershaw delivered my completed motor in good time and informed me that he'd had the cylinder head ported to his own specifications by Fred Walmsley, and that he thought it should be a "good 'un."

The wheels from Dick Hunt took a little time to be ready, but he was inundated with work and beholden to his castings supplier. When I did collect them, I was most impressed. The fuel tank supplied by Terry Baker was fine but the oil tank shape was miles out. I eventually sent paper patterns to him and, without complaint, he swiftly made another version that fitted perfectly. Sadly, Terry died in 2010, but his son-in-law, Richard Phelps, and daughter, Aline Phelps, still continue to make lovely products in the family tradition, trading as TAB 2 Classics.

The best laid plans, etc! The TTI gearbox arrived on time, and as soon as I had the motor I started to offer them up to the frame using a pair of Molnar Precision dural engine plates. Clearances were tight, and it had obviously been impossible to get six speeds into the standard gearbox shell. I found the gearbox to be wider than standard, and a right pig to position happily. A little metal had to be removed from the middle case of the gearbox and the engine plates before clearance below it could be had. Filing metal from a brand new, £4000 gearbox is worrying. Anyway, the objective was achieved, but every time the motor had to be removed from the frame I cursed that oversized gearbox shell, and inadvertently scraped yet more pristine paint from my frame. My Velocette Owners Club pal, Den Edwards had offered to paint the frame for me and a beautiful job he did for minimal cost: ta, Den (sorry about the occasional damage). Pete Swallow's forks and primary cover arrived in good time and fitted straight in, as he promised they would.

I certainly called in a few favours during the project, not least of which, involved Brian Barrow. He agreed to fabricate a high level exhaust system, but this turned out to be a right bugger! Several trips to and from his workshop eventually resulted in a lovely system, but I did try his patience. Fitting the larger Krober tacho within a standard Manx Norton cowling proved tricky, but Don Williamson designed and had made a lovely bracket, in titanium, at his factory, and it was the envy of all who saw it.

Phil Harding kindly helped me out by making a couple of special fittings in stainless steel, and Paul Duncombe fabricated a lovely alloy gear linkage, although it took us two attempts to get the dimensions correct. I don't think either of these skilful, self-employed engineers ever made much money out of my orders! You do need good friends in the racing game.

My eventual total spend would be around £23,000, but I did have a very high specification, brand new Manx Norton for that sum, so was not unhappy. Bob and I took the bike into his mechanics' training workshop one weekend in March 2007, and, after a bit of fiddling, got the bike running cleanly; it appeared to be oil-tight. Within the next two weeks we took the bike to a midweek practice afternoon at Mallory Park to run in the motor, followed by a 'no limits' track day at Brands Hatch. Both went well, making only small adjustments and refining the running of the motor at all speeds.

It was a bit of a strange experience to ride without a full fairing, but it did make me realise that I would have to keep my head down and my stomach slim so that I could position myself behind the small cowling's fly-screen! Bob was brilliantly attentive and as enthusiastic as ever.

The biggest mistake I made was at Mallory Park when I went out in a session and forgot to turn on the fuel tap as I left the warm-up area, having stopped the motor following a slight delay. There was enough fuel in the float chamber to take me halfway around the circuit, but then the bike just petered out. Not realising what had caused the problem — and anxious to get out the way of other riders — I dismounted and pushed the bike off the track and onto the grass just next to Edwina's Chicane ... and straight into about three inches of liquid mud. I was not best pleased: a lot of cleaning was required before I could ride the bike again. What a numpty.

In early April I found myself standing beside my Manx Norton as it roared away on full throttle on Chris Adams' dyno in Aylesbury. Quite surreal and nerve-wracking. The reading was 50bhp at the rear wheel, affirming Gerry Kershaw's opinion that it would be a good motor. A few phone calls had confirmed that our power output was similar to other standard Manxes, but a little behind the 55-56bhp of the front runners.

My first meeting at Brands Hatch in mid-April was on a hot, sunny weekend. The bike ran perfectly all weekend and, with full grids of 40 competitors, I was very happy with three 12th places and a 13th. The bike received a few compliments, with special credit for the gear change linkage; a couple of the riders thought it was quick. One of the best weekends of my life. Brilliant!

The rest of the season's meetings involving the Manx Norton were a learning curve. Oulton Park in May was good but, at the next meeting at Mallory Park, the bike suffered from vibration. Close examination found that slightly loose engine mounting bolts were the problem. The bolts had settled into the new powder coating on the frame, and slight vibes from rich carburetion had loosened them. I had an eighth place in my last race gifted to me by a couple of fallers — thanks lads!

In July, Bob and I travelled to Scarborough. Braking has never been my strong suit, and I came in for some banter from Bill Swallow who had witnessed my forks bobbing up and down as I braked for Mere Hairpin, near the paddock. Very embarrassed and red-faced, I gave myself a good talking to. I was slightly releasing the front brake as I blipped the throttle, and this had caused the fork movement. From that day I tried to lose this bad habit.

The multiple heavy braking points at Scarborough made themselves obvious as my front brake lever gradually lost its adjustment during the course of each session out on track. My four leading shoe front brake required adjustment, for which there is a special technique to do it properly, and Stacey Kilworth, a top classic racer, spotted me struggling; he very kindly showed me the ropes in this respect. I finished ninth in both races but a friend and originator of the Lansdowne Series, Richard Thirkell, had a massive accident in one race, as he travelled down the hill towards the chicane prior to the start and finish area. Coming down that section of track at high speed, his bike's front wheel lifted over a bump, which I think caught him out. Both Richard and his bike flew into the air, hit the banking and tumbled down the track. Miraculously, Richard suffered only serious bruising, but his bike was mangled. Thousands of pounds worth of damage. He was very lucky not to have been killed.

Following Scarborough we travelled to Castle Combe, but in the second race, the motor just cut out and I free-wheeled to a stop to await the recovery truck. With the help of other, more mechanically-minded riders, we diagnosed the problem as a sheared woodruff key on the mainshaft. End of my racing fun for the weekend — out with the red wine!

After returning home I poured out my problems to Don Williamson, and he generously offered to fly us and the motor in his light aircraft to Lancashire. I grabbed at the offer and we arranged for Gerry Kershaw to meet us at a hilltop airstrip in the countryside above Huddersfield.

The flight went smoothly and, after we had landed and taxied to the single hangar, a man appeared to find out why we had landed on his private airstrip. I recognised him to be Jamie Whitham, the well-known professional motorcycle racer, who, once he understood what we were up to, left us alone to unload the motor, have a brief chat to Gerry and return home. Don allowed me to take the controls for most of the return trip, piloting the straight and level stuff under his friendly guidance, though he was in charge of the take-off and very smooth landing. Being a four-seater, the aircraft had dual controls, so Don could have taken over at any point, if necessary. I thoroughly enjoyed my experience — no wonder so many racers learn to fly!

A couple of weeks later, I enjoyed a long drive up the M1 to meet Gerry at a northern services where he exchanged my repaired motor for some hard-earned cash.

In September I enjoyed a combined vintage car and classic bike race meeting at Donington, previous to the final meeting of the season at Cadwell Park. Despite not getting the gearing correct at

Donington, I still managed a couple of 13th places from full grids of 40 riders. The weather at Cadwell Park, Lincolnshire, in October was cool but dry, for what was to be a lesson regarding autumn race meetings. I was up for a 'grand finale' to my first season with the Manx Norton, but as I went out for the first practice session, with mist still hanging in the trees, I caressed the front brake lever as we cruised down to the hairpin, and the front drum brake immediately grabbed on fully, throwing me off the bike. This slid along on its left side with me tumbling along the track after it, very red-faced! Following riders filtered past me, wondering what on earth I had done to end up crashing there, just a hundred yards from the track entry point, and at such low speed ... A couple of them told me later they had only just avoided hitting me and my bike, as it all happened so suddenly. The damp atmosphere had got into the brake drum and the first application had caused the linings to grab the brake drum viciously. I had managed to keep my expensive crash helmet clear of the track, but now had lightly scuffed leathers and a very sore little finger on my right-hand.

With help from other riders I managed to straighten the bike enough to get out for a later practice/qualifying session, and completed three of the four races, after more repairs. Speaking to other riders I quickly learned that I was not the first racer to suffer this indignity, which usually happened in damp early spring or autumn weather conditions. Less grabby brake linings were now available, and fitting these was added to my winter job list.

A day or two after we got home I took myself off to the casualty department of our local hospital to be examined by a very gentle eastern European doctor, who took one look at my finger and told me: "You have a mallet finger." I asked if they would operate on this and he quietly informed me that the scar tissue an operation would leave would probably cause me more issues than the limp finger-end I now had. At least the finger would bend around the brake lever, even if I couldn't straighten the last joint because I had severed the ligament that does this. No one said racing wouldn't hurt, did they??

My first season with the Manx Norton had come to an end. We'd had ups and downs — but great fun, too.

CHAPTER 17

STORIES FROM THE MANX NORTON YEARS

I OWNED AND RACED THE MANX NORTON FROM 2007 UNTIL 2016: it proved very reliable, and I lived the dream of my youth. I could finish just within the top ten in my class of the Lansdowne Series, and enjoyed regular dices with Stuart Tonge, Pete Swallow, Nick Bedford, and Patrick Walker. I also chased — though usually failed to catch — Gordon Russell, Stan Woods, Charlie Williams, Mike Farrell, and Robin Stokes. In the early years Pete Swallow, Tim Jackson, and Andy Molnar competed for top honours on their 350cc machines, and in our mixed class races we enjoyed many tussles, as I out-powered them on the straights whilst they dived under me at every corner.

I made a number of detail changes on the bike as I learned from my pals the various ways to get the best from a Manx. Different exhaust systems appeared as noise limits at circuits became a challenge, and my original low-level system was soon abandoned in favour of a high-level version to allow more ground clearance. After a couple of seasons I realised that I could do well in the 'over 55s' sub class if I acquired every point possible, so I swapped my 18in wheel rims for more traditional 19in items, as good compound tyres in that size were just becoming available from Avon (extra championship points were awarded for originality). The top runners used electronic ignition systems, but I stayed with magnetos for several years because this again earned me extra points; until Bernard Murray, who was to share my bike at a Goodwood Revival meeting, offered to pay most of the cost of a new electronic ignition system, as he thought it would increase my bike's performance, and move us up the result sheet. Andy Molnar provided the kit but was of the opinion that the bike wouldn't be any faster, though it would start more easily and run consistently well, which proved to be the case. "Fit and forget" were his words.

Over its life my Manx utilised many parts purchased from Andy Molnar, who was, and is, very opinionated. I found him to be honest and usually absolutely correct in his advice, and he was good to me, supplying many parts over the years, and trusting me to send payment after delivery. When I announced my retirement from Isle of Man competition in 2009, aged 61, Andy said "You've made exactly the right decision to stop now. You won't improve on that third place. You have nothing to prove and are still alive!"

Pete Swallow and I had been pals for a long time due to our Isle of Man exploits, and we often parked together in the race paddocks, our wives chatting together and leaving us to our spanners. Pete's wife, Carol, is a little more hands-on than my Shelagh, and would have a go at Pete if I managed to beat him, especially when he upgraded his Manx Norton to 500cc. To be fair, she also actively encouraged me to be more aggressive, and I did try! Pete would calm me down in times of crisis, and I would encourage him when he had occasional moments of doubt. My notebook gleefully records every time I beat Pete, but there are not that many entries for this. I remember one meeting in 2014 at Silverstone on the GP circuit when I enjoyed four great races dicing with Pete. He and I swapped places several times during each race, and during one of them I just ducked under him at the final complex on the last lap to beat him to the line. "I didn't expect that!" he exclaimed, and Carol gave him some stick; he returned the favour in the next race.

TT star Stan Woods and his lovely wife, Sue, became good friends, along with Charlie Williams, another TT hero, and his smashing wife, Ann. Both men joined the Lansdowne Series a few years after I did, giving me much encouragement and sound advice. I think my Isle of Man racing history gave us all something in common, and respect was mutual. I am very methodical and plan everything prior to meetings, but I am not too good under stress. I remember several moments of panic caused by broken ignition wires and other issues that occurred between races, when Stan would see me flapping and wander over to patiently sort me out and calm me down. No wonder he is so popular with other racers.

One year Stan decided to enter the Classic meeting at Chimay. On our Manxes in the first race, we ended up side-by-side, flying down the very fast section that we called 'Armco Alley' (our bikes were on a par, performance-wise). As we approached the left-hand kink at the beginning of the tricky S-bend near the bottom of the hill, I made sure I was on the left-hand side of the track, as this favoured me for the exit. Stan had no option but to back off and I beat him to the finish.

After the race he came up to me grinning, and said: "You were a bit braver than me." In the next race, however, he made sure to beat me off the line, and all I could do was follow him home. Revenge was sweet, I think!

The two of us had a few good races over time, and I usually had to do the chasing as Stan was so good off the start line. Even if I qualified ahead of him on the grid you could bet he'd come steaming past, even before I was in second gear.

Pete Swallow — who has been racing longer than I have and is very competitive — has admitted to having the odd red mist moment. In 2011, I was closely following him into the very fast right-hand bend onto the straight at Pembrey called Honda Curve. Pete carries an old injury to his shoulder, and consequently isn't able to move around on his bike very much; short and slight, he simply wedges himself in and goes for it. As we exited the bend, I had a close-up view as his bike slid away from him at close to 100mph, and he and the bike dug grooves in the grass verge in a very untidy manner. Pete had known I was right behind him, challenging for position, and I think he just over-egged it. He and his bike were well bruised, and there was much debate about whether the tyre let go or his footrest dug in. Pete thought the tyre but I thought the footrest: he leant his bike further than I did exiting the corner as he couldn't physically lean off the bike very much due to his shoulder issue.

That wasn't the only time he was involved in an accident, either. In 2012 he was chasing Stuart Tonge in a practice session at Oulton Park as I followed. Unfortunately for them both, Stuart's bike had a problem and he suddenly lost speed, and Pete was so close behind him that he couldn't avoid Stuart's bike, ramming him at high speed. Both bikes were seriously damaged and their riders well-shaken and bruised. That ended their meeting, but I profited as it moved me up the results list. Later that year, on the first lap of a Lansdowne race at Snetterton, Pete decided that he could overtake a few of us on the inside as we approached Sears Corner. He did overtake us, but then couldn't stop for the tight hairpin corner apex, and slid down the track as his front wheel tucked under, probably when his brake locked on. More dents to his ego and the bike; I don't think it did his new Arai helmet any good, either. As a result, I think Pete began to question his racing judgement and ability, although we still retain our different opinions during discussions when we socialise, as we are still close friends.

One of my long-time classic racing pals is Duncan Fitchett; a top rider whatever machinery he chooses to compete on. At a meeting, again at Pembrey, I found myself dicing with Nick Bedford. Our bikes were equal with regard to performance, and we weren't far apart in ability around that particular circuit. During a lunch break I spent a little time chatting to Duncan, and mentioned racing with Nick. Duncan asked me what gear I was using for Honda Curve, the bend prior to the start and finish straight, where Pete had previously dumped it. "Fifth," I told him "clicking it up to sixth just before the finish line." Duncan said "If you really need to, kick it down to fourth as you brake slightly for the corner and rev the nuts off it, clicking it into fifth as you exit: you'll carry a little more speed."

Sure enough, in our next race I ended up right behind Nick as we approached Honda Curve on the last lap, so I did as Duncan suggested and slipped past Nick on the inside of the bend to beat him to the line. After the race I met Nick in the paddock, and he asked "How did you do that?" I'd promised Duncan I wouldn't tell anyone his secret so simply smirked at Nick and shrugged.

Stuart Tonge and I had a few good battles over the Manx years. Stuart prepared my Manx's motor after Gerry Kershaw cut back on his customer base. Stuart is a brilliant engineer, and his own bike is extremely quick, especially under acceleration, and he spends hours tweaking carburetion and ignition settings on a dyno to find optimum performance. I could sometimes 'do him' around the quicker bends, though he would often get me back out of the same corners. Early on, he had a go at me for diving under him at Paddock Bend at Brands Hatch, and was not best pleased when I said that he had left the door open. I get on really well with Stuart, and I'm sure he won't mind me saying he really hates being passed whilst racing. If you do manage to get past him he will try everything he can to get back past you quickly and with a vengeance. At another Brands Hatch meeting I managed to get under him as we entered Clearways bend on the Indy circuit. Sure enough, as we exited the bend, his bike's superior acceleration paid off and he swooped past me on my inside, getting a little too close as he did, his left-hand footrest clipping my front forks. The impact and shock caused me to wobble at high speed, and I thought I was headed for a serious crash. Thankfully, the Manx Norton's excellent handling saved the day and I survived to follow him home at the finish.

I saw Stuart after the race and quietly asked him whether it had been necessary to get that close to me? His reply was that I must have moved across his path ... We agreed to disagree on this, and remained friends.

In 2012 we had a Lansdowne round at Thruxton. I enjoyed the wide open spaces around that circuit, and unusually managed to beat both Stuart Tonge and Robin Stokes in a couple of the races. In the last race of the weekend I had a great dice with Roger

Munsey. Roger is a past Vintage MCC racing champion, who owns an indecently-fast Norton Domiracer replica. He has raced all manner of bikes, and often works on and parades rare machines for George Beale, the collector and sponsor. Roger and I had exchanged places several times during the race; as we approached the last chicane, I was setting him up for a final pass when I was baulked by a couple of slower 350 riders we were lapping. Roger celebrated and I felt miffed. Roger is such a nice chap who has raced for a lifetime at a very high level, and we've had many varied and interesting conversations regarding classic racing. Top bloke and great to reminisce with.

Gordon and Sally Russell are stalwarts in the classic racing scene. Gordon has raced and officiated at a high level all of his life, and both he and Sally are deeply involved in the organisation of classic events at top level, Sally often being our Clerk of the Course; a very responsible position. We racers have a lot to thank them for.

Gordon often races in the Lansdowne Series, where I can't usually get near him, though, in 2012, we were riding close together in a race at beautifully-sunny Oulton Park and for some time I was following Gordon around this lovely circuit (one of my favourites, as it is similar to an open road circuit) approaching Old Hall Corner at the end of the start and finish straight, I realised I was so close to Gordon that I could try and out-brake him. I proceeded to grab the front brake as hard as I dared, barely retaining control as I slipped inside him, just managing to avoid the slippery kerb on the exit of the corner to lead him down The Avenue towards Cascades corner. As we exited Cascades, he overtook me, and that was it: he just beat me to the finish line and I would never pass him again. Gordon congratulated me afterwards, smiling as he did so!

In a Lansdowne race at another meeting at Oulton Park, a British Superbike round, Gordon ran out of road when exiting Cascades, taking to the grass and demolishing a polystyrene advertising board before tumbling off uninjured. It was all televised, and he certainly took some stick for that.

Over the winter of 2012 I decided to fit a fairing to the Manx. Bernard Murray had quietly complained that 'our' bike didn't have a fairing when we had raced it at the Goodwood Revival in 2011. To be fair, most of the other bikes did have fairings as they are allowed for that event, and Bernard liked to race on equal terms. I always fancied riding with a Peel Mountain Mile fairing, so approached Pete Swallow as I knew he had raced with one. Pete confessed he had one left from a batch that he had made some years ago, and, under pressure, agreed to sell it to me, as well as make the necessary, quite complex, brackets. I left him to get on with this and had a chat with Dave Davis regarding a new low-level exhaust system to comply with Goodwood regulations, and which would fit within the fairing, utilising an open megaphone that, again, Goodwood regulations required. I knew that Duncan Fitchett used one of Dave's systems on his Norton, which looked the dog's bollocks!

A couple of visits to Dave's workshop in Wiltshire resulted in a lovely exhaust system, and the happy banter that all visitors to Dave's house enjoy. Dave is a highly qualified scrutineer and a very skilful fabricator, as well as one of classic racing's characters.

Pete quickly delivered the fairing plus brackets, and I spent several happy hours adjusting the parts to effect a satisfactory fit for everything. The bike looked lovely and drew many compliments for its period appearance when we raced it at Goodwood later that year. I loved riding with the fairing, and soon came to appreciate the protection it must have given to Manx Grand Prix and TT competitors over the mountain circuit in inclement weather. I spent a lot of money on the fairing and exhaust system, but they were worth every penny.

As we packed up our caravan to leave the camping site after that meeting, Shelagh threw two black dustbin sacks onto the grass. I assumed these contained rubbish, so placed them against the wire fence alongside other campers' rubbish. Unfortunately, one of the bags contained dirty washing that included my dress shirt, some trousers, Shelagh's overalls and best bras! (I was supposed to put *that* bag in the van, it turns out). I was not popular when, arriving home, we realised our (my) mistake. *Best* bras are not easy to replace, I'm told …

Richard Adams helped me greatly with improving the Manx, and always had my best interests in mind. After a few years' ownership it was obvious that almost all of the top riders had fitted improved interior dampers to their front forks, and Richard explained that it was not too difficult to fit Honda CBR600 internals, offering me a set together with fitting instructions at a very reasonable price. I soon had them on my bike, complementing a works pattern swinging arm that Richard had manufactured and sold to me a couple of years earlier. This component allowed for improved rear wheel adjustment, and made chain length alterations — when altering gearing and rear sprockets at race meetings — much easier. I don't think the bike became much quicker, but it was more refined at the end of my tenure, and easier to ride and maintain.

Generally, I didn't give much thought to hurting myself during the Manx years, but watching Pete get bashed about wasn't fun. In 2013, one of our Lansdowne riders, Karl-Heinz Kalbfell, died in an unfortunate accident at Brands Hatch, when he fell off and was struck by a following rider who couldn't avoid him. It cast a shadow over the paddock, naturally, and although I had experienced this sort of thing whilst racing on the TT course, some of our Lansdowne riders were very upset. Karl-Heinz was a great character and enthusiast, who is greatly missed by us all. My turn for some pain was soon to come, however.

Again at Brands Hatch, in October 2014 I was knocked off whilst braking for Druids Hairpin. Late braking has never been my forte, and just prior to the meeting I had seen a book advertised on the internet that I thought might improve my technique. It was entitled *A GP Winner's Guide to Riding Faster on Circuit*, and was by Simon Crafar. Amongst other tips, Simon gave advice regarding the best way to tackle a hairpin, and used Druids as an example. He advocated approaching up the outside of the course, cutting across at 45 degrees to touch the inside kerb at the beginning of the radius, then following the kerb and applying power whilst drifting out on the exit.

I took all this on board, and used the technique in the practice sessions and races for that Brands Hatch meeting, and all went well until the last race of the weekend, late on Sunday afternoon. I had followed a fellow Lansdowne competitor for a couple of laps and, watching his lines, decided I could possibly pass him on the inside at the approach to Paddock Bend, the corner prior to Druids hairpin. I achieved my objective quite smoothly, leaving him plenty of room to negotiate the tricky bend, and powered up towards Druids using Crafar's recommended racing line, as described in his book. As I leaned into the inside right-hand kerb at Druids, the other rider steamed up along my right-hand side, clipping my handlebar and front wheel spindle, knocking me and my bike flying; I hit the ground suddenly and very hard. He was going so fast he couldn't stop in time to correctly negotiate the hairpin. I think he was a little miffed at being passed, and was going to get me back as soon as possible, whatever the circumstances, but we'll never know the truth, as he remained adamant that I had caused the crash.

My bike slid along the track surface, damaging several sticky-out bits — tank, exhaust, footrest — and I landed squarely on my right shoulder. I managed to crawl off the track to the inside verge and, feeling very sore, felt around inside my leathers. My shoulder didn't feel right and bloomin' hurt: I presumed I'd broken a collar bone. The race continued without me, and when it had ended, I endured a trip in the recovery van, along with my bike, back to the paddock. Not feeling at all well, accompanied by Shelagh I took myself off to the medical centre, where a very nice lady doctor gently manipulated my arm and explained that I had ruptured my right shoulder ligaments. My arm was put in a sling and I was advised to visit my local A and E the following day.

Back in the paddock I was still not feeling great, so two or three lads helped Shelagh to pack our van and hitch up the caravan. A team member of the rider who had collided with me quietly advised that he had been close to the incident, and thought his rider had been out of order. A couple of others said the same, although one or two of my fellow racers had witnessed the incident and were of the opinion that it was just a racing accident. Nothing would change what had happened, so I just had to deal with it.

We left the circuit with Shelagh driving the van and towing a caravan for the first time in her life. It was getting dark and we had 50 miles of the M25 motorway to negotiate. I passed out a couple of times whilst we trundled along in the slow lane, and the third time I did, Shelagh just screamed at me, thinking I might have died. She was very worried and close to panicking, but managed to keep the van and caravan moving steadily towards home. I resisted dying and opened the window to allow the cold night air to keep me conscious. My son-in-law met us at the caravan storage depot and helped us unload the van when we finally got home, by which time Shelagh was in pieces and I was in plenty of pain. A sleepless night ensued.

Hemel Hempstead Hospital A and E confirmed the Brands Hatch doctor's diagnosis the next morning, and sent me away with painkillers and a physio appointment. I soon realised that my shoulder had significantly dropped, and would handicap future racing, so went for a consultation with a top shoulder surgeon at a private hospital. He thought he could improve things with an operation to pull my shoulder up and back into place, using a kevlar loop between my shoulder blade and collar bone. He was a motorsport fan and offered to do it on the NHS, which I gratefully accepted. A couple of weeks later I went under the knife to have a hole drilled in my shoulder blade and the kevlar loop inserted. I soon began some serious physio to keep everything mobile. The physiotherapist was brilliant, and explained that I would have to keep up the physio to maintain sufficient muscle strength to keep the shoulder blade in place. I still do some exercises at least once per week, and that's for life!

By the following spring I was able to ride again, and soon got back into the groove. By now a number of new riders were entering our Lansdowne races, and the 'old pals' atmosphere that I joined the Lansdowne Series for was not quite the same. A large proportion of the top runners were younger riders on highly-developed sponsor machines, who were prepared to take more risks, so I now struggled to make the top ten.

At Oulton Park in 2015 I experienced another near incident with one of these younger riders. I had passed him in a straight line, but he pushed past me a few bends later around the Cascades section, brushing my shoulder as he went by. This unnerved me, and I began to feel a little vulnerable as I was, by now, 67 years of age.

At another Oulton Park meeting the following year I found that my alloy fuel tank had split, so toured the paddock to try and borrow a spare tank. Richard Molnar, Andy's son, offered me a brand new one but asked me not to fall off and damage it. I kept my word but, as I returned the tank, I noticed that his Manx Norton had suffered recent damage which included a large dent in the fuel tank. He had fallen off in the final race of the day. I handed him the tank and said "I've looked after it, as promised." Richard grimaced and replied "I wouldn't have!"

I was still enjoying my racing and the 2016 season progressed in changeable weather. With varying results I raced at a chilly Cadwell Park, followed by a sunny Snetterton and a cloudy Oulton Park. The Manx ran well, but some of the familiar faces were not turning out as in previous years. Stan Woods had quite seriously damaged an arm in a fall at Brands Hatch; Pete Swallow seemed to have lost some of his enthusiasm for racing, and Charlie Williams had experienced a couple of 'offs,' so was cutting back on his competitive forays.

Pete liked Castle Combe but it was not one of my favourite circuits. The Lansdowne Series often raced there, however, and 2016 was no exception. The circuit is based on an old airfield and is virtually flat, utilising the old perimeter track and a couple of chicanes. The start straight does go downhill into a slight dip about 400 yards after the start line, where the track bears slightly right at this point.

The track is quite wide, and allows for a clear run down into this dip, where riders funnel through, all ideally wanting to be on the inside of the track to gain an advantage up the other side of the dip towards a left kink and the first proper right-hand bend. The infield is open grass field and the outside of the track has a small grass verge, then spectator earth banking.

Our race on the Sunday started well but ended badly. Pete Swallow had qualified on the third row of the grid with me immediately behind him. It was a lovely hot sunny day, and both of us were looking forward to some good racing. We completed the warm-up lap and, when the lights went out, everyone really went for it, with a couple of the quicker riders, who had qualified badly, pushing past us. I maintained station behind Pete as we approached the dip. All of the riders ahead of me appeared to converge on the inside racing line, and the first two rows cleared off, but I suddenly realised that the three riders immediately ahead of me, one of whom was Pete, were all trying to ride on the same piece of track, which wasn't going to work.

Just as I clicked my bike into fourth gear approaching 100mph, the three bikes became entangled. One bike reared into the air, another spun round on the track, and all three riders were thrown from their machines in one untidy mess. I wrenched the throttle shut but was travelling too fast to take much avoiding action, though did manage to veer to the left, clipping one of the bikes, which sent me towards the left-hand verge and banking. Once on the grass I tried to steer back onto the track whilst braking, but the bike slid away from me, and we slid along the grass, eventually coming to rest against the verge, the bike on top of me. I extricated myself from beneath the bike and looked back. What a mess. One of the bikes had broken its yokes and the front forks had become detached. All three riders were lying in the track, and marshals and medical staff were rushing to attend to them. I had a very sore right ankle but was otherwise unhurt; my bike sustaining only a few dents.

Shelagh and Pete's wife, Carol, plus a lot of rider team members had been watching from a point after the start/finish line, and saw the whole thing, later describing it as 'horrific.' The three riders seemed to remain in situ for a very long time, with everyone soon realising that they were seriously injured.

I picked up my bike and helped the recovery team load it into a van that would deliver it back to the scrutineering bay. I then walked back to the paddock, hoping to find Shelagh there; however, our part of the paddock was deserted, and our caravan was locked, so I made my way to the medical centre to find out what had happened to my racing pals. On arrival, I found Shelagh and Carol waiting anxiously, and they told me that Pete was in a very bad way, having been knocked unconscious. Both of the other riders involved were also seriously hurt with multiple fractures.

After what seemed a very long wait the medical team opted to airlift Pete to the local hospital, and Carol followed him there, driving their van. There was only one space for a casualty on the helicopter, and it had been a difficult choice for the medical staff between the rider with the most seriously broken limbs and Pete, who had a suspected head injury. What a worrying time for everyone. Pete did recover, though he suffered an eyesight problem for at least a year afterwards. The other riders each eventually made a good recovery and carried on racing, but it had been a dreadful experience for everyone. Understandably, Pete decided to hang up his racing boots — but I decided to carry on, although my ankle injury turned septic, necessitating several hospital visits as it took a while to heal.

That September I decided to enter a race in an IHRO event that was part of a mixed car and motorcycle race meeting at Hockenheim. I approached a grasstrack racing pal of mine, Phil Speed, to broach the possibility of him coming along as my mechanic. We had stayed in touch over the years and enjoyed each other's company, and Phil eagerly accepted, suggesting that we use his motorhome that had a large 'garage.' I gratefully accepted his offer as this was a much better proposition than towing my caravan. Phil is an experienced foreign traveller, and he planned the route, leaving me to ensure the Manx Norton was in good order and ready for a good thrashing!

We enjoyed a happy, sunny drive to Germany, arriving slightly early at the circuit, so indulging in a couple of beers and a very nice meal at the circuit café. We set up in the paddock alongside my Bavarian pal, Reinhard Neumair, and his wife, Gabi. A number of my old IHRO pals were also parked up nearby, and English, Dutch, German and Swiss competitors shared banter and alcohol very happily.

My bike seemed to be in good form, and I enjoyed the practice and qualifying sessions whilst trying to learn the circuit. The stadium section was awesome but the rest of the circuit was pretty boring and straightforward. Phil acted as 'mum' and produced a lovely meal at the end of the day.

We both slept well with Saturday dawning sunny. I had a great race, overtaking a couple of other riders to eventually finish seventh. I had made a good estimate regarding gearing, and the bike and I finished the race in good order, looking forward to a repeat performance in our final race the next day.

Ah! Heavy rain at dawn was destined to continue for most of the day. We were a long way from home, and witnessing several fallers in the races before ours made the decision not to race that much easier. I don't enjoy racing when all you can sensibly do is ride carefully in order to remain upright and not crash. Other riders returning to the paddock said that the surface was like ice. The Hockenheim circuit is mainly used for car racing, and there were events at this meeting, all of them leaving rubber on the racing lines, which allowed water to remain on the surface, making it very slippery.

I wanted to end the season on a high note, and the previous day's race had provided this. Phil totally agreed with my decision to miss our race, so we packed up whilst a depleted field of competitors took to the circuit — I was not alone in opting out. Reinhard rode well and finished towards the front of the field but came back in saying it had been treacherous, and we had made the right decision as he hadn't enjoyed it at all, concentrating solely on not falling off.

Phil and I travelled home pondering what motorcycling delights 2017 would involve; little did I know what radical changes the winter would bring!

CHAPTER 18

MY LITTLE ITALIAN BEAUTY: THE AERMACCHI

AFTER I SOLD THE AERMACCHI TO GRAHAM GODWARD IN 1978, HE raced the bike for a few seasons and used it for a couple of Classic Manx Grand Prix races. We spoke whilst I was spectating at one of these, and I learnt that the swinging arm had cracked during one practice session, which necessitated having it welded for the race. Graham ultimately bought a Yamaha two-stroke racer and sold the 'Macchi, sometime in the early '80s, to Dave Dock, a classic racing pal of mine.

Dave raced the bike in several Manx Grand Prix events, and also a few other meetings with moderate success, as he was not one of the 'quick' boys. We kept in touch and I asked him to contact me if he ever wanted to sell the 'Macchi. Dave was a carpenter (not a mechanic) and maintained the bike to a practical level but didn't modify it at all, thank goodness. My pal Bob Johnson and I met up with Dave at one Snetterton race meeting in about 2006, and he asked our advice as the bike was not handling well. On checking more thoroughly, Bob, who was very experienced at suspension setup, found that only one fork leg had oil in it, whilst the other was bone dry. Problem solved!

The bike looked a little unloved but otherwise okay. Dave had it in the original style Aermacchi red livery; when I had bought it in 1976, the paintwork had been Francis Beart green. I changed it to blue and Graham Godward changed it yet again to yellow. We all have our personal tastes, I guess? Originality didn't seem to matter in those pre-classic days.

In 2013 I was looking for a new 'project' and began thinking about my old Aermacchi ... maybe now was the time to try and get it back and give it the odd race outing? A phone call to Dave Dock confirmed that he still had the Aermacchi, but that it hadn't been raced for a number of years. I arranged to go and see him and, whilst there, saw the bike. After a bit of to-ing and fro-ing, we managed to agree a deal for me to buy it back at a reasonable price. The motor was partially dismantled but the rest of the bike was complete, and much of it was still original; the welded swing arm was visible. Fortunately, I had kept some large photographs of the bike, taken when I first owned it, and these enabled me to check that a lot of the bike was still as it had been all those years ago.

As to be expected, all of the fibreglass bodywork had been replaced, and the fibreglass fuel tank changed for an alloy version. Even an exhaust pipe that had been made for me by Richard Peckett was still with the bike. One half of the crankcase had been replaced, but the very rare and original Dell'Orto carburettor and float chamber were with the cylinder head. It had been in Dave's garage since 2008: due to ill health, it was highly unlikely that Dave would be racing again. After some difficult negotiations with Shelagh, I was granted permission to spend rather more on my project than originally planned.

I returned to Dave's a couple of days later to pay for the bike, and the deal was concluded with photographs taken for posterity. At home, I soon had the entire bike stripped down, and found that Dave had already had some cylinder head repairs done, following a dropped valve incident. The head and a re-bored cylinder and new piston were in a box that came with the bike. A useful phone call to Aermacchi racer and Manx GP comrade Dave Smith brokered a deal for him to rebuild the motor, and a trip to Dorset was undertaken a week later to deliver all of the motor parts to his workshop. I then began the longer task of fettling the rest of the bike. It was time to call in some favours and plunder the bank account even more!

I started work on the chassis. The front magnesium Fontana hub looked tired, and the rear alloy Ceriani hub looked as if it could use a spa day! I delivered them to another engineer friend, Dick Hunt, who specialises in manufacturing and repairing classic motorcycle drum brakes, amongst other components. I was worried about a deep scratch in the spoke flange of the Fontana hub, which Dick said he would get professionally crack-tested: it was indeed, a crack, and Dick said he would machine off the spoke flanges and shrink on aluminium ones. Tricky work, but a permanent fix. I also asked Dick to renew all the brake linings, rebuild the wheels with stainless spokes, and generally fettle the linkages. Quite a list — I hoped my bank balance would stand the strain. The high quality wheels and brakes on an Aermacchi are pivotal to its performance and appearance, so it just had to be done. Dick is a master craftsman, and I knew I would ultimately get a brilliant job, but I'd have to be patient.

The motor soon came back from Dave Smith. It had needed a new big end and very expensive con-rod, supplied by Aermacchi guru Dick

Linton, plus a couple of other parts, but Dave said it had gone together nicely. I had a little while to wait before I could test his workmanship! The frame appeared undamaged so I removed all the ancillary parts and took it to my local powder coater. The owner, Steve Jerome, thought he could match the traditional Aermacchi red colour, but we agreed to just blast and undercoat it first. I then had second thoughts and decided to return it to the colour it had worn until I changed it to blue — Ford Ludlow Green — as used by the famous tuner Francis Beart.

Beart had sourced the bike, probably from Syd Lawton, sole importer in Britain of Aermacchis, and maintained it for the first owner, Theo Louwes. I had emailed Louwes regarding his ownership of the bike, but his English was not wonderful and I could only extract a certain amount of information from him. Beart had painted it in the green finish that he always used on his own bikes, for Louwes. I spoke to Steve about this, who said he couldn't match the green colour in powder, and my best bet would be to get some two-pack paint mixed and have the frame sprayed over his powdered undercoat. Interestingly, some rock-hard original red-coloured paint could be seen within the steering head, which seemed to prove that all Aermacchis were delivered in red, and Francis Beart had indeed changed the frame colour.

Whilst all this was going on I had been in contact with Ken Halliwell from Liverpool, who Dave Smith had recommended as a source of Aermacchi fibreglass parts. Ken agreed to mould a full fairing, mudguards, and a seat for me in Ludlow Green, but said it would take a few weeks. He kindly sent me a colour sample, and I found a local paint retailer who mixed up a litre of paint plus hardener as close as possible to the correct colour. I then approached another long-time motorcycling pal of mine, Den Edwards, a retired professional vehicle paint sprayer, and he agreed to paint my chassis parts in his small home workshop. Den completed this task within a couple of weeks, and a great job he did, too.

I had attempted to identify a correct modern paint code for Ludlow Green and had contacted another classic racing friend, Dave Varney, who owned the original Beart Aermacchi. He kindly sent me a colour sample he had matched to the original bike's paint, but warned me that there was no current car paint 'Iban' colour code for the old Ludlow Green. Ken Halliwell's green fibreglass wasn't a million miles away from Dave's sample, so I decided to get my paint mixed to Ken's colour: at least all the parts of my bike would match!

I spent a great deal of time in my shed refurbishing the carburettor, ignition parts, forks, and other small parts. I sourced new handlebars and levers, plus a steering damper from Italy, and also ordered a rear sprocket carrier conversion from the same company, as all the sprockets

I acquired with the bike were knackered, and the conversion allowed the use of more easily available sprockets. When I bought the bike it had non-standard handlebars and controls, and a non-standard hydraulic steering damper.

The alloy petrol tank that came with the bike had some 'gravel rash' and needed a little TLC. Originally, the bike had a fibreglass tank, but this had disappeared in the mists of time! My racing pal Pete Swallow is a genius with alloy, so I asked him to try and fettle the existing tank, and make me a small alloy oil catch tank for the engine breather. Within weeks Pete had sorted the tank and made me a beautiful catch tank.

My engineering/bike pal Paul Duncombe agreed to make me footrests and linkages (when the bike was in rolling chassis spec), and I also asked him to mend one of the exhaust pipes that came with the bike. Brian Barrow, my fabricator friend, modified a second exhaust pipe to utilise one of his silencers as I needed a silenced system for test days.

Things were progressing well, though the wheels took forever as Dick Hunt was very busy. A year passed and eventually the job was done. The bill was quite reasonable considering the amount of very specialised work involved. As soon as I got the wheels I put the chassis together and was able to measure and order cables and a few other fittings. I then took the chassis to Paul's premises, and he quickly knocked me up a beautiful set of footrests and linkages exactly as I wanted them. (That's a lie: he actually had to programme his CAD milling machine, which he said took forever, and I could never pay him enough to cover his time ... ta, mate!)

The fibreglass had arrived and within another couple of weeks I also had cables. I'd had any useable nuts and bolts re-plated, but bought and made a number of others, as some of the originals were very tired. Most of the engine plates and brake torque stays were original and still bore Beart's rotary polishing marks. Parts of the motor also had numbers stamped on them from the time of Beart's ownership. Beart had cut off the ends of the rear seat support tubes to lighten the frame, and I made and fitted some alloy plugs in the open ends to prevent water ingress.

I bought a six-volt battery plus a spare, and numerous carburettor parts to ensure the bike would start and run efficiently. I renewed the small amount of wiring, and bought a new rear tyre; badgering Pete Swallow into selling me a good used front tyre he had just taken off his own bike to try a tyre with a different tread pattern. Dunlop had ceased production of the tyre I needed, so I was unable to buy a new one.

I already had a suitable Krober rev counter that fitted straight onto the existing original front fairing bracket, and ordered some inexpensive fairing fittings (in the end I made my own fittings but used the design as a basis). I also bought some lovely original-design natural rubber handlebar grips from Italy: a bit of an extravagance but they looked great. I found a new ignition lever at an auto-jumble, and also bought some free-flowing, original-type 'old stock' petrol taps on eBay. It was coming together! My engineer pal Phil Harding offered to make some nice rear axle nuts and a couple of other small parts that needed replacing, and a great job he did. We were there!

After a bit more spannering I was ready for the first test at a 'No Limits' track day at Donington in early July, and Shelagh came along as helper. As soon as we started the bike, however, the exhaust pipe filled with oil. Bother! Mark Neate, organiser of the 'No Limits' track day, kindly waived my entry fee and it was back to the workshop for us. I thought that I had blown something in the motor and phoned Phill Sharp. Phill, a good racing friend and Aermacchi expert, had offered to help with any issues, and had a motorcycle business in Surrey, so not too far away from me.

I took the bike to Phill and he found that the 'tuner' who had modified the cylinder head after the previous blow-up had ported the inlet tract and broken into an oil chamber. Phill sealed the hole with plastic metal and rebuilt the top of the motor for a very reasonable charge He also managed to ride the bike on roads roundabout for a few miles to ensure it ran reasonably properly enough to test and run in at a race circuit. Good chap!

The following week I took the bike to Mallory Park and ran in the motor in, although not taking it above 7000rpm. It seemed to run quite sweetly.

In late July, Shelagh and I took ourselves off to Chimay in Belgium with the Aermacchi and Bob Johnson's lovely TAB Honda 350. The Aermacchi ran well in the first race on the Saturday until asked to go over 7000 revs, when it began to misfire, with very rich carburetion. I didn't have smaller main jets for the rare 35mm Dell'Orto SS1 carb, and couldn't buy or borrow any in the paddock so, by Sunday afternoon, I had the bike in the van, planning a dyno session on our return home. At least I'd had a competitive ride on the bike — my first since 1978.

Puzzling over the baffling carburetion at my local friendly MSG Dyno setup in Aston Clinton, I suddenly realised that when I had originally owned the bike we had to use a 'soft' sparkplug to warm up the motor before switching to a harder (higher heat range) plug for the race itself. What an idiot I was! We had diligently warmed up the bike, keeping the revs below 3000rpm to prevent breaking the piston rings, before putting it on the dyno, and never gave a thought to swapping the race specification sparkplug once it was warm. My Manx Norton had electronic ignition — sparks and current to spare — so never needed a plug swap. A quick swap to a clean race plug and the Aermacchi's motor revved freely up to 8000 revs. Problem solved! The first plug had oiled-up slightly at low warm-up revs, but this was enough to prevent the motor revving cleanly; the primitive original six volt ignition not providing a strong enough spark to keep the plug clean.

A week or so later I took the bike to the Donington Classic Festival and rode it in a 'stars' parade, having dutifully warmed it in the correct fashion. The Aermacchi drew attention and lots of compliments: it was a joy to ride, and I felt proud that I had returned it to original trim. My Lansdowne racing pal Duncan Fitchett drooled over it ... he'd always yearned to own one, he said, and if I ever wanted to sell it would I give him first option? I readily agreed, but without any intention of parting with it, yet.

A couple of weeks later Bob and I took his Honda and my Aermacchi to Gedinne in Belgium and, in lovely sunshine, I enjoyed a couple of enjoyable IHRO races on the 'Macchi (and some great races on the Honda). The bike ran and handled beautifully. The Fontana front brake was seriously efficient and nothing went wrong. The bike again attracted a lot of attention and looked a peach. I didn't have to use a silencer in Belgium, and the exhaust note of the short stroke motor certainly caused a stir. I rode carefully, trying to recall what it had been like all those years ago. No wonder these bikes had performed so well in Grands Prix.

This was to be my last ride on the Aermacchi, as my blood condition took off and that was that. I was, however, satisfied that I had preserved a very original and special example of the model, and no one else would have had the knowledge to get the specification correct.

The year following my Gedinne races, once again I took the bike to the Donington Classic Festival, as I had arranged for Clive Ling, another Lansdowne pal, to parade it for me. Clive really enjoyed his ride, and returned proclaiming that the front brake was the best he'd ever used, and the bike felt fast. Duncan was there, so I mentioned that if he was still interested I might want to sell the Aermacchi. I could only store it in a windowless shed and, frankly, couldn't bear to look at it if I couldn't ride it. It would break my heart but I would be happy if it found a good home and was ridden occasionally.

Duncan subsequently paid me a fair price for the 'Macchi, and has paraded it in France, where it ran perfectly: when not in use it has pride-of-place in his lounge ... my lounge was always too small for that! The bike is in good hands and, as Duncan is a generation younger than me, he will derive years of pleasure from it.

CHAPTER 19

GOODWOOD REVIVAL ADVENTURES

MY INVOLVEMENT WITH THE LANSDOWNE SERIES BROUGHT ME into contact with a group of riders who regularly entered motorcycle races at the annual Goodwood Revival race meeting. This race meeting is primarily for classic racing and sports cars, but a motorcycle event has been included since the event's inception in 1998. I fancied adding another historic race circuit to my CV, and Goodwood, located near Chichester, is almost unaltered since it was used for racing in the 1950/60s.

Originally known as RAF Westhampnett, it was a fighter airfield built during the war as a relief airfield for RAF Tangmere. One of the airfield circuits utilised for motor racing after the Second World War, the first car race meeting, on the perimeter track 2.4-mile circuit, took place in 1948 and the last in 1966. I believe the only motorcycle race to have taken place at Goodwood Circuit during this period occurred in 1952. The circuit was attractive to me because it had no chicanes and was fast and flowing, which suited my road racing style. There wasn't a lot of run off around the bends, but I was well used to that, having regularly raced on circuits on the Isle of Man and at Dundrod.

Early in 2009 I began networking with the people involved in the Revival, particularly Gordon and Sally Russell, my friends from the Classic Racing Motorcycle Club, and was lucky enough to get an entry, with ex-TT star Trevor Nation as the 'star' rider on my Manx Norton. I was a stand-in as someone had pulled out at the last minute: I had let Gordon and Sally know that I would keep the dates free in case I got 'the call,' which, happily for me, came!

Each bike has two nominated riders: usually the owner/entrant and a star rider selected by the organisers. Over the years, Barry Sheene, Wayne Gardner, Freddie Spencer, and Kevin Schwantz have starred alongside the cream of modern and classic motorcycle racers. I was in serious racing company!

There were two practice sessions on the Friday and a race around lunchtime on both days of the race weekend. A Le Mans start

— where riders run across the track to their already-running bike held by the other rider — was incorporated into both races. I was scheduled to finish the Saturday race, with Trevor completing the Sunday race. Only 30 bikes are accepted for the event, and have to be of pre-1966 specification.

Trevor was brilliant to work with, and knew all about properly setting up race bikes. He helped me refine my suspension settings, and we enjoyed a good meeting as my bike ran well with a best result of tenth in the Sunday race, Trevor lapping five seconds faster than my best time. Class will out!

I struggled to get an entry for my own bike in the 2010 event as a number of Manx Nortons were already entered and a varied field of machines was the objective. A last-minute offer of a ride sharing the beautifully original 1939, ex-Noel Pope Velocette Mk 8 KTT belonging to my Lansdowne friend, Seb Perez, saved the day for me. Seb has a number of original classic race bikes, and I felt very privileged to be trusted to share the Velo with him. I knew Velocettes well, and had ridden another pal's (Pete Miles) Mk8 once before for a few parade laps of Donington circuit. Girder forks and a single sprung seat whisk you back in time, and it took a little while to get used to the bike at speed. I found gear changing on Seb's bike tricky at first, then realised that if I sat well back on the pillion pad the gear lever fell in the correct position for smooth gear changes. We had a very pleasant, trouble-free meeting and finished 13th in both races; lap speeds well down compared to the previous year's effort on a much later specification bike.

My Goodwood credibility had increased following two good years, and I managed to get another entry in 2011, entering my own bike with ex-TT winner Bernard Murray as my partner. I carefully prepared my Manx Norton and prayed for a nice dry meeting. My prayers were not answered, however, and showers were set for the weekend.

Bernard is a really nice chap but is a worrier, and he had me double-checking everything, making it a busy weekend of spannering. I didn't mind: a number of bikes always break mechanically, and good preparation reduces the chances of this. I needed to be regarded as a finisher not a failure if I wanted to continue to be considered for future entries.

The old cars that race at Goodwood often deposit oil on the track, and with both of our races taking place on a damp surface, caution was essential if we were to stay on board. Bernard didn't enjoy the slippery track any more than I did, and mid-field in both races was the best we could achieve: 11th in the first race and 17th in the second. The changeable weather played havoc with the bike's carburetion, and despite trying everything I could to sort it out, never quite got the bike running cleanly over the entire rev range. A bit frustrating and tricky when racing on a damp surface.

Sharing my bike with ex-racing stars was very nerve-wracking. I always wanted the bike to perform perfectly, of course, but racing isn't like that, especially at the Goodwood Revival. The paddock shelters are open at the front to spectators and the weather, and there isn't a lot of room for tools and a bike bench. Each allocated shelter has to accommodate two bikes, their team members, and whatever kit they've brought along. Spectators frequently interrupted us whilst working to ask questions, and as many of them were 'car people,' these weren't always very sensible. Neither is there lighting so if the problem we were trying to remedy was serious and needed time to fix, it could get quite gloomy and difficult to see as evening approached.

For 2012 the organisers had set an age cut-off date of 1954. Being determined to get a ride I began looking around for a suitable mount. My engineer pal, Phil Harding, owned 'Woden,' a very special motorcycle originally built by the famous Brooklands racer and sprinter Francis Williams in the early 1950s. It utilised a Manx Norton chassis, and was powered by a prototype 500cc V-twin JAP motor. The motor, which had never been developed or mass produced by JAP, had been displayed at the Earls Court Motorcycle Show in 1949. Some years later the bike was bought by Ernie Woods, the Auto Cycle Union Chief Scrutineer, and was converted by him to road race specification. It was raced — though failed to finish due to an oil leak — in the 1969 TT, ridden by Ernie's son, Steve.

Phil had bought the bike at auction, and I managed to persuade him that it ought to be used in anger, and if this could be at the Revival, it would only enhance its value, as well putting it on show to a huge audience. After a few serious pub discussions with his brother, Derek, Phil decided that he would become involved, and whilst he and Derek prepared the motor and transmission, I had the bare rolling chassis in my workshop that, with Phil's guidance, I race prepared.

We started work on Woden early in the year, but the months raced by and the bike was only just finished in time for the Revival in September. It looked and sounded wonderful with its twin, open-ended exhaust pipes, and attracted a massive amount of attention in the Goodwood race paddock. Phil and Derek had to answer all sorts of technical questions from spectators about the bike, but were justifiably proud to be there.

I was again paired with Bernard Murray, who I had primed regarding the bike's value, and the fact it was unlikely to be competitive as its power output, in its undeveloped state, was low compared to that of some of the opposition. We were there to enjoy the ride and return the bike to Phil in an undamaged state. The event's organisers like to have a varied grid of machines, with a number of fast, competitive bikes as the main attraction, plus more unusual but not necessarily quick bikes for additional spectator interest. It is supposed to be a spectacle, not a serious race ... but you try telling the riders that!

The practice session took place on a wet and oily surface and neither Bernard or I enjoyed ourselves. After only a couple of laps of the qualifying session Woden disgraced herself as the ignition timing gear slipped on its taper, sending the ignition settings haywire. Bernard had to pull into the pits as the bike was running so poorly. The bike couldn't be fixed quickly, so we would have to start from 28th position on the grid, which wasn't as bad as Wayne Gardner, whose very special BSA Gold Star had suffered problems as soon as he went out to qualify. He would start one place behind us.

Phil and Derek spent the next few hours with Woden's motor in bits, lapping the magneto gear taper to try and ensure it would stay put in the races.

Saturday's race went well and, although we finished towards the rear of the field in 17th place (there are always lots of mechanical retirements in this 'older' class at Goodwood, as the bikes tend to be original and fragile rather than replicas), everyone was delighted that the bike had performed perfectly, resulting in even more spectator interest. Sunday's race was a repeat performance and we finished 19th, which gave us an overall position of 14th from the two races out of the original field of 30.

Probably due to a slight oil leak, the gearbox sleeve gear bush had tightened a little during Sunday's race and as Phil pushed the bike into the parc fermé after the race, it squeaked a little and made the bike difficult to push. Good job for us the race had ended when it did, as a gearbox seizure could have had one of us down the track with a damaged bike. You need a little luck, I guess!

For 2013 it was back to the later-specification bikes, and I received a proper invitation to compete on my Manx Norton. Bernard was to partner me again, and kindly offered to pay most of the cost of an electronic ignition system for my bike as he believed it would give us a little more power. Bernard always looked carefully at the opposition and wanted our bike to have the equivalent specification.

In the Lansdowne Series races we could race with a small front number plate cowling only and no fairing: for the later year class at the Revival fairings were permitted, and Bernard asked me to try and get one. Goodwood is a very quick circuit and I could see that a fairing would benefit our top speed, so I took his suggestion on board, ordered and fitted the ignition system, and went fairing shopping.

Historically, I had always wanted to race a Manx Norton fitted with a Peel Mountain Mile fairing, as they protect the hands from weather and look so traditional (I relate the purchase and fitting of this in an earlier chapter). Once fitted, the bike looked wonderful. For Goodwood I ran the low-level exhaust system that Dave Davis had made for me, and utilised the open straight megaphone he had also provided at my request.

The bike looked and sounded brilliant, and elicited a lot of kind comment from Goodwood fans. The weather played ball, and Bernard and I enjoyed a great race meeting. Our best speed through the speed trap in the now-single practice/qualifying session was 118mph, which compared well with the opposition. After qualifying I decided that the bike was slightly under-geared, and set to changing the necessary sprockets, leaving Bernard to go off to a champagne reception for the 'stars.' After the stress of riding I was a little tired, and somehow selected the wrong sprocket, only realising my error as I finished lock-wiring everything. Consequently, I had to repeat the procedure so was well-knackered by the time I had finished. Bernard was oblivious to all of this; how I wished that I was the 'star' rider!

Both of the races were conducted on a 'just dry' track, and the bike performed faultlessly. On the Saturday we finished 11th, but had to accept a 20 second time penalty, when Bernard — enjoying himself too much — left it late for the rider changeover, and missed the permitted time window by a few seconds. We were relegated to thirteenth.

Sunday was a repeat but, with more finishers, we achieved 15th place only, and 11th overall for the two races. Our speed trap result improved to 121.5mph, and everyone went home happy, except for Shelagh (remember the story told earlier of me throwing away the black bin bag which contained her best bras?) and Tim Jackson, my Lansdowne sparring pal, who was knocked off Alan Cathcart's

beautiful and original Matchless G50. A very dented fuel tank plus
other general damage was the result, and Tim didn't fare much
better: walking wounded and very miffed!

Woden was the subject of more attention for the 2014 event. Phil
Harding had lapped-in all of the magneto driving gear tapers, and
given the motor some TLC and minor modifications. Bernard Murray
and I were to share riding duties again for what would end up being a
lovely sunny dry weekend of racing. The bike ran well but didn't appear
to be any faster than previously, which our lap times confirmed. We
finished 16th and 17th in the two races, giving us an overall result of
15th: not bad for probably the slowest bike in the race.

I made a very poor start in the Sunday race as I couldn't get the
bike into gear after running across the track. Woden's clutch only
engages at the end of the lever travel, and in my anxiety to get away
quickly, I made a complete hash of the whole thing, leaving me at the
very back of the field. Fortunately for us, several bikes broke down
in both races, so our results were better than we deserved.

Phil was a little disappointed with the bike's performance,
and promised a programme of engine development for its next
competitive outing; more compression being the priority. On
our return home he immediately commissioned new cylinder
head castings, as the original items wouldn't accommodate the
modifications needed for the compression hike: a better inlet tract
angle for the carburettors was also deemed beneficial.

I couldn't get an entry for my Norton in 2015, though was
fortunate enough to get a very late call to replace World Superbike
Champion Troy Corser on a 1954 RS54 BMW, supported by the works
BMW team. Troy had left his visa application too late, apparently, and
I was recommended to the team by Mike Farrall, another Lansdowne
racing pal. Mike knew all the BMW team as he had raced alongside
them at a number of continental race meetings, and also owned an
early racing BMW. He told the team that I was 'a safe pair of hands'
for a bike valued at over £150,000! I was asked to try not to fall off,
and had to sign a contract before I rode the bike. An English version of
the contract was not available, but I signed it anyway; goodness knows
what would have happened if I had written off the bike? A short while
later the team leader, who spoke perfect English, sidled up to me and
informed me with a smirk that I had just signed a contract to buy
a Bosch washing machine! (I should confess here that Mike Farrall
was the team's first option as replacement rider, but he was already
committed to sharing a very fast Rudge with TT star Charlie Williams,
and stood a much better chance of a good result on that bike.)

The weather played ball and made my rides safer, my partner being German motorcycle journalist Ralf Schneider; an experienced racer and a really nice chap. The bike, though, didn't want to play. It had seemed fine in practice, although not particularly fast, and I spent my laps trying to keep the bike upright to avoid grounding the horizontally-opposed motor's cylinder heads around Goodwood's long fast bends. The only tyre available for the narrow 19in front rim was a very soft compound ribbed pattern, and we were quickly tearing the outer ribs from it. The warm weather and abrasive track didn't help here, and Ralf was quite concerned. I think he was more used to racing modern superbikes on much larger, nearly slick tyres. I, on the other hand, had raced all sorts of old bangers so slightly strange handling was normal for me.

After the first race Ralf complained about the handling but when the German team lads checked out the bike they found scratch marks on the rocker boxes, and thought that Ralf may have been leaning the bike slightly too far, the cylinder heads touching down and upsetting the bike's handling. No wonder it felt strange to him! Our lap times were very similar, though, so this can't have made much difference.

Another problem was that the bike seemed to lose power slightly after only a few laps. Much discussion ensued, and the team's English — though German-based — mechanic, John Bostin, offered to strip the carburettors and change the settings. I was sure that the magneto was breaking down as it got hot, and it was ultimately agreed that this probably was the cause of the power loss. John and I got on famously, and I learnt that he had competed at a high level in grasstrack racing when a younger man. He knew my engineering pal Paul Duncombe from the grasstracking: it's a small world!

The bike had run well for the first two or three laps, so I was sure the carburettor settings were not at fault. A spare magneto was not available, so we were lumbered with a poorly-performing bike for race two. Never mind: the BMW lads found tickets to the big formal Goodwood party that Saturday evening for Shelagh and me, and the alcohol consumed there took the edge off our problem.

Ralf and I did our best on the Sunday and brought the bike home safely. The team thanked me profusely, and I think we put on a good show for the fans. The front tyre just about survived, and we were not the last bike over the finish line.

2016 was to be my last Revival ride; on Woden but with Clive Ling, another Lansdowne friend, as my partner. Bernard Murray opted for a quicker mount that, sadly for him, turned out to be not as good as Woden. He had to endure multiple mechanical failures sharing the famous 'Fan Norton' with my friend Roger Munsey, when first they holed a piston early in the qualifying session, and then the gearbox experienced problems that turned out to be terminal in Sunday's race.

Due to a delay in production of new cylinder head castings, Woden had the same 'slow' specification as in 2014. This unique bike, however, was very popular with spectators, and the organisers seemed unbothered by the fact that we were bound to finish near the back of the field.

Qualifying on the Friday went okay, and we achieved similar lap times to our previous outings there. Clive soon got used to the bike; just happy to be part of the spectacle. He really enjoyed his racing and fitted in wonderfully. Saturday dawned wet and stayed that way — very miserable, really. Several bikes failed but Woden ran well and we finished 21st from a field of 30. Sunday's dry race was a bitter disappointment to everyone as the magneto drive gear again slipped on its taper and, with the ignition timing haywire, I had to retire the bike after just four laps.

Clive never got to ride in this second race, and Phil and Derek were not at all happy. Clive, typically, just smiled and brushed it off. We packed away the tools and enjoyed a couple of beers together, discussing possible improvements for 2017. No point in dwelling on the failures.

The brothers thought that the reverse loading on the magneto gear when changing down the gearbox at racing speeds tested the taper too much, and decided to add a keyway to the shaft for future outings. When Phil originally bought the bike it had a distributor-type ignition system, but he had modified it to drive twin BTH magnetos, as these were always fitted to larger capacity V-twin JAP motors, and were more reliable than a distributor. Two newly-rebuilt magnetos, with their strong magnetism, were too much for the morse taper's grip to the drive gear.

Two steps forward and one back? That's racing!

CHAPTER 20

THE SPANNER MEN

DURING MY EARLY YEARS IN RACING I MANAGED EVERYTHING myself, but once I decided to venture to the Isle of Man and into Europe, I needed more than Shelagh's excellent catering skills.

In 1978 I was still very much on my own on the island, though was fortunate to share the garage at Union Mills with Derek Chittenden, who was running his Hejira race bikes from there. Derek and his lovely wife, Sally, soon became our great friends, and our kids played together when the opportunity arose between practices and races. Derek is an extremely skilled fabricator and mechanic, and the Hejira single cylinder racers he manufactured featured unique square-sectioned frame tubes, together with many other special parts. I pestered him for help when any problems occurred — and I had plenty of issues, as you've read. Fortunately for me, Derek kindly offered to be my official mechanic for the race. My toolkit was child's play compared with his, and I blagged and borrowed from this for the entire fortnight. We are still in touch and see each other now and again; the children now have their own families, of course.

In 1985 I used my Velocette Owners Club pals as unpaid help; they really had to work for the pints of Okells bitter I bought them as a reward. Paul Rose joined us for practice week, and Derek Cheesman, Terry Chalk, Bob Fensome, and dear old Pete Clements joined us towards the end of practice week and for race day. Paul added 'recovery vehicle driver' to his CV, and that Velocette was stripped so many times we lost count. All of their combined knowledge and enthusiasm kept the Velo going, though, and we had several evening sessions in the unlit garage near Hutchinson Square where we had digs. Lead lights and torches had to suffice in the absence of mains electricity, and we soon became experts at cylinder head and clutch removal and replacement. Paul was a tower of strength during practice week, providing a lot of encouragement when problems began to get me down.

The bike had been very reliable on short circuits, and I was concerned that all of the careful pre-MGP preparation in my lovely new garage/workshop at home would have to be pulled apart in a gloomy grubby garage. Without Geoff Dodkin's 'spares kit' and Peter's other parts it would have been a total failure: just goes to show that you can't do it solo! Thanks, lads. I wouldn't recommend campaigning a Velocette around the TT course.

Our first Seeley effort at the MPG in 1990 was almost a disaster. Derek Cheesman and Pete Clements did come over to the island later in practice week, and stripping and cleaning the motor, sourcing replacement parts and various other jobs following the big end failure, could not have been achieved without Derek's professional approach. By the time he and Pete arrived, I was a little frazzled, but with John Goodall's guidance and many 'team' hours in the garage, the bike did come together in time to qualify and finish the race.

The following year the 'Charlie Sanby saga' occurred. I had hoped to team up and share problems with Charlie but this was not to be, and I relied on my CRMC pal, Roger Imberg, to look after me. Roger was a CRMC 350cc twins class champion on his home-tuned and very fast Honda K4. He harboured ideas about racing on the island, and wanted to sample paddock life: an eye-opener for him, as it is for any first-timer. Roger achieved his ambition several years later, and won a coveted MPG replica.

One of his favourite tales about me concerns him following me through the twisty Glen Helen section of the TT course one evening during practice week. He claims I was lifting my head slightly when cornering to avoid hitting it on the rockface around one bend in that section. I think I was just being extra careful, but Roger compliments me on having the confidence to take the section in that style. His Honda K4 was a quicker bike than my Seeley 7R, but I knew that section like the back of my hand and held my bike flat out through there. He also says he knew from that moment that he should primarily stick to short circuit racing.

During this practice week I met up with my pal, Paul Marks. A Jet Ski enthusiast, Paul had brought his powerful Kawasaki-engined Jet Ski to the island, and offered Roger and me a ride. After several pathetic attempts in Peel Harbour I managed to get the hang of it, and with the reassurance of a buoyancy aid and wetsuit, became quite proficient. I'm a poor swimmer and also cautious, so never went out too far into the large harbour. If you fell off, the Jet Ski lay on its side and slowly circled the rider until he climbed back aboard, so no real worries.

Roger was less confident than me, but felt compelled to give it a go. He fell off a lot, consequently pulling a muscle in his back. This was the type of Jet Ski that you stood, not sat on, and it required a good fistful of throttle to get it going and keep it upright. After several failed attempts — and struggling with his painful back — Roger did get aboard, but was a fair way out by then, and he began to panic slightly. He did eventually stay on the machine long enough to return to dry land, but vowed that this was his first and last Jet Ski adventure!

Roger and I are still the closest of friends and our families frequently socialise together. Roger had stayed with me in our boarding house in Hutchinson Square in Douglas, but for race week our wives flew over, and Roger and Pam transferred to the allegedly-plush Mannin Hotel. Pam took one look at the dilapidated state of their room and demanded Roger ask for their deposit back, and they moved to another, much nicer establishment further along Douglas seafront. I think it cost 'careful spender' Roger a few extra quid, but happy wives mean happy husbands! The Mannin closed down a couple of years later, and stood derelict for many years until being totally refurbished quite recently, so Pam's assessment was correct.

In 1992 Derek Cheesman and Dave Carter became my regular MPG companions. Dave was a faithful addition to our team for a long time, and willingly gave up the MGP fortnight to experience the trials and tribulations and my tantrums for many years. A surveyor by profession and a few years older than me, Dave was very much a vintage motorcycle enthusiast. He was most methodical, and would take notes, fetch and carry, clean everything, and usually buy the first round, so was an all-round good egg! Often, at times of stress, he would say it was 'Okells time,' and suggest that a break would do us good. I wanted to press on regardless for hours on end, but Dave kept me grounded.

In the early '90s Dave stayed in a guest house a few doors up from us in Hutchinson Square. He had stayed there for years when spectating, and the landlady reserved a small room at the front for him every year. When I was ready to go to the garage after breakfast I would stand outside his guest house and shout up to his open window. He was usually reading his morning paper (Dave was an avid *Times* reader and crossword addict) and would grudgingly put it aside to come down and start work. I was a hard taskmaster.

In 1994 I travelled to the island with long-time friend Pete Rust, who I had known from the early '70s, and who was a keen motorsports fan, especially car rallying (you'll recall he helped me out with the Lotus Elan rebuild). Pete was an industrial mechanical technician, and could turn his hand to anything. I think Dave Carter could come over for race week only that year, so Pete accompanied me for practice week; his wife, Lyn, and Shelagh joining us later. Pete was an able and willing assistant, but one comment he made when Lyn joined us, which I mention in an earlier chapter, has stayed with me: "They just don't stop talking about bikes!" he exclaimed to his wife. I admit it, of course; it's like an addiction.

Pete and Lyn number amongst our closest friends, and we still see them regularly as they live nearby. I still go to Pete if I have any electrical problems: he really is a whiz in that regard. Motorcycling pals stay pals for life, I guess.

Derek Cheesman, like Paul Duncombe, taught me a lot about being fastidious, and never accepted second-best workmanship. Being a time-served motorcycle mechanic gave him a very broad knowledge of all-things mechanical, and many times he would come up with a good solution to a problem or breakdown. He could also think on his feet, and in moments of crisis was the man to have beside you. Derek had completed National Service in the '50s, and called a spade a spade, which suited me fine. He loved regaling folk with stories from that era. One year on the island, he caught me checking the tightness of the rear axle nuts on the G50 Seeley, which he had replaced. He looked offended, and I felt the need to explain my actions. I told him that before I launched myself down Bray Hill at 130mph, I had to be certain in my head that everything critical on the bike was tight, and any risk of mechanical failure was minimal. I could understand his hurt feelings, but it was difficult for me to relinquish this responsibility after years of taking care of myself. Always after that Derek would ensure that I checked his workmanship or the tightness of any important parts, and we developed a really good mutual understanding. He would finish whatever task he was doing, and insist on handing me the spanner to check his work. I never doubted his work, but needed the reassurance of having checked myself before risking my life around that highly dangerous TT course. Once the throttle was wide open and the next corner apex in view, there must be no doubt about the machinery.

Derek retired and moved to Lagos in Portugal in 1996. He and his wife, Stella, had holidayed there for many years, and bought a lovely little villa in a nice estate above the town. He bought a red Renault Trafic van to transport the few important belongings he wanted to take with him and, rather than complete the complicated procedure of importing the van to Portugal, offered to sell it to me at a knockdown price. The only snag was I had to get out there and drive it home. Dave Carter offered to come with me, and so, in February 1997, we flew out. The weather in Portugal at that time of year was splendid, and I have photos of us in shorts and sun hats.

The journey home across the centre of Portugal went well initially as the weather was good, although some of the roads were in dire need of a decent resurface. We crossed the French Massif Central in sunshine, but as we left that area, it clouded over and the end of our second day consisted entirely of heavy rain. The volume of water caused the windscreen wiper fuse to blow at least twice, and visibility was terrible. We managed, though, and enjoyed some good French dining in nice hotels along the way; Dave taught me to enjoy moules marinière (mussels cooked in white wine and garlic). I kept that van for several years and it served me well, giving little trouble. Thanks, Del.

John Walker deserves a chapter to himself. He would never claim to be a mechanic, but we have been pals since our teenage years, and remain close. John was an insurance broker in the city, and taught me how to enjoy alcohol to the full. He was, and is, an expert in this. He tells me hilarious stories of his working life and a more reliable friend it would be hard to find.

John has owned motorcycles for most of his life, and has blundered through the mechanical issues they have thrown at him. He's not competitive, but has consistently encouraged and helped me throughout my racing years. We travelled to many foreign circuits together, and whilst I did the serious spannering, John looked after our other needs! He can cook, which is one of my failings (probably due to being married to an expert), and can always find a reason to test the local alcoholic beverage. He's a brutal car/van driver, and there's many a time I have winced as he's crashed through the gears of my various vans. John's wife, Linda, is an angel: goodness knows how she copes with his foibles.

Bob Johnson arrived in my life in 2003 when I met him at Lloyd Coopers motorcycle shop in Hemel Hempstead whilst buying an Arai tee shirt, and we are still close pals. Bob was an army staff sergeant with REME for many years and fears nothing mechanical. When we met he was managing the workshop for Lloyd Coopers, a Honda dealership. Our joint enthusiasm (addiction) to road racing led to the TAB-Honda K4 project, plus other involvements over the years. Without Bob's wonderfully laidback attitude to all things 'tricky,' I might have thrown in the towel several times.

When it comes to money, however, Bob is a disaster: he will never be rich because he is so generous with whatever money he has. The way he reacted when the 400cc Kawasaki threw tantrums was incredible: he simply dropped everything and gave his all to try and make it succeed.

Bob has a weakness for red wine, and I have many a thumping headache to thank him for. One race weekend at Snetterton, the TAB-Honda just would not run cleanly, and after a terrible Friday practice session we took to the bottle and went to bed late, slightly the worse for wear, anticipating a slow drive home in the morning instead of racing. Bob obviously had a restless night, and woke up early, determined to fix the problem. I was seriously hungover following a long session in the Snetterton bar, plus a couple of bottles of Bob's finest red the previous evening, and was not keen to get involved. Bob persevered, however, and a loud, joyful shout suggested he might just have fixed the fault. I was instructed to get my 'effing leathers on' and get the bike onto the grid. I made it just in time, and had a great race — which of course resulted in Bob insisting that I could go faster if I drank more!

A couple of years later, we were on the island with the aforementioned Kawasaki. Fortuitously, I was one of the first two riders to go out for practice that year because, as I waited in the warm-up area queue with dead engines, we were photographed by the local press, a radio commentator bestowing fame upon us as the first two riders to practice at the 2004 TT races. Almost immediately we were called to the start line, so I pressed the starter button to call the engine into life. Nothing happened, I began to sweat and tried again. Still nothing. By now the organisers were anxious to get things going, so I was pushed aside and another rider took my place on the start line. I was shouting and screaming at the bike in temper and frustration when Bob arrived alongside, casually flipped the kill switch to the 'off' position, pressed the starter button and the bike sprang into life. My older single cylinder machines didn't have kill switches, so I never gave this a thought. That cost me a round of drinks in the pub later that day. I never was good in situations where things go wrong unexpectedly, and I still get stick about that incident. Soon afterwards Bob bought me a polo shirt with the phrase: 'We like angry — angry is fast' emblazoned across it!

Bob and his wife, Anne, still come to race meetings with us, although I've learnt not to share sleeping quarters with him. We were scheduled to race the TAB Honda at Chimay in Belgium one year, and I had — foolishly, as it turned out — accepted Bob's offer to travel over in the small Fiat motorhome he owned. All went swimmingly until bedtime after a few glasses of red. Bob had the only bed and I was allocated an airbed on the floor ... which was fine until he began snoring loud enough to wake the entire paddock. I tried everything, including wearing my moulded earplugs, to shut out the racket, but to no avail. In the end I shouted at him using the worst swear word I could think of, whereupon Bob woke, deeply hurt that I should use such language to him. Since that day he has had various treatments to try and stop the snoring, including an operation, which have helped, although he still snores a bit. He still insists that I was rather rude to him!

Spannermen: everyone needs a good 'un!

CHAPTER 21

SPONSORS – THE LIST IS ENDLESS!

RIGHT FROM THE START IN 1976 I WAS FORTUNATE ENOUGH TO have sponsors who helped in various ways to keep me racing. The Hertfordshire Constabulary Motor Club always found a way to direct a few pounds in my direction; very few police officers could afford to compete in motorsport, and yet the hierarchy of the central sports fund never objected to my annual appeals for assistance. Many of the other sports and social clubs (golf/choir/shooting, etc) received far larger grants than motorsport, however, so my conscience was clear.

I also made sure our club was affiliated to The Federation of British Police Motor Clubs, which was also a source of generous sponsorship, and although this dried up in more recent years, I wrote numerous articles for its magazine, became the general secretary, and continued to receive some backing in return.

The lovely blue paintwork that appeared on my Aermacchi in 1977 was courtesy of Terry Jones, proprietor of TAJ Motors in Rickmansworth. As a locally-based officer, I often requested his recovery service when dealing with traffic collisions, and his paintshop returned the favour. Terry and I got on well, and at least once he knocked out a small dent in my panda car during duty hours, saving me having to report a 'polac' (police accident), that would have put me off the road whilst it was investigated. Several members of my shift at 'Ricky' nick also used his services for this purpose, though there were times when even his considerable skills couldn't disguise a heavy bump, so 'fessing up was the only option.

A few years later, another police recovery company, Shaw Brothers in Markyate (owned by Steve and Russell Shaw) provided me, free of charge, with a stolen/recovered 50cc Honda scooter, minus bodywork and registration, frame and engine numbers. The numbers had been removed by the thief and, with no means of identification, the bike's owner couldn't be established. It ran perfectly and, with its easy-to-use automatic gearbox, I used it as paddock transport for a number of years. Several of us even managed a full lap of the old, longer Assen TT circuit, after practice had finished, whilst I was competing in an IHRO race at a Grand Prix meeting.

Shaw Brothers had some wonderful, huge recovery vehicles and, whilst I was with the traffic department, I spent many happy hours, often in the middle of the night, watching them demonstrate their skills, hauling huge, crashed lorries up motorway embankments. A few years later another police recovery business, Adams Recovery, based in Aylesbury, helped me out a bit. My networking contacts really paid off.

Geoff Dodkin became a very good friend and adviser whilst I was competing on the Velocette. He would supply whatever parts I phoned for, without requesting immediate payment, and, as I have related, lent us a brilliant spares kit on a sale-or-return basis when I took the Velo to the Isle of Man. Without doubt, Geoff discounted almost all of the parts we needed for racing purposes, and his guidance when preparing the bike was invaluable.

Around this time, Pete Clements, my partner in the Velocette project, was also a partner in a motorcycle business called RIP Spares (RIP for each of their forenames), based in Potten End, near Hemel Hempstead. He and another Velocette Owners Club pal, Ron Clowes, were the active partners with a third 'sleeping' partner, who I never met, called Ivan. Another Velo pal, Terry Chalk, became involved in the business at a later date, and he and Ron supplied Pete and me with anything they could at trade prices, or less! Many of the parts for the Velo racer came via RIP or through its contacts.

Another Velo Club pal, Alan Wright, also owned RIP at one point, but in the early nineties he ran a 'pirate' Porsche spares company called EWP Spares, based in Markyate. Alan helped me for several years; mostly, I suspect, via some quite profitable cash deals. He is the best wheeler-dealer I have ever known, and built up his business so well that it became the go-to outlet for genuine and pattern Porsche parts. I think it was ultimately a real nuisance to Porsche.

Alan lived in Slip End, near Markyate , and was pals with a nice chap called Pete Stockdale from the same estate. Pete had been sidecar ace George O'Dell's original passenger until George crashed the outfit in the Isle of Man TT, and Pete sustained serious foot and ankle injuries that ended his racing exploits. When I first wanted to go racing on the continent, Pete lent me his bright yellow Ford Transit van, and even went as far as to lend it to me for at least one Manx GP meeting. Prior to this I had been lucky enough to occasionally be able to borrow vans (usually very tired, quite old Mercedes vans) from the owner of a van hire company in Hemel Hempstead. The owner, Rob Osborne, was a racing enthusiast, so as long as his oldest van was not out on hire for the weekend I could borrow it. I'm not sure I was ever insured, though ... I think I hired a van for the first couple of meetings and then Rob offered me the free deal. Top bloke, but he did go broke eventually.

Through my traffic police pals I was introduced to Keith Collow, Shell Oils' competition manager. Shell had been involved in sponsoring certain police motoring events, and Keith happened to live in Hertfordshire, as I did (and do). I met Keith whilst on duty at a couple of these events and really enjoyed chatting to this very nice man. I can't remember whether I asked, or he offered assistance but, from the early nineties, I enjoyed a free or very cheap supply of Shell R40 oil. My Manx Grand Prix racing opened a number of doors for me as so few bike racers were competing on the island, and the classic races still attracted a fair amount of publicity. I used Shell oil for a number of years until Keith retired.

By this time, I was on very friendly terms with the staff at my local family-owned motorcycle dealer, Moore's of Hemel Hempstead. Dave Moore was an ex-TT rider who had raced alongside Mike Hailwood in his early years. I loved listening to his tales of racing in the classic period. Moore's was the agent for Silkolene Oils, and Dave pointed me in the direction of the local rep, John Cartwright-Howell. John lived near me, and a gentle nudge from me resulted in lower-than-trade prices for Silkolene R40. John looked after me for a number of years, directing me to suitable gearbox and fork oil products, and often supplying generous samples for free! Both Keith and John were real gentlemen enthusiasts, and, over the years, must have helped many riders operating on a shoestring.

Please bear with me as this list is becoming lengthy, but you'll realise that I was good at finding sponsors, and made great friendships through these deals. Many friends threw something into the pot without ever asking for specific results: they simply wanted to be involved, knowing they had helped in some way. Already mentioned in previous chapter are the wonderful bikes that Don Williamson and Bob and Anne Johnson supplied to me, the only proviso being that I enjoy myself and try and come back in one piece. Once a year Bob's pals, Brian and Linda Loader and Dave Peirson, would make a donation to Bob, which helped him to keep the Honda K4 in top spec. When Derek Cheesman began to receive his old age pension in Portugal,l he would send a few quid towards my running expenses, and Stuart Jukes, now living on the Isle of Man, did likewise. Dave Carter, my long-term spanner man, often slipped me something just before we set off to the Isle of Man, which we probably spent in the island's pubs over the fortnight we were there. When he was with us my old friend John Walker would readily help me to spend this beer money, but always added his own generous contribution. Such good friends.

My local Velocette Owners Club awarded me a small grant at its AGM for a number of years, and one of my pals there, Eddie Faulkner, paid a couple of repair bills for my Seeley race bike via his van hire company. Every little bit helped me to keep the bikes running safely and quickly. They all knew I was competitive and generally finished at the top end of the field, although unlikely to win. I kept them all supplied with nice racing photos (often kindly taken by Rusty Lee from Sport-Pics, who sent me wonderful photos at discounted cost for many years), and informed them of any good results (I kept the poor results to myself!).

For several years a biking friend, Roger Brown, who owned a powder coating company in Hemel Hempstead, painted my bikes for me. His powder finish was brilliant, and if I ever paid for anything it was hugely discounted.

In the early nineties I managed to find a suitable guest house in Hutchinson Square in Douglas, on the Isle of Man. They let me use their scruffy garage, and Shelagh and I stayed there for a number of years. Joyce and Ian Noble, from The Allerton Guest house, made us most welcome and, after the first year, I had to pay for Shelagh only, whilst I stayed for free. I never checked, but I think Joyce may have received a grant from the island authorities towards sponsoring a rider. Shelagh's sister came over for a week one year, and Joyce let her sleep in the bathroom on a campbed as no other accommodation was available. I've no idea what she paid for that 'first class' room. Joyce was a Geordie and somewhat careful with money: I had to ask for the bathplug if I wanted to soak my aching muscles in her bath, and the meals she prepared were a little basic, though adequate (especially as I wasn't paying for them). I don't think that running a guest house during the short Isle of Man tourist season was ever going to make her wealthy, so I understood her frugality.

Bush and Pat Kerruish, my Manx friends, let me use their warm and well-lit garage located in Tromode, near Douglas, for several years without payment, and gave me the keys for the house, allowing me to come and go as I pleased, never doubting my honesty. Very Manx.

Soon after I got involved with Don Williamson (he who sponsored me for tyres prior to providing the Petty Norton and then the Paton), he introduced me to his Manx-based friends, Julian and Marie Harper, who owned a lovely Victorian villa in Derby Square in central Douglas. We stayed in this house for several years with Dave Carter; what luxury. Don was also staying with us, and one morning, Shelagh noticed water dripping through the ceiling onto a very large and valuable antique dining table. Don appeared to have trodden on a loose bathroom floorboard, and a nail beneath it had pierced a water pipe for the central heating. After a certain amount of panic and calls to Julian, who was staying in his other house in Alderney, a plumber turned up to plug the leak whilst lovely, unfazed Julian calmly sorted out the massive insurance claim for furniture, carpet and ceiling damage. Julian also bunged a few bob into the race pot over the years, so grateful thanks again.

Friends and contacts helped out in different ways, often via their businesses, and usually just because they wanted to be part of the racing game. In the early nineties, another friend of Alan Wright's, Terry Smith, helped me via his insulation business, as did David Speed through his Automatic Number Plate Recovery company. Dave Whitby, a neighbour who, at that time, was a partner in a Hemel Hempstead-based garage, helped me out for a couple of years, and I don't remember actually having to ask him to. Through his financial advisory firm, Velocette Owners Club pal Roger Yates paid some of my bills for many years, and after Don Williamson sold his own high tech engineering business, he somehow managed to persuade his pal, Terry Grubb, to become involved with my racing via his specialist gear technology company. If I needed any very technical machining Terry would help me out, using his computer-controlled engineering machines.

I never had to race on worn-out tyres, as I soon learnt that if I asked someone to sponsor me for just a pair of tyres I had a good chance of success. My friends — Pete Sharples, David Dawson, Gordon Hayward, Mike Fotherby, and Phil Harding — all keen motorcyclists — owned their own businesses, and helped me out in this way. Bob Davies, another lifelong motorcyclist, became a good pal. He runs a garden machinery business in Kings Langley, and has helped me buy numerous items that I needed, which his firm could supply at seriously discounted prices. I enjoyed rebuilding a BSA Gold Star for him, that he still treasures.

Bob Johnson had good connections through the motorcycle trade, and both Colin Saunders of Saunders Motorcycles in Knebworth, and Gordon Heal from Lloyd Coopers Motorcycles in Watford helped with various discounts. Bob Johnson also tapped-up Nick Wilde from a local insurance broker, and used his connections with Mark Neate, who ran No Limits Track Days, to get discounted testing sessions at various venues.

I made sure that I always wore good leathers, and thereby hangs a good tale. Prior to riding my sponsored LC Yamaha to the Pyrenees in 1985, I went to the Motorcycle Racing Show at Alexandra Palace in search of a new pair of leathers. I approached Martin Pell of Interstate Leathers and asked for sponsorship and, blow me, he agreed to supply a made-to-measure pair. Goodness knows how that deal worked, payment was never mentioned, but sure enough the leathers arrived on time. Perhaps he thought I could influence the constabulary purchasing department which, of course, I couldn't, and wouldn't try, anyway.

My next set of BMJ (Barbara Miles) leathers came to me in 1992, courtesy of Pete Clements' widow, Gladys. 'Glad' insisted that Pete's hospital promise of a new set of leathers should be kept, and I proudly wore the royal blue leathers for the next ten seasons. My grasstracking engineer pal, Paul Duncombe, had directed me to Barbara as she made Simon Wigg's speedway leathers. Barbara had never made leathers for road racing, and they had to be altered a couple of times to fit comfortably in a racing crouch, but they were made from really good leather and looked the business.

For the 2003 TT, ten years later, I decided I ought to look the part. On another visit to the racing show I spotted a pair of Jurgen van den Goorburgh's leathers hanging on the Dutch MJK Leathers stall. They were cut in a perfect racing crouch, and the colours were wonderful. The British agent, Graham Falke, offered a good discount if I had extra MJK decals on the leathers and, with slight alterations to the colour scheme, I soon owned a new set of full-on GP leathers, which I still have. I was so pleased with them that I bought another plain black set from Graham when I started my Lansdowne racing.

I can't finish here without mentioning Robin Packham, who owns Falcon Shock Absorbers, and has supplied me with his shocks for years. In the early nineties I encouraged him to get into the classic road racing scene, and his shocks have now become very popular. I initially used them on my grasstrack racing bikes, and we soon became firm friends. Robin will do anything to help riders, and is probably too generous for his own financial good! A lot of the top classic road and off-road racers now use his equipment. I met Robin through Paul Duncombe, who, over my racing career, contributed so much, always willing to properly engineer parts I needed, and often refusing adequate payment. We remain close friends, and I'm proud to be godfather to his son, Stefan.

Yes, I certainly became involved with all sorts of businesses!

CHAPTER 22

THE FINAL LAPS

TIME AND AGE WERE CATCHING UP WITH ME, AND I DEVISED A cunning plan for when my racing days were over: I would try to become a scrutineer (or, as known in the modern era, a Technical Officer) so that I could remain connected and useful to the motorcycle racing fraternity. My police background helped with being assertive, and my own bike preparation for racing in the Isle of Man had required great attention to detail. I always encouraged scrutineers to have a good look at my bikes: even fastidious mechanics and riders can become distracted, and forget to add that bit of lock wire or a split pin.

I enjoyed the banter with the scrutineers, especially at the Manx Grand Prix, where, unexpectedly, I was once asked to take a breath test prior to morning practice. As I had driven my team to the pub the previous evening, I hadn't taken alcohol, so was reasonably confident I would pass. The smiling scrutineer quietly whispered to me: "Don't worry, you'll pass it okay, we're not after you!" Apparently, one of the riders was known to be relying on a little Dutch courage before tackling the mountain course, and the scrutineers were targeting him, though needed to appear impartial by checking other riders also. Needless to say, one rider was quietly excluded from racing that year.

I also experienced the flipside of this approach when, at one pre-race scrutineering session at the MGP, a pedantic scrutineer decided that the rear disc brake of my Seeley 7R was inefficient, so would not let me race unless I improved its performance, despite the fact that I had completed every practice session during practice week and been scrutineered without issue. I began to sweat, realising there was nothing I could possibly do at that stage to make the brake work any better. As the race was due to start in an hour's time, in desperation I approached the Chief Technical Officer, who I knew quite well, and asked his advice. He took me aside and suggested I removed the brake pads, and cut a couple of shallow slots in each to help disperse any dust; he also said to bring the bike to him for re-examination. Of course, adding the slots did nothing but his quiet consideration was a fine example to me, and I shall never forget his kindness. The brake did, of course, work well under racing conditions anyway; it just lacked leverage when used statically.

Motorcycle racing scrutineers are licenced by the Auto Cycle Union, the governing body for motorcycle sport in Great Britain. The scrutineers are not responsible for the safety of machines, although they do provide an additional safety check: their purpose is to ensure regulation compliance. Ultimate responsibility for a machine lies with its rider. I queried this, as I was not too keen on being sued if I failed to spot anything amiss. To get each rider through scrutineering takes several minutes, and there is simply not enough time to tick off a safety checklist to be 100 per cent sure that every preparation detail is perfect. An initial cursory look at a bike soon tells the scrutineer if he is likely to find faults or issues. A clean, immaculate machine usually passes through without issue; though, as I have said, it is still possible for a detail to be forgotten or missed.

When I first enquired about training for scrutineering I was told I should simply turn up and have a go, whilst being shadowed by a qualified scrutineer, and the CRMC Chief Technical Officer kept a watchful eye on me for the first few meetings. I found him easy to work under, and we soon established a rapport where I would ask him if I wasn't sure about anything. Sidecar outfits were something I had to learn about: the basic safety stuff is the same, but the braking systems and a couple of other items are different to solos. I soon found that if I queried things with the experienced sidecar boys themselves they would guide me through any doubts I had about what needed looking at. They've had their bikes checked numerous times, and willingly showed me the ropes as they were keen to ride on safe machinery. I had enough knowledge to check out the basic mechanical systems and, although they have to remove the streamlining for us to check the bikes, a number of items are still very difficult to get to and check thoroughly. Once again, a scruffy outfit takes far longer to check than a clean and tidy one.

Recent updates to regulations are often bones of contention, and if a rider hasn't ridden for a couple of years it's not uncommon to find they have failed to modify their bike. Common sense usually sorts out these issues, and if it's possible to modify the bike before practice the rider is advised to go away and do the job. If it's a very minor thing they may be allowed to compete, but warned that the issue must be resolved prior to the next meeting.

Of course, these rejections can cause friction, and I had one rider curse me and threaten to go home, rather than fix a small problem. He'd already been rejected by another scrutineer for having incorrectly-shaped race numbers on his bike, and been sent away to replace them.

On re-presenting his bike — to me, this time — I noticed that his rear wheel sprocket guard was loose because it had a broken pop rivet, leaving it held in place by one rivet only. I told him I was very sorry for having to reject his bike again, but the guard would have to be properly secured, and the bike re-examined again before he could practice. This was the final straw for him and he stormed off. The Chief Tech was watching this develop and came over afterwards to compliment me on the way I had dealt with it. I was polite but firm — easy for an ex-copper!

Having had my own bikes scrutineered for the last forty years means I have a good idea of the items to check. A step back to take a good look at the machine provides an overview of its general state of preparation. Plenty of lock wire indicates that the rider is aware of safety issues. Worn tyres, an oily bike, or unrepaired recent crash damage are warning signs of problems ahead. Most riders are very proud of their bikes, and present them in good condition, but it never ceases to amaze me that some regard a scruffy bike as some sort of 'badge of courage.' Conversely, I've also examined spotless mint-condition bikes and found locking split pins missing from vital brake components; the riders mortified that they'd missed this when preparing the bike. Profuse apologies and thanks were followed by them taking away the bikes to quickly sort the problems before re-presenting them.

I've had riders produce bikes with footrest ends ground away following previous crashes, leaving a very sharp edge that, in close combat, could easily injure another rider. These riders sometimes claim that the bike has been in that condition all season, and no one else has ever queried it, but I just politely tell them to find a file and smooth the edges and then submit it again as: "I won't pass it in that condition. We have the power, you see? No signed pass sticker, no racing ..."

The best laid plans, etc ... in February of 2017 my blood condition decided to cause problems: no pain, just a sore knee and a slight, but persistent cough. A visit to the doctor and a couple of scans revealed a deep vein thrombosis in my left leg, and multiple small clots in my right lung, so I was rushed to hospital. I was prescribed strong anti-coagulant drugs for life, and given very firm instructions to give up motorcycling racing. My doctor wouldn't sign my racing licence application form, anyway, so that was that — grounded. There was to be no more racing and I was advised not to even ride on the road, as one bang on the head and I would be in serious trouble, as nothing would stop a bleed on my brain. (A no-brainer, eh?)

I attended two ACU scrutineering seminars in February, and I sold my lovely Manx Norton, my super Velocette MAC, and my van and caravan, replacing them with a small motorhome: no bikes to transport now! During the early part of the racing season, Shelagh and I travelled to all of the Classic Racing Motorcycle Club race meetings, and whilst I scrutineered the bikes, Shelagh learnt how to examine riders' clothing, so we were now both involved. We were made most welcome, and really enjoyed the company and banter of other officials.

My health problems had to be managed but, apart from having to rest my leg occasionally, I could get by. By mid-summer we were well into the scene, and I decided to offer my services as a technical officer at the Classic TT festival, the Manx Grand Prix on the Isle of Man in late August. I was warned it was a bit full-on, and that some of the procedures were different, but my assistance would be welcome. I booked a ferry knowing that I could stay with my youngest daughter, Katherine, who lives there with her husband, Simon, and their three children. Shelagh was unable to travel with me as she had other family commitments at home.

I decided to drive to the outskirts of Liverpool, stay the night in a B&B, and catch the morning Sea Cat from Liverpool to Douglas. Sound asleep in the digs at six in the morning, I was woken by my mobile phone receiving a text message. The Sea Cat had struck the quay in Douglas, causing some damage to the bow area, and my sailing and any others for the foreseeable future were cancelled! I was advised to call the booking office in Heysham at 8.30am. I didn't fancy hanging onto a phone whilst the world and his dog tried to get alternative sailings so I drove to the ferry terminal in Liverpool, where I was advised that the next sailing with space went from Heysham three days later. Bother! I did accept this provisional booking but decided to drive to Heysham and wait on standby, hoping for space to become available on that afternoon's ferry sailing. I certainly didn't want to drive back home to Hertfordshire, and then back up again a couple of days later.

I raced up the M6 to Heysham and found that I could indeed go on standby as the third vehicle in the queue. I spent a couple of hours chatting to waiting passengers, mainly bikers, and then two coaches full of foot passengers arrived, having been transported from Liverpool. I sprinted to the booking office only to be told that although car space wasn't going to be a problem, passenger numbers might be for safety reasons. I tried to stay calm, and hung around the booking hall. Just before the end of loading they told us that four extra cars would be allowed to board — phew, just made it! The Steam Packet Company did ultimately add a freight boat to its sailings which took a lot of the waiting lorries, so most people did travel a few hours or a day later than scheduled.

Arriving on the island, I drove straight to the paddock as I was now late for the early clothing inspections and signing-on procedures. I was soon indoctrinated, and met some of the 'regulars.'

I already knew the Chief Technical Officer: Peter Maddocks from the CRMC and my Manx Grand Prix racing, and Gordon Thorpe, our own current Chief Tech, was also there, enjoying a working holiday. I felt well at home. I was warned that the next day, Saturday, would be manic as it was the first day of practice, and all the riders would want to be out on the course to get their eye in and start qualification.

This was dead right: approximately 400 bikes, including those from numerous other countries, were presented each day, and although there was a full team of scrutineers, there would be little time for rest. As the practice week period passed, I learnt to pace myself, and fortunately, there were enough of us to allow for several short breaks. Our scheduled hours were from 3.00pm until 8.00pm each practice day, and from 8.00am until 5.00pm, or later if required, on race days. All assistance is voluntary; there are no wages!

Six rows of bikes passed through the two bays, and bikes being examined were moved through two at a time in each row; there were about a dozen scrutineers (technical officers) working at any one time. All ages were represented, although most of us were over 60, with two younger ones and a couple middle-aged. When an older chap popped his head into the office to offer his services for the following year someone quipped that it would reduce the average age to 74!

The system — and items checked — are slightly different to the procedure at short circuit meetings, and it was organised so that an official would not examine the same bike two days running to obviate habitual errors. Peter (and Gordon) kept a keen eye on me, and quiet friendly advice was on hand if I forgot to or didn't realise I hadn't checked something. After the first couple of days Peter told me I was doing a very good job: the pressure was off.

The TT course tests bikes to the maximum, and I felt a great responsibility to ensure that all of the machines I checked were safe to race. I was fastidious and double-checked anything I doubted. Tyre direction indicators need to be checked, as the slick tyres used on modern bikes don't have tread pattern. The design and size of these markings vary, and most are tiny and hard to locate. Some of the paddock tyre fitters rub a piece of white or yellow chalk over them to more readily identify them, which makes things easier for us. Hidden behind fairings, making them tricky to see, oil filters and sump plugs must be wire locked. The various makes and models of bikes are all different, and the filters not all located in the same area of each bike's chassis. I had a lot of items to check, and spent half of my time on my knees when examining each bike. My pencil torch came in handy.

By the end of practice week I was a little tired (race days are a little easier as there are fewer bikes to check, and we had more time to examine them), but what a pleasant way to be involved in the racing. I made a lot of new friends and soon acquired the nickname 'Classic Bloke.' I was the only one wearing CRMC green overalls, and I drew a few humorous comments when I got out my small brass rod and began 'pinging' the spokes on the classic bikes' wheels (the best way to check for tension). I was asked if I wanted to 'ping' the cast spokes of the modern bikes!

During my stint there I did find a few horrors, and made a number of suggestions regarding bike preparation. The other techs soon realised that I was a very qualified and experienced rider/technician, and adopted me without question. I ate my fair share of the free toffees and sandwiches that appeared on a regular basis. Tea, coffee, soft drinks and water were also provided, and the ladies involved on the admin side mothered us — it was a lovely experience which I will happily repeat.

CHAPTER 23

THE TZ YAMAHA, AND TODAY

THE DEEP VEIN THROMBOSIS I SUFFERED IN 2017 MAY HAVE PUT a stop to my active motorcycling, but I remained involved through scrutineering.

After a couple of months of inactivity, gradually recovering my health and acclimatising to drugs for the thrombosis, I got angry with myself and made a decision. As far back as I can remember, each winter I have rebuilt classic bikes for friends and acquaintances to pay for my racing activities. Suddenly, I was no longer racing, so had no need to fund raise, and my motivation had disappeared. I grasped the nettle and, bearing in mind my love of pure racing motorcycles, went looking for a TZ Yamaha Grand Prix race bike.

Through my Lansdowne Series racing on my Manx Norton, I had befriended TT stars Stan Woods and Charlie Williams. I was also pals with Em Roberts, who had worked for Maxtons (Ron Williams owns suspension specialist Maxton Engineering, and for a number of years produced a chassis kit for racing two-stroke Yamahas). Em built and prepared Charlie's racing two-strokes, one of which was a Maxton Yamaha. I had sold all of my racing kit apart from my precious original Aermacchi GP race bike, but realised, eventually, that keeping it in a shed all year whilst someone else enjoyed riding it was not for me. My racing pal Duncan Fitchett had shown an interest in buying the bike if ever I wanted to sell, so I gave him a call. After a brief and pleasant discussion a deal was struck and he now owns that lovely bike. I gather it lives in his lounge!

My love of classic racing and my engineering background had always led me to covet real racing bikes, not converted road bikes. I realised that the generation after me was not interested in '60s single cylinder racers such as my Norton, but was fascinated by the racing two-strokes of the '70s and '80s, which meant primarily TZ Yamahas. To justify it to my wife, any purchase had to be a good investment, so I sold the idea to her on that basis, and she fell for it: anything to get me out of the house, into the shed, and out of her way, I guess.

I did some research and discovered there was a new race series for this type of bike, covering GP racing two-stroke machines. Called GP Originals, initial plans were to organise three race meetings in the 2017 season, catering for both 250cc machines up to 1984 and 350cc machines up to 1981. Yamaha ceased to produce a 350 after 1981, and I was advised to go for a 79/81 TZ 350 F or G model. I was told that plenty of spare parts were available for the period of bike I was looking to buy, whilst sourcing spares for the later 250s was tricky. The decision was made; no point starting with a 100cc handicap, anyway — I'd go for a 350!

I contacted Charlie, Stan and Em and sent them shopping. Em found me a Maxton-framed bike, but chassis spares are very difficult to source as Maxton hadn't made any parts for some years, and Yamaha parts don't fit the Maxton chassis, so that went on the back burner. Stan emailed me with details of an alleged 1979 350 TZ that a dealer friend of his would sell for £8500, which seemed a reasonable price. I asked Stan to get some photos for me and checked my bank account. Fortunately, I had spent a couple of months listing all of my racing Norton spare parts on eBay, and sales of these provided a starting fund. I did have some money from the sale of the Aermacchi, but owed a large proportion of it to the family's funds, from which I had borrowed to buy it. Stan said that if I didn't buy the TZ, he would, and would strip it down and check the motor before I made any commitment. He's a good friend, is Stan.

The photos showed a complete bike fitted with some obviously new fibreglass. I copied the photos to Em, who said that as far as he could see it looked okay, and the price was reasonable. I then arranged to visit Stan in Cheshire to view the bike, maybe buy it and bring it home.

All race bikes that have been well-used end up with replacement parts all over them. I knew this, so didn't expect to find a completely original specimen. When I arrived at Stan's, he had the motor dismantled all over his workbench, and a rolling chassis stood in the corner. The chassis appeared in reasonable order and the wheels were in-line. The fuel tank looked good, and although slightly dented here and there, the expansion chambers were perfectly serviceable. It had a super electronic rev counter and original spoked wheels, albeit with a Honda front disc brake instead of the original Yamaha one.

Stan let me gaze at the motor parts. He commented that it had what appeared to be a set of new gearbox internals, an updated clutch, good condition carburettors, and its cylinder and head were in good order. If he was me, he said, he'd put it back together and run it for a meeting or two to see how it went: if I wasn't happy, he would gladly keep it himself as a winter project. I bit the bullet and paid him the money. I now owned a TZ Yamaha. I called in on Em on the way home and, after a brief examination of the pile of bits in the rear of my estate car, he declared it "probably alright for the money you've paid"!

I had already decided to give the motor to Lea Gourlay, a racing friend who specialised in servicing and tuning TZ Yamaha motors for the classic racing fraternity. I first got to know Lea whilst racing Don Williamson's Paton in 2008/9; he had since had a serious accident whilst racing on the fearsome Dundrod road circuit, the resulting injuries forcing him to quit racing, and concentrate on his motorcycle work. I travelled up to Worksop to deliver the motor to him soon after I bought the bike. Lea looked over the parts and quickly found that the motor was in poor condition, and well-worn. The crankcases were scrap as the main bearings had turned in them; fortunately, spare sets were available at a reasonable price. The cylinder had been over-ported, so performance would be an unknown quantity until we tried it out. Lea agreed to sort the motor for me as soon as he had time during, or soon after, the busy racing season. I had also taken some of the chassis parts to show him, and he told me the rear wheel was from a 250 TZ, but that this would be an advantage as it allowed an offset sprocket for using a wider rear tyre. The expansion chambers might have been Swarbricks, but he wasn't sure. We would have to see how they worked with the ported cylinder.

Unhappily, the further we dug, the worse it got. The ignition system was an original Hitachi — very worn and not fit for serious use, but could be kept as a spare. My lovely rev counter was illegal for the GP Originals Series or CRMC racing as it was too modern. The forks were 1978 TZ E but very similar to the F and G types — just 1mm smaller in diameter, so usable. The fuel tank had been welded underneath, and the tap itself was damaged. I went home slightly depressed. It was no one's fault, but I'd hoped for a better set of kit — and there was worse to come.

The frame was powder-coated, and when I had it blasted clean, numerous welded repairs were visible. The bottom rails had a really horrible repair, and around the headstock were several other smaller welds. The frame was straight, but clearly showing its age, and further investigation of the now visible frame number confirmed it as a 1978 TZ 250 E, identical to a 350 E specification frame, but not an F from 1979, nor a G from 80/81 as originally claimed. A short while later, Lea phoned to say he had stripped the crank and its centre was cracked three-quarters of the way through. A £1000 replacement would be required ...

I obviously needed a new frame if someone else was going to risk their life on it, and the motor was going to cost a small fortune to sort out. The welding beneath the powder coating was almost invisible, and I never showed the crankcases to Em. It took an expert eye to see that the main bearings had turned, so Stan would never have known. Despite all my experience, I had bought a pup!

After realising that I had made a bad purchase, I got on with sorting out the mess, and began ordering replacement parts. I took advice from the CRMC's eligibility expert, Gordon Russell, and visited Harris Performance in Ware, Hertfordshire, to order a replica Yamaha frame. I met Lester Harris, who could not have been more helpful. I had a tour of the lovely modern engineering facility there, Lester relating how they had made numerous TZ Yamaha racing frames over the years, as the originals were so prone to breaking. In the classic period, apparently, some of them had fractured after only one race meeting!

Lea Gourlay had confirmed that my alloy swing arm would be suitable, and I took this with me to Harris, which agreed to build me a replica 1980 TZ model G Yamaha frame, and fit my swing arm into it. The frame would come with slight permissible modifications to allow rubber mounting of the motor. It would come complete with engine plates, and I was assured that all of my other original Yamaha parts would fit straight onto it. Delivery was promised for November, and I paid a deposit (I thought).

A month later I had a call from Lester to say that they had received several orders for similar frames, and were going to CNC-machine some of the smaller frame parts as this would produce a better engineered frame, but delay delivery until December. I still had plenty of other parts to source, so this didn't cause me any issues.

After polishing the rims, I gave the wheel hubs and rims to my pal, wheel builder Dick Waldron, and he rebuilt the wheels using stainless spokes. The original fibreglass seat and front mudguard were damaged, so I bought new 'lightweight' parts (a front mudguard and a seat unit, plus a complete two-part fairing), and had them painted, along with the original fuel tank, in traditional Yamaha race design by another classic racing pal, Nigel Banks. Via an online TZ forum, I sourced the correct paint codes and dimensions which I forwarded to Nigel, who was well pleased with the information that he could use for customers also. Nigel quickly produced some brilliant paintwork.

I bought a lot of smaller TZ Yamaha items from Vince Cundle at Fondseca, who has an online shop selling all manner of TZ parts, and has been very good to me. Vince was a mine of information, and helped me avoid mistakes: he even managed to find me a pair of original front discs that Lea had recommended I try and source. Vince sold me a very nice (and expensive) replica temperature gauge, and ordered a new Mestre French crank for me that arrived quickly and I delivered to Lea.

My bank balance was taking a beating, which I felt was bound to get worse — and it did! Lea soon phoned to confirm that my original Hitachi ignition system was too damaged to use, so I ordered a new ignition kit and had that delivered directly to him. In the meantime, I bought a more traditional rev counter and ordered some Avon tyres. Bob Davies offered to supply me with some expensive racing sparkplugs, which I gleefully accepted, and he ordered them through his garden machinery and tool supply business. I soon got a call to collect them. Ta, Bob!

Lea had advised me on tyre specifications, and as the rear one I ordered was contrary to Avon's recommended fitting (it had a slightly different profile), it would only just fit into the swing arm. I queried this with Lea, who said that when he'd first fitted one to his race-winning TZ, his rider asked "Why haven't we used these before?" Enough said. I asked Lea about possible issues if it wouldn't fit at the front of the swing arm, and he explained that the TZ's wheel base was too short anyway, and it would wheelie very easily. It would be better, he said, to always have the wheel located towards the rear of the chain adjustment, providing a longer wheelbase, which would prevent some of the wheelies. Lea's advice has been invaluable, and has saved me from making numerous and possibly expensive errors.

A call from Harris Performance in late December 2017 to say that my frame was ready was most welcome, and I hurried to the factory to collect it. It looked lovely, and my swing arm fitted well. I met Nick, the craftsman fabricator who had built the frame, who turned out to be an Isle of Man racing enthusiast, and knew some of the Paton race team lads I had met during my last years of racing at the Manx Grand Prix. The price of the frames had increased since I placed my order, but Harris kept to its original quote. I thought that the engine plates and mounting were included in this price, but unfortunately not. Then, a week later, I received a call from Harris, apologetically advising that the deposit had never been taken from my credit card, so I owed an additional £500! Never mind, press on, it's only money.

On a happier note, as promised, my forks and other items fitted perfectly. The frame was a really good replica, which Nick told me utilised better steel, slightly thicker tubing, and a strengthened design generally. I had specified attachment bobbins for the footrest hangers as the original frames had welded-on tubes that were prone to accident damage. Lea had offered to make me alloy footrest hangers and footrest linkages to suit the bobbins. These would bend, rather than the frame, in the event of a crash.

Lea suggested I use a 'crossflow' radiator, and agreed to make one for me, and supply a new rear brake master cylinder, as the one fitted to my bike was in very poor condition. The rear brake caliper was damaged, so I bought a new one, and also a pair of rear wheel adjusters, as mine had been weld-repaired. I also bought a new rear shock absorber, as I didn't feel it would be sensible to race on a 40-year-old hydraulic suspension unit. If I was going to go racing properly, I wasn't going to mess around!

At the end of the 2017 race season, I had approached a racing friend, Clive Ling, to ask if he was interested in racing my TZ at a couple — say three — meetings a year. We would combine it with events he was already racing at, and I would be scrutineering there also. Clive asked for time to discuss it with his lovely wife, Donna, and soon came back to say he'd love to be involved. Clive had a good reputation as a safe, quick rider who didn't often crash — just what I wanted. I'd been previously involved with him riding Phil Harding's Woden at the Goodwood Revivals, and we liked each other. Our wives also got on well, so that was another hurdle jumped!

By now I'd sold my lovely VW Transporter van, and bought a small motorhome; everything had changed when I'd had to give up racing, and I didn't think I'd need a van anymore. I looked around the race paddocks and realised that a small box trailer would suffice, so went shopping, eventually buying a really nice one from a firm in Norfolk.

In mid-March 2018 it was snowing; my shed was freezing and I'd decided against any spannering! I'd spent the previous two months gathering together the final parts of the TZ jigsaw, and had collected some complex alloy front brake disc spacers and rear wheel spacers that a friend, Roger Walker, had kindly machined for me. Roger is a long-time Velocette Owners Club pal, and a very skilful and fastidious engineer. We had chatted at a Mallory Park race meeting the previous year, and he had offered to make any parts that would assist my project. I made a note of that offer and, when I realised that my small lathe hadn't the chuck capacity to hold the material for the front spacers, called-in Roger's offer. Within a week he had delivered exactly what was required; refusing any payment.

Lea called to let me know that the motor, fitted with a few hundred pounds worth of new electronic ignition system, was ready, and I quickly drove to his Nottinghamshire home to collect it and pay the bill. As promised, Lea had also made me a nice new alloy radiator, a set of footrests, gear shift and brake linkages plus hanger plates that I collected with the motor. He had also modified my carbs, set them up ready for use, and replaced a broken float chamber.

Whilst we were chatting, Lea queried whether I had modified the front forks in any way. I told him that I had carefully rebuilt them as standard, whereupon he quietly suggested they would benefit from having more modern dampers installed, explaining that the modern tyre compounds available to us were much stickier than the original 1980s tyres, and my rider would suffer from tyre chatter.

Lea's workshop was surrounded by racking, holding all manner of bits and pieces and I asked him if he happened to have any spare dampers. Yes, he said, he did, but explained that they required machining to get them to fit inside Yamaha fork legs. Agreeing to modify my forks, Lea wryly commented that his customer waiting list was getting longer, as I kept saying yes to anything he suggested! Arriving home with the motor, I quickly posted my forks to him, and within a couple of weeks, I was a few more pounds poorer, but in possession of a modernised set of forks.

Lea had provided me with approximate dimensions for brake hose lengths and I ordered two front hoses and a rear one. Snow in early March delayed delivery, but they fitted perfectly. I had swiftly mounted the motor in the frame, and Harris Performance provided optional spacers that allow sideways adjustment of about 8mm to compensate for chain alignment issues. Lea had insisted I use the widest rear tyre possible, which meant that clearance between the tyre and rear chain was minimal, as was clearance to the alloy swing arm. A bit of spacer juggling was going to be required to get optimum motor positioning.

I decided I would use the thinnest rear chain I could, and contacted Andy Forsdick, from whom I often used to buy chain, at Kempton Park Autojumbles. Andy has been in the chain business all his life, and used to work for Renold Chains. He advised me to use a Regina thin plate chain rather than the usual heavyweight type, and assured me it would be strong enough for Lea's predicted 70bhp-plus! This saved me a couple of millimetres and would hopefully ease my little problem.

Lea had previously suggested I use a Dave Swarbrick exhaust system as he thought it would work well with the tuned cylinder I had. The bike did come with some battered exhaust pipes of unknown origin, well past their sell-by date, having been repaired in several places. I had phoned a very helpful and pleasant Dave in February, who promised delivery in three weeks time. He was as good as his word, and a full system, complete with silencers, arrived via courier.

The rear brackets were not welded on, as all bikes differ in exhaust fitment, and I asked Clive if he would complete the fitting, which fortunately he was happy to do. He was anxious to see the bike he was to ride, anyway. I took the bike, in my trailer, to Clive's home workshop in Norfolk, and watched in awe whilst he spent around five hours skilfully gas-welding on the rear ends of both pipes, and adding strengthener plates that had been provided with the kit. The pipes ultimately fitted perfectly — and looked brilliant. I did virtually nothing to help as my racing pal Bob Johnson, who also lives in Norfolk, had offered to come and join the party. He knew Clive well, and 'too many cooks,' etc, I let them do the clever stuff and confined myself to providing encouragement and sarcastic humour, with Clive's wife, Donna, providing welcome refreshments.

I wanted to fit a handlebar lever-operated choke system to the carburettors as this would assist with cold starting, and also used to enrich the mixture near the end of a long straight to prevent potential seizures. I managed to buy a complete kit — not cheap, but relatively easily fitted after a little careful cable trimming. Both Lea and Vince advocated a later V-Twin Yamaha quick-action twist grip, so out with the wallet and wait for the postman. I didn't want Clive to find fault with my bike when he rode it, so felt it easier to fit the best parts from the off rather than later on.

I also bought a very expensive, but accurate, replica TZ 750 temperature gauge, plus a nice mounting bracket for this and the new white-faced Scitsu tacho I'd purchased earlier. I had to spend a day in my shed fabricating a rather complex rubber-mounted holder that would fit onto the mounting bracket for the temperature gauge, but I was anxious that it shouldn't vibrate and get damaged.

When I closely examined the two front discs and their carriers that I'd bought from Vince I found that, although serviceable, one of them was not a racing item but the road version, with a slightly heavier inner disc carrier. The discs were original Yamaha parts from a later 1990s model TZ: the best available and legal for our racing class, I'd been told. Seeking perfection, I did a spot of searching on eBay and found some more discs for sale in the USA. I thought the price was 250 dollars for a pair as the listing showed two discs, but when I contacted the vendor he explained that the advertised price was for one only. After some lengthy email exchanges to verify condition, and that it was definitely a 'race' disc, I again bit the bullet and paid up. The disc duly turned up but the bobbins connecting the disc to its carrier differed from the one I had bought from Vince, and looked worn. I then found a great little company in Wales that specialised in motorcycle disc brake services, which replaced all of the bobbins in both discs at a very reasonable price, and in good time. Now I had a matching pair of the best available discs.

Lea had complained that the new replica TZ Yamaha ignition system had taken some serious fettling to fit onto the crankcases, and I found another issue when trying to fit the CDI box to the front of the frame ahead of the headstock. I had opted for the more traditional-looking (and more expensive by £100) CDI box, but the manufacturer couldn't supply any of the correct fixing grommets, so Lea again came to my rescue by digging into his stock of used parts. I really wanted to keep the bike at least looking standard, hence the traditional paint job, wire wheels, swing arm, and other original smaller parts, where practical.

When I tried to fit the clutch cable I was unable to get enough free play, and found that the adjuster within the left-hand engine cover was thoroughly seized. I tried reasonable force without success, so rather than smash it to bits, I sourced and ordered another original from the USA ... not too expensive at £35. In the meantime, I soaked the seized item in WD40 and left it for a few days, before having another go, when, you've guessed it, the adjuster freed off. Aagghhhhhhh! I really do know how to waste money.

The spending seemed never-ending. After fitting the larger-than-standard alloy radiator, I wondered whether my beautifully-painted standard TZ fairing would fit around this. A quick call to Lea, my mentor, and he confirmed my worst fears: I would have to buy another, wider fairing. A racing pal of Lea's could provide one, so I dipped into my nearly-empty pocket yet again. A listing on eBay resulted in selling the original fairing, which did recoup some of my earlier expenditure but I was still going to lose out financially, as I now had to get Nigel Banks to paint the new one.

Tyre fitting was fun. The front went on fine, but the rear was a right so-and-so! I had recently sold my aged, heavy-duty compressor and Bob Johnson, my racing pal, had let me have his smaller, more practical one as he needed a large one for his paint-spraying activities. Unfortunately for me, my new acquisition wouldn't provide enough pressure to blast the huge rear tyre into position on the rim. I used masses of genuine tyre-fitting grease and removed the valve core, but one portion of the bead refused to slip into position. I resorted to taking the wheel to a small motorcycle workshop in my town, where the lad there had the solution, as he'd fitted plenty of his own racing tyres: after several failed attempts he resorted to using WD40, which did the job, the tyre suddenly sliding into position with a huge bang.

In early May, I attempted to fit the fuel tank and was horrified to find that it wouldn't go over my new shock absorber, as the spring was resting against the tank. I sourced an unpainted replica tank via Vince, who said "try it on and pay me if it's okay." This was better than my original, but would still need alteration. I gave both tanks to Clive Ling, who decided that we might as well alter the original, which he thought he could do without damaging the paintwork. Vince was very good about me returning the unpainted tank, and Clive ultimately did a neat alloy welding job on the underside of my original tank. Sorted!

Fitting the tacho and temperature gauges had been straightforward but the thread for the temperature gauge sender, in the alloy cylinder head, was very shallow, and I was not confident that it would remain watertight, even though I had used PTFE tape on the thread. The temperature gauge was also tricky to fit into the plastic instrument fascia, but a bit of fiddling produced a good flexible mounting (this would all come back to bite me).

Later that month, I was scrutineering at a classic endurance race at Donington Park, at which Lea was also going to be. Although, at this stage, the fuel tank was not finished, I took the completed bike along and Lea fired her up for the first time using his own fuel tank. She fired at once and seemed fine. Both Lea and I were well pleased, although I did feel that the clutch lever action was very heavy. Wandering round the paddock and looking at other TZs, I chatted to several owners, one of whom said he had a remedy for the heavy clutch lever. He had extended the actuating lever for the clutch push-rod, which transformed the lever pressure required. He had raced his TZ on the Isle of Man, he told me, and had to find a remedy to this problem or would never have managed the four laps. I swiftly modified my TZ's actuating lever — that was another problem sorted!

I spent more hours adjusting and fiddling with various fittings, and ended up quite satisfied with the bike. Clive suggested we take it to a track day at Cadwell Park in early June, so on a cool damp day, we met up there. Bob Johnson came along too, to provide moral and mechanical support. The bike actually ran well, but the temperature gauge sender leaked water as I feared it would, so only a few laps were possible. Clive loved the bike though, and at least we had successfully tested the chassis and motor. The leak needed an engineering fix, and a few days later my toolmaker pal, Phil Harding, designed and made a brass insert that resolved the problem. Phil also made me an oversized cylinder drain bolt as the thread for that was also very worn. Thanks, Phil. Clive mentioned that the fairing seemed a little low, and might need repositioning slightly, but he thought the bike was quick and handled well.

Clive and I agreed to enter the TZ at a GP Originals race meeting at Oulton Park in mid-August, so I concentrated on perfecting the preparation and adjusting the fairing position. Our plans were never realised, though, as, tragically, Clive lost his life whilst competing at an endurance race in Chimay in Belgium, late in July. Everyone was devastated. Clive was a great friend to me and many others, and even today we are struggling to come to terms with his sudden death.

Clive was a racer, through-and-through, so I knew that he would want me to continue with the TZ. I could no longer race myself, but needed to maintain that strong link to classic racing, so decided to take the bike to the CRMC Classic Festival in early August to see if I could find a replacement rider. It wasn't going to be easy as Shelagh would have to approve of my choice, and

I wanted a mechanically-sympathetic rider. I spent many hours looking at old programmes, trying to pick out a name, with Ian Bain being the only contender. Ian was a very quick, safe rider, a Liverpudlian pal from my Lansdowne Series racing days. He was the perfect build, and a great mechanic, too. He was also a real British Vintage enthusiast. I approached Richard Adams, the series organiser, and asked his opinion of Ian. Richard said that Ian would 'never ride a Japanese bike,' but I might as well ask him as he was competing at the meeting.

To my surprise and great delight Ian bit my hand off when I asked him, and we arranged to get him out on the bike in a feature parade the following day. John Davidson, who I have known for years, was in charge of entries, and looked kindly on my request for a late entry. I took the mickey out of Richard about his Japanese bike, praying that the bike and weather would perform for us. Ian rode the full session in red-hot sunshine, and the bike ran beautifully with no water leaks. He came back wearing a broad smile, saying it was the best set up bike he'd ever raced: very quick and with handling and brakes that he loved. Wow! I was almost tearful.

The initial plan had been to race the TZ a couple of months later in October, but the weather was dreadful, and we walked away from that idea. The bike stayed in my nice warm shed all winter, with Ian and I deciding that its first competitive outing would be at a GP Originals event at Oulton Park in April 2019. I had built up a comprehensive spares stock, and delivered the bike to Oulton Park with jerry cans of fuel and bags of enthusiasm!

Unfortunately, it was another really wet weekend, and although the bike ran reasonably on the rather damp Saturday qualifying session, it obviously didn't like the pouring rain on the Sunday. Ian completed five of the six scheduled laps in the first race, but pulled in with the carburettor slides sticking open. A throttle that sticks open on a 70bhp Grand Prix bike is very dangerous, and he made the sensible decision to pull out. The second race was no better, so the bike was consigned to the van in disgrace. Many of the other riders had similar issues caused by their two-stroke fuel emulsifying.

A few weeks later, we took the bike to a CRMC race meeting at Pembrey in South Wales for what proved to be a bright, but cool race weekend. Four races and a practice session were planned, and Ian and I hoped for a better event. Practice, and the first two races on the Saturday went well, although there was a slight water leak from the temperature gauge sender, and Ian said the clutch seemed to be slipping. He qualified mid-field, though. The bike was certainly fast, he said, which would take a little while to get used to, but he loved riding it. I was a happy bunny!

The third race on the Sunday didn't go so well. Ian noticed another water leak and pulled in early with steam coming from one exhaust pipe: not a good sign. Ian assured me he could fix anything mechanical, being very experienced on two-strokes, having ridden Greeves motorcycles in competition for many years. He also runs an engineering machine shop, so is totally equipped.

Family issues gave Ian some serious problems, so it wasn't until mid-July that work commenced on the TZ. Ian found that an O-ring seal had failed on one cylinder head, so machined the head's surface to guarantee it was flat; also re-cutting the seating for the temperature gauge sender.

After examining the top end of the motor, Ian assured me it was in very good order, and the pistons were showing very little sign of wear. He complained that he couldn't find anything else to fettle on the bike, and said I had done a good job on the rebuild, which was a big relief to me as the responsibility of letting someone else race your bike is heavy.

Ian entered the bike for the big CRMC classic event at Donington in early August, both of us hoping that the bike would at last run properly and be leak-free! The weather forecast was good, but very humid, and so it proved. Ian told me he didn't intend to take any risks, and wanted to get used to riding the bike. The Yamaha has a lot more brake horsepower than his Manx Norton (which he was also racing at Donington), and weighs about a third less. It also has twin front disc brakes that really work!

Practice went well. The bike was fine, Ian said, though not revving out in fifth or sixth gears. Discussions took place and, acting on advice from experienced TZ riders, Ian dropped the carburettor needles one groove to weaken the fuel mixture. This didn't work, unfortunately, and he pulled in after a couple of laps of the first race as the bike was not running well, and was worse than it had been in practice. I went off to speak to Lea Gourlay. His own TZ had been problematic, and he advised me to increase the main jets by three sizes. I relayed this information to Ian who made the necessary alterations. On Sunday the bike performed faultlessly in the first race and Ian finished in tenth place. A brilliant, safe result. Thanks very much, Lea. Everyone was tickled pink. There were no water leaks and the clutch had worked perfectly.

The second race was run late in the afternoon when the weather had changed slightly. Ian finished a strong sixth, and said the bike was really quick, had handled perfectly, and he couldn't believe how good the brakes were. It hadn't run quite as cleanly as in the previous race, but we put that down to the change in weather. Rain was on the way!

The TZ Yamaha project had delivered: my rider loved the bike, and I felt the expenditure had been worthwhile. Steady, safe progress is being made, and my partnership with Ian is working well. He has a brilliant sense of humour, a lovely family, and is great fun to work with. He even offered me the job of gofer/ mechanic at the Goodwood Revival, which, I'm pleased to say went so well that he has booked me for 2020!

After Donington, Shelagh and I went to the Isle of Man for the Classic TT and to visit my daughter, Charlie, and her lovely family. I spent a lot of my time scrutineering, whilst Shelagh played nanny. I wanted to advance my scrutineering career, and had asked Peter Maddocks, Chief Scrutineer for the Classic TT and Manx Grand Prix, if it was possible to be trained in engine measurement whilst I was there. This would add another tick to my CV, and increase my usefulness at future race meetings (engines may be measured if there is a protest regarding cubic capacity or some other irregularity). Peter arranged for me to measure the first three finishers in each of the classic races under supervision (routine procedure at the Classic TT). My knowledge of engineering helped tremendously with this, and I had no problem with the different makes of machine. The V-twin Yamaha that had won the classic lightweight race was the most difficult, as I had to lay on my back to measure the dimensions of the forward-facing cylinder. Before I left the scrutineering bay on the last day of classic racing, CRMC Chief Technical Officer Gordon Thorpe, who was also officiating at the event, took me aside to say that he and Peter would recommend I be promoted to senior scrutineer status. I was delighted, and really made up to be considered capable of taking such responsibility. (I've since received my ACU licence, suitably updated.)

Life goes on. My medical consultant suggested I try a different drug, administered as weekly injections instead of daily tablets, to treat my blood condition. Since changing, I feel better generally, and my blood levels are well-controlled, which has encouraged me to consider returning to riding a motorcycle on the road, albeit with due care. No racing, though: been there; done that!

A widowed family friend had kept her husband's 1959 Triumph T110 since his death from cancer six years previously, and offered it to me for a very reasonable price. It was an easy decision to say yes. The bike had been totally dismantled, in boxes, for 40 years, having been the mount they used for their honeymoon in the '60s. The reconstruction is progressing well, and I hope to have my first ride in spring 2020.

Motorcycles are in my blood — it's a disease — isn't it ...?

CHAPTER 24

THE LAST WORD

MY FRIENDS SAY I'M A PAIN IN THE BACKSIDE, BECAUSE I'M SUCH A perfectionist, and I admit it: I like things to be right. Throughout my racing years, I spent hours examining the various individual parts of my bikes. I was never happy with second-best, and would make a part two or three times before I was fully satisfied that it was safe to use — and efficient. Paul Duncombe taught me this approach, and it has become my way of life. I suffer from attention deficit issues, and eventually discovered that the only way to work was to make copious notes and lists. Much of this book has been sourced via those notes, and I have used an A4-sized blue notebook since 1998. I started a new one for the Yamaha; before that it was smaller notebooks that fortunately, I kept.

I lack the confidence and expertise to build my own engines, but was lucky enough to work with a number of really expert tuners/engine builders, including Francis Beart, Les Kempster, Tony Baker, Geoff Dodkin, Nick Payton, John Goodall, Jerry Summerfield, Gerry Kershaw, Ken Garfield and Stuart Tonge, plus Lea Gourlay more recently. I must also include Don Williamson and Steve Linsdell in this group: their engineering expertise with the Paton made it so reliable. Bob Johnson deserves a mention, as his skill and perseverance whilst developing the TAB Honda ultimately made it a quick, very competitive race bike.

Bob seems to happily work in an apparently chaotic workshop, but mine must be spotless. I have a large, carpeted, tidy shed and the garage is the 'dirty' area for machining. No cars in there! I hate mechanical failure, and spend hours drilling and lock wiring components so that they can't come loose or cause issues. I love Loctite, and will often just gaze at the bike I'm working on, looking for potential problem areas that need a locking mechanism. Good preparation is everything to me, and I have picked up a few compliments over the years from scrutineers. I never failed to finish in any of my 39 Isle of Man TT course races because of bad preparation. I'm proud of that. I only had five DNFs, all caused by engine problems except for the Petty Norton's fuel tank disaster!

I took everything except the kitchen sink to race meetings, and would often lend tools and spares to other riders. My van was always full. I bought and carried loads of unnecessary spare parts I was unlikely to ever use — but I *might* have needed to, in which case they were no use at home in the shed! I hated the idea of driving miles to a race meeting and then having to go home early due to a mechanical issue, or for lack of a spare part.

I have taken advantage of every one of my friends. They have all, at one time or another, been dragged along to race meetings in the UK and Europe, to act as pushers and gofers. They have all willingly obliged, also frequently putting a few quid in the race fund, sharing the driving, and often providing alcohol and banter to everyone's delight. Thank you, all.

I'm quite capable of maintaining my race bikes, and enjoy working on them. I have always checked tappet settings and ignition settings, and occasionally removed a cylinder head to fix the odd oil leak, but beyond that I generally leave race motors to the experts. I have, however, restored numerous road bikes for friends, including rebuilding the motors. Anything to help the racing budget! I will strip a racing gearbox and am most methodical, taking digital photographs as I go, as I don't trust my memory at all. I've spent a lot of money sourcing the best parts for my bikes and paying my engine tuners: I'm sure I could have owned a much better house if I hadn't raced classic bikes.

My lovely wife, Shelagh, has been a tower of strength, and without her support I would never have achieved anything. She has sacrificed an awful lot to help me succeed. I really have pushed our marriage boundaries. I know that numerous times when I've been tearing round the TT course, the clock above my number on the huge, start line timing board has failed to show my true location, or has stopped, causing her to think I might have had an accident. Watching our progress from 'The Grandstand' on the Glencrutchery Road must be agony for racers' families. I'm sure I couldn't cope with that sort of pressure, yet Shelagh has encouraged me in every way, and never failed to trust my judgement. My three daughters, Amanda, Julie and Charlie, have also been totally supportive and are my biggest fans. I love them all so much.

Shelagh and the girls have been nagging me for some years to write a book about my racing adventures, as have my pals, including Alun Thomas, a friend from my police training school days, who kindly offered to proof read it. Well, here it is. Thank goodness I'm still here, and able to remember it all. What a lucky chap!

INDEX

239